What others are saying about Escaping Emotional Entrapment:

"If you want a happier, healthier relationship, this book offers practical advice to help you achieve just that. A building block for an emotionally enriched life."
John Gray, *"Men Are from Mars, Women Are from Venus"*

"Gaining emotional control empowers you to make choices that are normally out of reach. Using humor and insight, 'Entrapment' is a straightforward, common sense approach to bring out the very best in you."
Denis Waitley, Ph.D., *"Psychology of Winning"*

"Positive emotional energy is the fuel of success and happiness. This book shows you how to become a complete optimist in every area of your life."
Brian Tracy, *"The Psychology of Success"*

"A well thought-out, thorough and valuable approach for anyone who wants to improve their life."
Robert G. Allen, New York Times #1 Best Selling Author

"The mind and body are intricately connected. Emotional fitness plays a dramatic role in the ability of a person to practice a balanced lifestyle, maintain a healthy body and even recover from physical illness. Dr. Rutley provides an extraordinary approach to cultivating a resilient state of mind."
Jerome Perera, MD, University of Toronto

"Daniel Rutley's Escaping Emotional Entrapment is an excellent self-help book that clearly and succinctly states some of the principles of Rational Emotive Behavior Therapy and other sensible procedures. It can help with emotional problems."
Albert Ellis, PH.D.,
Presiden

Enjoy the Escape!

Daniel Kulley

Escaping Emotional Entrapment
Freedom from negative thinking
and unhealthy emotions

Daniel Rutley, Psy.D.

Visit online:
www.DanielRutley.com

Pax Publishing
Las Vegas, Nevada, USA

Escaping Emotional Entrapment
Freedom from negative thinking and unhealthy emotions

by Dr. Daniel Rutley

Published by:

Pax Publishing
7465 Ullom Dr.
Las Vegas, NV 89139

Printed in Canada
Fourth Printing 2010

Canadian Cataloguing-in-Publication Data

Rutley, Daniel, 1957 –
  Escaping emotional entrapment: freedom from negative thinking and unhealthy emotions

  Includes index.
  ISBN-10: 0968740901
  ISBN-13: 978-0968740903

  1. Self-actualization (Psychology)
  2. Emotions   I. Title

BF637.S4R878 2001   158.1   C00-900827-6

Dedication

To my father, Malford (Jeff), who was my most influential teacher and whose warm personable nature I most wanted to emulate. To my mother, Noella, who has always encouraged and supported my insatiable curiosity and is the definition of love and kindness in my life.

To Dina who is the personification of friendship and whose devout loyalty, generosity and love knows no boundaries. Without your loving support and faith in me, this book would not have been completed.

And, to Chris, who helps me to remember what is important. You model elegance in spirit and form. This book was in waiting until you.

Professional Acknowledgments

I would like to acknowledge the psychologists, theorists and teachers who have influenced my thinking in the development of this book: Paul Avery, M.A.; David Burns, Ph.D.; Raymond DiGiuseppe, Ph.D.; Wayne Dyer, Ph.D.; Paul Hauck, Ph.D.; Denis Waitley, Ph.D. And Brian Ferris, Ph.D. whose distinctive flare has provided inspiration and his many stories have been adapted in this book.

I would like to extend a special acknowledgement to Albert Ellis, Ph.D., founder of the Albert Ellis Institute for Rational Emotive Behavior Therapy, whose pioneering work has allowed countless therapists to effectively assist their clients in leading happier, healthier lives, and whom without this and many other books would not have been written.

Personal Acknowledgments

I would like to thank the multitude of people whose advice and comments have been indispensable in producing this work. Megan Harris and Basil Maxwell for their preliminary input. Also Chuck Lorre for allowing me to use his "vanity card" number 45. And to Richard Bach who wrote Illusions. Two people who have helped me in immeasurable ways and I am fortunate to call friends: Linda A. Johannesson - your creativity and wit continues to amaze me; Don Hunter - thanks for being there to assist, you are one in a billion. I am especially grateful to James Campbell for the hours of work performing the initial editing and sharing his always creative and stimulating perspectives. Also praise to Karen Stedman whose skillful editing has made this a better and easier book to read. And Gaelyn Larrick and Shannon Bodie at Lightbourne who were wonderful to work with. And a few of my most influential teachers who have added quality to my life and thus, this book: Frank Bartle, Graham Forst, Stan Persky, Bruce Alexander and Paul Avery. And a big thanks to Al.

And, in particular, Dina McDermott for her indispensable assistance and advice in every step in the development of this book. A special "Thank you" to Lidia "Chris" Parfeniuk who has been a source of inspiration and provided invaluable feedback.

Table of Contents

Section III

Section IV

Section V

Section VI

Warning - Disclaimer

Escaping Emotional Entrapment
Freedom from negative thinking
and unhealthy emotions

Dr. Daniel Rutley

**For FREE video clips, articles, newsletter,
and more, visit online:**

www.DanielRutley.com

Escaping Emotional Entrapment
"It's About You!"

This book is *about* you. It is about your feelings, your attitudes and *you* maintaining a positive direction in life.

Do you want to be more centered with a greater sense of confidence, be happier and more fun-loving? Do you want to have more energy and feel more enthusiasm yet be at peace within yourself? If you want to feel stronger and be in greater control so you will be free to advance in any other area of your life that you choose, unencumbered by negative unhealthy emotions...then this book is for you. If you *really want* to make a change, you can!

By developing better emotional control and breaking free of the unhealthy emotions that bind you, you can learn how to create a change that is so powerful it will literally change your life for the better. By becoming emotionally fit you will be happier, more fulfilled, centered and content, and better able to cultivate long-lasting healthy relationships.

Emotions rule! No matter what you are doing, if you are having a panic attack, in a fit of rage or sunken into the abyss of depression — your emotions will win out — your emotions will rule.

If you ask yourself what is more important, what you know or how you feel — you understand that what you know does not matter if you feel bad. Like with physical health, if you do not have a strong and stable positive emotional outlook, the quality of your life drops dramatically.

Emotional Control vs Practical Advice

A myriad of therapists, counselors and well-meaning friends will give you advice on: developing your spirituality, the importance of relying on your intuition, enhancing your parenting skills or improving your relationships. As valuable and well intentioned this practical advice might be, seldom will it be followed if you are in significant emotional distress.

The average person finds spirituality elusive when anxiety mounts over unpaid bills. Human beings have an almost infinite ability to talk themselves into anything, thus an *overconfidence* in intuition can be problematic if it is influenced by insecurities. The best advice on child rearing and relationships goes out the window if the person has poor emotional control getting angry, anxious or jealous easily. When in distress, the sound practical advice found in many self-help books, heard on TV and obtained from credible sources goes unheeded. Have you ever given wonderful advice to a friend only to have him or her ignore it?

The problem for many people is that they do not realize how severely their emotions impact their life. The decisions that people make are more determined by their emotional states than any other single factor. People often think, "It's a logical decision" and that is why they made it. But if an option does not *feel* right, most people will not take it regardless of how sensible it is. The selection most people make is the one that *feels* right — logical or not. That is why we often observe others coming to conclusions that are clearly illogical and seem utterly absurd to us. This divergence occurs because *we* see their options and their decision in an *un*emotional light. Emotions guide and color our decision process. This happens without being cognizant of it. Subconsciously. Below our level of awareness.

The Essence of Emotional Entrapments

When people have been tested, it's found that their choice of mate, career, vacation, music and lifestyle plus much more are all impacted significantly depending on their emotional state. We are not normally conscious of how much our choices are altered by emotions. This is because our choices — whatever they may be — seem right, fit right and are congruent with our emotions *at the time*. Nothing seems out of place...*at the time*...until sometime the next morning when your feelings have changed and you think, "Why did I do that?"

If a woman is feeling unassertive and unconfident, this will guide her life into a very different direction — personally and professionally — than if she were feeling stronger and more daring. The problem is that after a while, wherever we are, it becomes comfortable. Natural. Seems to fit...sometimes even when it is uncomfortable, like in a difficult relationship. There's a tendency to develop a "that's just the way it is" attitude. We get into a rut, stuck, comfortably uncomfortable and do not know how to get unstuck. This is the essence of emotional entrapment.

But this is not the way it has to be. Emotional entrapments like depression, anxiety and anger are more like bad habits that are subconsciously developed, nurtured and raised without any conscious desire or intent.

Simply put, we were not taught emotional control as children. Do you remember sitting down with your family and your father saying, "Okay family, I'd like for us to talk about the dynamics of how to control our emotions"? It didn't happen. They did not teach it in school or in your religion, and we sure did not learn it from our friends or siblings. No one knew how to control emotions.

In the mid-1900s, psychology knew very little about emotional control. There was a fair amount of study on how to change behavior but not emotions. Today, there is an immense amount of available information on emotional control. We can now break free and escape emotional entrapments. Liberate ourselves. Learn to soar like an eagle instead of being destined to hug the ground like a tortoise.

After giving a lecture on the dynamics of escaping emotional entrapments, an elderly man came up to me, introduced himself and said, "You know, I've lived over 80 years and it never came to mind that I could make a *decision* to change my emotions." That is what this book is about: Learning to control your emotions so that you may choose a full spectrum of healthy emotions. You can choose to be passionate or pensive, ecstatic and excited or calm and relaxed. Yes, how you feel really can be a choice. Now you are going to learn what countless generations before you did not know.

This is a book about choices. Choosing how to think. Choosing how you feel. Ultimately, choosing how your life will continue to develop. How you think and feel will determine the choices you make and the actions you take.

Escaping Emotional Entrapment: Freedom from negative thinking and unhealthy emotions is about delivering you from the emotions that can enslave you. These emotions bind you, sometimes subtly but *always* impact the direction of your life significantly *and* negatively.

Depth and Breadth of Experience

This book is written with you in mind. It is strategically written so you can clearly and easily see how to understand yourself and gain better control over your emotions.

Escaping Emotional Entrapment combines a diversity of disciplines that will help you view yourself and your life with greater depth and breadth. Escaping Emotional Entrapment embraces both the spiritual (examining the "spirit" of who you are) and the scientific (accepted, reliable constants within our physical world).

A collaboration of complimentary disciplines in my life affords me a unique outlook that is shared in Escaping Emotional Entrapment and provides for improved and synergistic learning to you, the reader. Individual psychology permits an understanding of how we can deceive ourselves *and* how to grow beyond ourselves. Social psychology examines how groups work, while anthropology and history presents a wide base of cultural understandings across time for perspective. Combine these with my love of the physical world (i.e., physics and astronomy) then add philosophy as a foundation for guidance and stability and this is the background for the development of Escaping Emotional Entrapment. Because this is more than a profession, it is a way of life for me - it makes me uncustomarily qualified to act as your guide through the labyrinth of your emotional world.

With over 20 years in counseling, teaching and lecturing, I remain interested, curious and fascinated with people…always wanting to pass the information I learn onto others. Have you ever been to a professional of any kind — physician, lawyer, investment broker — and they talk to you using the terminology of their profession? I have and it's frustrating and often belittling. This book is for you. No jargon. Just plain language and good communication.

It's from a particular context or framework that we view ourselves and our world. From time to time, and especially if we are in distress, it becomes important to "reframe" our outlook on life so that we develop into happier and more productive people. Inside these pages you will find a reframing of our most common emotional entrapments into healthier emotions and ultimately joy, fun and fulfillment. Reframing gives you the advantage of looking at life differently, adding to the number of ways you can think about your experiences. This contributes to a greater psychological flexibility, a vast behavioral liberty and an immense emotional freedom.

Thinking and Feeling Intertwine

We have three primary colors. Psychologically speaking, we have three primary irrational concepts. They are:

Insistence

Amplifying Negatives

Assessments of Self-Worth

When we utilize these philosophies, we get ourselves upset or distressed. Depending on the combination and to what degrees each of these concepts are applied will largely give us the full spectrum and variation of emotional entrapments.

The three primary unhealthy emotional groups that other unhealthy emotions stem from are: depression, worry/anxiety and anger. These three areas are the focus of <u>Escaping Emotional Entrapment</u>. Those who experience other intense unhealthy emotions will also derive significant benefits from applying the concepts herein.

"It's About You!"

Jealousy, which is another strong unhealthy emotion, most often consists of anger masking significant amounts of anxiety (insecurities) and qualities of depression (self-pity). By reading and applying the principles in Escaping Emotional Entrapment, jealousy will minimize significantly though it was not discussed directly.

Each person is unique and has a unique relationship with his or her problem area. There are dozens of doorways that lead to the solution of any given emotional entrapment. You will find an abundance of examples and illustrations throughout; each designed to enter a different doorway.

To assist you in getting the most out of your reading time and to aid you in relating to the material, there is a "Section Preface" at the beginning of each section. This contains a short one-minute exercise to help you apply what you are reading to your personal life. Or it may provide you with ideas or thoughts to keep in mind when reading that section. It is important not only to read but to *read actively* — in other words, apply the material directly to you and your own life. In this way, you can make Escaping Emotional Entrapment more personal and meaningful to you.

Wisdom Never Goes Out of Style

Escaping Emotional Entrapment takes you through a series of stages. Each stage will help you develop the necessary skills to make the required change so that your life is far more enjoyable, productive and playful. Now aren't those the primary goals we have in life?

Throughout each chapter there are practical applications or chunks of information that you can instantly apply and practice to make your desired change long lasting or permanent. By showing you how to escape emotional entrapments by design — systematically — you can also learn how to solve or avoid them in the future. In this way, you can live with less emotional upset and to some degree, with fewer of life's difficulties.

"It's About You!"

Most practical problems (relationship conflict, death of a loved one, loss of a job, paying bills, etc.) are accompanied by an emotional problem, such as depression, anxiety or anger among others. These emotional problems actually make solving the practical problem more difficult.

Unfortunately, most people attempt to deal with the practical problem first, in an effort to feel better. This is often ineffective since many lifestyle problems are out of our control *or* are next to impossible to solve while we are emotionally entrapped. For example, it's difficult to increase or improve communication, trust and sexuality with a partner when you remain hurt and angry. By alleviating the emotional entrapment, you can relax and view the situation from a different perspective. Solving the practical lifestyle problem then becomes more probable. Everything is easier when seen from a position of strength. By the time you complete Escaping Emotional Entrapment you, ideally, will be well on your way to leading a happier lifestyle.

My goals in writing Escaping Emotional Entrapment are: to leave the reader with as few self-defeating behaviors and negative emotions as possible — particularly depression, anxiety and anger — and to increase productive behaviors and positive emotions, such as joy, fun and a sense of personal fulfillment. It is also important for the reader to develop an attitude of being self-aware as to ensure continued positive emotional freedom. It will become self-evident that there are other goals interlaced throughout these pages, such as self-acceptance, self-interest, self-direction, flexibility, tolerance, commitment, fun and fulfillment.

The Past is Silent

This book is rather uncommon in the array of self-help books because of what it is lacking. It will become apparent to anyone who has read a number of other self-help books that Escaping Emotional Entrapment focuses almost entirely on the present and the wonderful possibilities of the future. (The only exception is a forgiveness/self-acceptance exercise that puts your past to rest and starts off the first section.) What is lacking is any discussion about your childhood, your parents or how the past has treated you. The past is just that, past. What you make of today is what is important.

"Isn't the past important?"

Most definitely it is. But the past does not determine your future. You do!

You see, when a *significant* event in the past occurs we learn a lesson *and* develop an attitude from it. If the lesson or attitude is a good one (i.e., Although things went badly for me and I made mistakes, I can still like myself) then emotional health and growth follows. If the attitude is irrational or does not make logical sense (i.e., Because things went badly for me and I made mistakes, it means I'm a worthless, useless person) then emotional distress follows.

All therapies attempt to create an attitudinal change. If your attitudes have not changed at the end of therapy (or Escaping Emotional Entrapment for that matter), then the process was not successful. Instead of creating change by taking a detour through your past, my attempt is to create an attitudinal change by directly focusing on current attitudes that are causing distress and interfering with your happiness today.

If you are in emotional distress, your attitudes will be the primary source. When I talk of emotional distress I am referring to *sustained unhealthy negative emotions,* such as depression, anxiety, worry, guilt, and anger. These contrast sharply from healthy but negative emotions, such as sadness, remorse, concern, annoyance, irritation and frustration.

Unhealthy emotions help to keep you stuck, immobilized and you will feel trapped in them. By contrast, healthy negative emotions make their mark in your memory to help you learn to avoid the situation in the future; the discomfort created provides the impetus to make change. Healthy negative emotions are appropriate in intensity and duration to the problem, and when all is said and done, you have benefited and grown from the experience. It is self-evident that fun and fulfillment are healthy.

Escaping Emotional Entrapment starts with the foundation to all mental health: a generous dose of self-love and unconditional self-acceptance. The following section explains how emotions are created and how you can gain excellent control over them. There are three basic irrational areas of thinking that tend to produce emotional entrapments. Each area and how to free yourself from these mental entrapments will be discussed in detail in Sections III, IV and V. Sections VI through VIII will look at the three primary emotional entrapments — depression, worry/anxiety and anger that create the myriad of other emotional entrapments that are so commonplace. While Section IX focuses on making life fun and fulfilling, the last section "Bringing It All Together" is a review and quick reference guide to escaping emotional entrapments. There is a "how to" guide at the end of each section called "What do I do?" followed with "Section Highlights."

FUN-damentals of Emotional Freedom

I do not know if you have ever been to see a therapist. When I would go to conferences or symposiums, I found many therapists rather...stuffy. They were usually so serious. I know psychology and clients' issues are important, but being serious, solemn and somber helps no one to feel better.

Oscar Wilde once said that "Life is too important to be taken seriously." I believe he was right.

This is why after more than twenty years as a therapist, I have transformed my role to one of a "Personal Emotion Trainer": training individuals to gain excellent emotional control. It's my belief that psychology can do far better than just helping someone not to be depressed, not to experience anxiety or not to get angry. Psychology can be used to advance each individual's primary goal: to be happy and have a long, fun and fulfilling life.

The founder of the Humanistic movement of the 1970s — Abraham Maslow — believed that if you were going to study the human being, it was important to study the high achievers as well as those who struggle through life. It allows for a basis of comparison and provides a goal to aim for. Escaping Emotional Entrapment is designed to help you take the struggle out of your emotional life and at the same time to provide you with the tools to enhance and enrich your daily experience.

If I went to a therapist and she was not having more fun than me, I would question how much she has to teach me. With over two decades working as a therapist myself, I am acutely aware of how important it is to do the anti-depression or anti-anger work. What I have found is that people who are depressed are not playing and laughing enough. People who are angry are taking themselves and life far too seriously.

Remember that *importance* does not equal *seriousness*. Your vacations, I assume, are important to you, but God forbid that you treat them seriously. So I would invite you to read a light-heartedness into the most important words on the pages herein. Perform the section exercises with a playfulness and you will go much further.

Adults almost seem hesitant to be playful and most definitely do not treat "play" as a way of life. The philosopher Voltaire said,

> *"God is a comedian playing to an audience that's afraid to laugh."*

Do not be afraid to be childlike and to laugh at the absurdities of life. Do not be afraid to look inside and ask the difficult questions either. You will find the answers to be truly freeing and empowering.

Michelangelo said that in a mound of clay the statue of perfection already exists, he simply removes the clay that hides the masterpiece. Escaping Emotional Entrapment is about removing the emotional clay that hides a masterpiece: you.

You really are a masterpiece, unique and exceptional in many ways. Believe in yourself. Trust in yourself. And in the same vein as Socrates: Know yourself...there is no-thing and no one more important to know.

Daniel Rutley

"It's About You!"

Section I

Forget Me Not
I'm in love again!

Section Preface

Before reading further, take a moment of quiet time to complete this simple exercise:

Get yourself nice and comfortable. Now think back to when you were a child and you did something wrong or when someone got very upset with you. How old were you? What did you look like? How did you feel at that time? Keep this situation in mind.

Now close your eyes and go to a place, fictional or real, that is safe, warm and serene. Make yourself comfortable there. Look around. In the distance, notice a small child. Call this child over to you. This child is the younger you.

Sit with this child and explain that you are from his or her future and you've come back to say that everything is going to be all right; that you forgive this child for anything that happened and that this child is now safe and will remain that way. Compliment, praise and with emphasis, reassure this child that everything is going to turn out okay.

Do this right now for the next minute or so; then continue reading.

In the Beginning...

There is a historical and biological account for our deeply rooted desire to be loved or approved of. As we emerged from our primordial state, the desire for love or approval was a characteristic that would help ensure the survival of the individual. If you had the desire to *acquire* love or approval, you would be more sensitive to others and develop a greater social conscious. This would help you develop alliances that could be beneficial to your survival, and thus help you to pass along your genes.

In modern society, survival in order to pass along our genes seems like a moot issue, but our desire to love and be loved is as strong as ever. This emotion of love has driven men and women mad with desire, inspired paintings, songs and poetry, instigated wars and has been the impetus for many of the world's greatest achievements.

There are many advantages to being loved or approved of. If our neighbors like us, it makes living next to them more enjoyable. If your boss approves of you, then you have a greater likelihood of getting a raise. Others will help you, support you and provide you with friendship and comfort. Let's be honest: loving and being loved can feel wonderful and captivate our heart and mind in ways that few other emotions can, as expressed by Elizabeth Browning's Sonnets from the Portuguese:

> How do I love thee? Let me count the ways.
> I love thee to the depth and breadth and height
> My soul can reach, when feeling out of sight
> For the ends of Being and ideal Grace.

The vast majority of people seek out love to various degrees. Virtually all people are happier with it than without it. Although being loved has its emotional and practical benefits, why do some people seem to absolutely *need* to be loved, while others enjoy it when it arrives but don't particularly crave it? The answer to that question resides in one's ability to love one's self and have unconditional self-acceptance. And that's what this section is about.

Chapter 1

Loving is an Active Process

Periodically throughout this book, I will refer to unconditional positive regard and acceptance. Dr. Albert Ellis, founder of Rational Emotive Behavior Therapy, was one of the first to publicly promote the concept of unconditional positive regard in the 1950s. As long as this concept has been around, it is still not a staple in our attitudes. For the sake of clarity and good communication, I'd like to define what I mean by these terms.

> *Unconditional Positive Regard:* An attitude toward oneself or another that one deserves to be treated in a humane way and without malice or cruelty. While consequences to one's behavior may occur, the consequences are applied without malevolence or the desire to harm. The individual is deserving of the respect afforded to all human beings by virtue of being human.

A person is arrested for selling drugs. While you may disagree with his behavior, you maintain an unconditional positive regard for him, i.e., he deserves to be treated in a humane way.

> *Acceptance:* A rational philosophical position of accepting the "sinner and not the sin" — acknowledging the whole person while possibly disagreeing with the person's behavior. Similar to positive regard, the focus is on the individual and not the behavior — choosing to accept that all people are fallible.

While you may accept an individual and maintain unconditional positive regard for him, this is separate from your love for him. As an example, I may accept that Hitler was a human — a very disturbed human. It's hoped that as a civilized society, it does not lower itself to his standards and thus treats him with positive regard, humanly and without the malevolence that was so much of his character. With this said, I would choose not to love him.

Loving is an active process. It involves your thinking, feeling and behavior. It's time consuming.

Healthy intimate love advantages you. This is why your love for any individual may change dramatically whether or not her act of transgression impacts you or another. Let's say a friend of yours is having an affair. How much you may or may not choose to maintain your love for her may depend on whether or not she is having the affair with your spouse.

How much and even whether or not you choose to continue loving someone depends on a variety of factors that suggest there are limits or boundaries to healthy intimate loving. If so, what about unconditional love?

The Inappropriateness of Unconditional Love

The term "unconditional love" has two very separate meanings depending on the precision of the definition. The true meaning refers to exactly what the phrase says: one's love is *completely* without any conditions whatsoever. The other, more appropriate meaning implies unconditional positive regard, acceptance and an ongoing love with *few* exceptions.

The latter meaning consists of healthy limits or boundaries combined with a willingness to emotionally support, provide assistance or feel positively toward another with nonjudgmental acceptance of the person.

When I speak of unconditional love, I will use it in its strictest, most literal sense — unfortunately, many people attempt to live by this definition believing that achieving unconditional love is next to Godliness. When I speak of *unconditional love, unconditional positive regard and acceptance*, I will be using the definitions above.

There is a widespread belief in the concept of unconditional love. It is something that we have been taught is an ideal to strive for. Unconditional love on the surface sounds like a wonderful concept in theory. The concept is that you will love another without conditions, fully and completely, no matter what. Sounds wonderful when you're in love with that brown-eyed boy or that blue-eyed girl. How romantic. How giving. How foolish.

"Foolish? Why?"

Love for another person *had better* be with limits. This is not true with positive regard or acceptance. There is an old saying, "Good fences make good neighbors." The essence of this is that it's important that we all have definable boundaries of what we will and will not tolerate in our relationships *and* in all areas of our lives.

Treat me nicely, wonderfully, lovingly, considerately, respectfully and I'll love you. Treat me badly without tenderness, respect or consideration and I'm out of here…at least emotionally. Let's take a more extreme but very real example of an abused wife.

She walks into the hospital with broken bones or a black eye. The social worker there tries to console her, and after listening to this woman's many stories asks her, "Why don't you leave the guy?" "But I love him" is the woman's answer.

Love can be an incredibly powerful motivator. It's important to set limits of how you wish to be treated and to be crystal clear where those limits lie. If you are not, how will anyone else know? It's important to have clear boundaries as to what you want and what you will accept and will not accept.

Loving is *not* a passive act on your behalf. When you are at first *falling in love*, loving seems effortless — but it is not. It is an active process that can actually be energizing, but loving isn't passive and doesn't *just happen*. In a civilized society and with a healthy philosophy, all people deserve a sense of respect or positive regard as humans, but when it comes to you loving another, it is important that it be conditional.

If another person can treat you like a doormat and you bounce back behaving in loving and thoughtful ways, there is nothing for the other person to lose by treating you badly. I am not suggesting that you withdraw love or kindness at the first act of minor disrespect, but I believe there are limits and these limits need to be conveyed to others *if* you want others to respect those limits. You can convey the message: Treat me well and I will love you and treat you well. Treat me badly and I will withhold my love, and if necessary, I'm out of here.

Why would you continue to put energy into loving someone who is abusive to you — physically, emotionally, verbally, mentally? Why choose to love someone without setting limits? You would not give this advice to your child, your sibling or your best friend. Don't take it yourself.

When you tolerate bad behavior from another you directly, though unconsciously, send a message that it's okay to treat you that way. The other person — often without thought — obliges and continues to treat you badly. This is bad for them as they develop or reinforce a habit that will negatively impact on their life over time.

This is the message when one loves unconditionally: "It doesn't matter how you treat me, I will continue to show you love and kindness." This is an unhealthy position because if the other person treats you badly and you encourage that bad behavior by responding lovingly, this will hurt that person and you. A rule of thumb: behavior that is rewarded tends to repeat. Thus, it is important that bad behavior not be encouraged. The onus is on you to be treated in ways you like and not to reward others for bad behavior. If others don't respect your limits, then the onus is *still on you* to take action to make sure you *are* treated the way you like.

From an outside perspective, you would view someone who continues to adore his or her abuser as a form of unhealthy or "artificial" love *and* having a lack of respect for himself/herself. To put it bluntly, *unconditional* love is an immature, infantile and potentially dangerous concept. It amazes me how many psychologists, poets, songwriters have written about and promoted this idea. It is so prevalent in society that unless one thinks about it, this attitude toward love can go unchecked for a lifetime.

"But I will always love my child unconditionally."

For the vast majority of parent/child relationships, this is as close to true as possible. The limits and tolerance for your child's behavior is high. Partly because you, hopefully remain in a position of influence and authority over your child, regardless of his age. But realistically, unconditional love for your child had better not *truly* exist either. Setting personal limits as to what you will tolerate, is healthy for the both of you. It's important that you be a good model and let your child know you have limits. Let's take a rather extreme example simply to make this point.

If your child grows up, takes you down to the basement, ties you to the floor and tortures you for 10 years — my guess is that sometime over that 10 years your love for your child will diminish. The extremeness of this example illustrates that we all *really do* have limits. The question is, "Are your limits healthy ones?" Having boundaries is just a wise concept to adopt and an especially good one to model for our children.

Put the most energy into those areas and relationships that benefit you because you can't love everyone. Keep in mind that I'm not referring to a sense of "love of your fellow person" but a close, intimate, active form of love. So choose to passionately love those people that you *carefully* select who are closest to you and who treat you wonderfully...always making your limits clear.

The Appropriateness of Unconditional Love

There is one particular person I suggest that you passionately love, always treat superbly with a sense of acceptance, respect, compassion and without limits, *regardless* of his or her behavior. That person is YOU.

While it's important to apply conditions to loving other people, the one person that it's important to love unconditionally is you. As a culture we tend to do the opposite. We are much more forgiving of other people, but with ourselves, we are our own worst critic.

Here's a bit of a tongue-in-cheek example of how we can be our own worst critic. It was a "vanity card" that immediately followed a popular television sitcom: Chuck Lorre Productions #45

AN OPEN LETTER OF APOLOGY

Dear Me,

Over the years, I have resented you for not being athletic enough, brave enough, funny enough, smart enough, talented enough, handsome enough, rich enough, admired enough, educated enough, New York enough, out-going enough, quiet enough, old enough, young enough, loving enough and loved enough. I have demanded perfection from you and have found you wanting. The result of this obsession with perfection has been to make you terrified of failure and ridicule, angry at any and all obstacles, and finally, incapable of enjoying the bounty that was not only around you, but within you as well. Well, all that's about to change. From now on, I'm going to make every effort to love and accept you as you are. But since bad habits die hard, I'll start with something easy. From now on, you're old enough.

                    Affectionately,

                                     Me

One reason we tend to be so self-critical is because we only get to observe the behavior of other people, but we have much more information about ourselves. We know our own history intimately, our thoughts, feelings, motivations, hopes, fears and desires. Having all this information makes it effortless for us to be self-critical. With the lack of information about others, it's easy to see them more simplistically.

We tend to allow much greater leeway to others than ourselves. In the Bible it says, "Thou shalt love thy neighbor as thyself." If this was really true, most people would go and beat the hell out of their neighbor.

It's important to be more tolerant, forgiving and accepting of ourselves. Why? Because there's no logical or practical reason not to.

You see, if you don't like another's behavior, then you can get that person out of your life. There's no need to maintain relationships that drag you down, are unpleasant and don't advantage you in life. This is why you apply conditions to having them in your life. If you don't like the weather? Move. Don't like the government? Vote in another. Unhappy in your marriage? Divorce. Don't like your job? Get another. You can change or leave anyone or anything with sufficient creativity, thought, time and effort. If you don't like something, make a change.

The only thing you can't leave is you (barring suicide, which is not generally a good option because there are always ways of making tomorrow better). You are stuck with you. Like it or not. So, you might as well like it.

Imagine yourself in a small two-person pup tent. You are staying over night and all night long the other person is jabbering, "You did this wrong. You really messed up over there. You are a real screw up. You can't do anything right. Remember the time you...." Got the idea? By morning you'd want to kill the person. Most people live their life, to varying degrees, like they are living with a critical person in a two-person pup tent, day in and day out. Relentless! No wonder why emotional entrapments such as depression, stress, anxiety, worry and anger are so common.

When it comes to other people, unconditional love is a flawed concept. When it comes to ourselves, it's simply logical. If you can't get away from a situation, then it makes sense to learn to adapt to it. Learn to accept it and make it work for you. And, hopefully, you'll learn to enjoy it because you're going to be there a long time. This is true of lifers in prison.

If you were in a 6' by 9' prison cell with another person, and you were going to be there for the next 30 years, you would eventually find a way to adapt. Guaranteed. Would you find a way to adapt *and* be happy? Well, that's another question. If you're going to be there for 30 years, you might as well attempt to find a way to enjoy yourself. It would take a lot of mental gymnastics on your behalf, but you could do it!

Since you are born an imperfect human being, you might as well accept that and attempt to accept this condition of life, accepting your life, your "self" and enjoying your existence to the fullest. It just doesn't make sense not to.

The moral of this story is to accept and love yourself, completely and unconditionally. If you make mistakes, you can take responsibility for them, learn from them, rectify them and make amends. But do not at any time beat yourself up for them. Guilt, embarrassment and shame are the feelings most associated with self-denigration. As Richard Bach says in his book Illusions, "Live never to be ashamed if anything you do or say is published around the world..."

From a religious perspective, it seems unimaginable that God would create an imperfect being and then expect us to hate ourselves for being imperfect. When we criticize ourselves (and not just our behavior) we are criticizing God's creation. We all have a right to make mistakes, commit errors in judgement, act emotionally, illogically, irrationally and foolishly. We have a right to want what we want, to like what we like, to think what we think, to fantasize what we fantasize. We have a right to accept and love ourselves regardless of our behavior and regardless of whether or not others approve. We have a right to love ourselves without conditions. It's the right thing to do. It's the moral thing to do. Self-disdain will never give us positives that can't better be brought about by self-love.

Chapter 2

What Do You Need Love For?

We all enjoy the feelings of being loved by someone we care for. From almost our first breath, we seek love.

It's important that your parents love you when you are an infant — you could be in big trouble otherwise. Acquiring love and friendship from other children allowed you to develop social and interpersonal skills. As an adult, obtaining love and approval provides comfort, support, assistance and a whole array of advantages from sex with your partner to a promotion at work.

From our earliest days we have been bombarded by concepts of love and how much we need it, require it or desire it. Unfortunately, fostering "the need for love" in our children is something society does well. Television which accounts for much of our children's education, depicts commercials that strongly suggest, "Buy our products if you want to be loved and accepted. You are *not* good enough the way you are."

At a party, you have got to have that brand name beer, wear that brand name shirt and those designer jeans. You just simply aren't good enough unless you wear your hair in the latest style, use that 7-day deodorant, have a carcinoma tan and use the "extra brightening, take-the-enamel-right-off-your-teeth" toothpaste.

The message is really not all that subtle. The problem is that because it's so common and it's everywhere, we have come to ignore the perniciousness, the destructiveness, the insidiousness of the message: "You *need* others' love and acceptance. To get it, you *need* our products."

As children, we develop an understanding of the world by watching others. So many parents ooze out of every pore their *need* for love, that it is naturally transmitted to their children. "Mom and Dad have a *need* for love. It must be pretty important. I guess I must *need* it too." Kids watch parents get upset when they don't get what they want. Emotional entrapments like anger, anxiety, depression and jealousy are common and relate to people not getting the love they think they *need*. These messages are almost everywhere from movies, to dime-store novels to the so called "love songs."

It's been estimated that 87 percent of all songs are about love and relationships. Of these songs, 92 percent contain lyrics that express forms of unhealthy love or relationships. Listen to any popular love song and you are sure to hear lyrics that express the following ideas. (In parenthesis is the healthy equivalent.)

I can't live without you.
(I can live without you but greatly enjoy your company.)

You are my everything.
(I am my everything, but you enhance the quality of my life.)

Without you I'm nothing.
(I value me with or without you.)

I need your love.
(I want your love but don't require it.)

I can't be happy without your love.
(I can be happy without your love but prefer having it.)

I need you by my side.
(I would like you by my side.)

When you're sad, I am sad.
(I would like to support you when you are sad but
I will remain happy.)

Somehow we have developed an attitude that "I *need* your love and *can't* live without you," is romantic, instead of clingy, needy and simply unhealthy. It seems to me that if someone needs my love, I'm trapped. If I don't give them what they need, I get to play the bad guy.

Here is an example of a healthy and unconventionally romantic expression of love:

"I want you in my life. I don't *need* you but have found that you add quality and value in my life. You are the one I freely choose to be with. You intrigue me and have captured my heart. I love you and would invite you to join me as we travel through life. I will always be happy, but I would be happier if you would be by my side."

Would I feel miserable because she didn't *need* me or my love? Not in the least. This is an example of a healthy expression of love and, for an increasing number of people, a healthy expression of romance. Why? Because there is no compliment in having others *need* your love. It could have been anyone's love. You're just the fly who got caught in the web. They just think they *need* to be loved and you just happened by and were in the wrong place at the wrong time.

"But don't we all need love?"

When I am speaking of needing love, I am referring to adults and not children. There is an old, very poorly done study that concluded that if children don't get love they will die. This is a myth of the worst sort. What does tend to happen is the child grows up with all kinds of emotional, relational and social problems, but they do not die. For a child to grow up emotionally healthy, a display of love and caring combined with forms of physical love is nearly imperative. So when I speak of the "need for love" I am speaking with regards to an adult and NOT a child. Children are not capable of the rational organizational thought that allows an adult to have much greater emotional control.

The desperate need for love and acceptance is something that has been so ingrained in us from birth on, that it would be a rare person indeed that would *not* go into distress at some point if they received enough rejection. A *totally* healthy person would, for a time, feel sad, regretful, sorrowful and grieve the loss of the love that they deeply wanted. Realistically, even the healthiest of people of today would get into major distress at some point if their partner left them, their children hated them, their parents rejected them, their friends wouldn't talk to them, they got fired from their job, their church ostracized them *and* their dog wets on their leg. There is a line for almost all people, and when it is crossed, they will go into distress.

Your level of emotional health in this area is proportional to how much rejection or disappointment you can withstand without going into distress. You will likely feel sadness and sorrow — this is a healthy response to loss, but emotional entrapments like anxiety, anger, jealousy or depression are not.

If everyone you know rejected you today, and you were ostracized from society, would you avoid distress and remain in the healthy range of emotions? If not, you fall into 99.9% of all people.

So the question is begged, "Why do you *need* to be loved?"

1) We know that you don't need to be loved (as an adult remember) to be happy. Many people were happy before they met their partner and when their partner leaves, they fall into a deep depression thinking they will never be happy again. They were happy before meeting their partner, they can be happy again.

2) To feel good about yourself? Nope. Feeling good about yourself had better come from you and not someone else. If your self-love is dependent upon another, then it's not self-love but other-love. Hopefully, you loved your "self" and your existence before you met your partner, why not now?

3) To achieve in life? While you might at times require help from others to advance or accomplish certain tasks, it's their help that you require and not necessarily their love.

So why do you require love from others? The answer is that you don't. You may want it. You may desire it. It may feel wonderful to know that the person you love also loves you, but you don't *need* it. You won't die without it. While it may add quality and a certain fulfillment to your life, it is *not* a necessity.

Simply put, you need what you need but you don't need what you want. Being loved is a want, a desire, a preference, a joy to be sure, but it is not a need.

In fact, there are no emotional "goodies" to being loved. You know this one to be true if you have ever had someone love you that you did not like. The goodies only exist if you do the loving first. The real benefit is in the loving, not the *being loved*. The only people who go into great distress as a result of not being loved are those people who are not loving themselves adequately. Other people's love reassures them that they are okay. Other people's love helps them keep their deepest darkest secret at bay: that they really are worthless — but if someone loves them then maybe this isn't true.

What if I told you that a week ago I asked 10,000 people to love you today? Would anything change in your life? No. Having others love you gives you nothing of worth. It's when you love others that count. The golden rule of love could be: "Love unto others as you would have them love unto you." People who believe that they *need* love have a backwards variation of this golden rule: "If I love unto you, then you damn well *should* love unto me." The focus has changed and is now on them receiving love and not on them giving love.

The best way to *avoid* receiving love is to advertise that you, without a doubt, completely and totally need, must have and require love. No one needs, wants or desires a needy person in their life. *You* are responsible for giving *you* the love that you desire, *not* someone else. If you won't give love to you, why *should* anyone else?

So the solution is simple, treat yourself with all the love, caring and thoughtful tenderness that you would like to receive from others. Model for them how you wish to be treated by treating yourself that way first. Others may not always be around to give you love and since you will be, then you can always provide it yourself. (See page 38 for specific examples.)

*"Learn to love yourself
and you'll be loved forever."*

Chapter 3

Self-Interest vs Selfishness

There are many self-depreciating ideas that we have been raised with, such as "be humble," which is defined in *The American Heritage® Dictionary of the English Language* as: Marked by meekness or modesty in behavior, attitude, or spirit; low in rank, quality, or station; unpretentious or lowly.

Why is humility considered a good quality? Why aren't we allowed to speak with confidence about our achievements? Because we were taught that that would be arrogant or boastful. While it can be, it need not be. We tend to go to extremes. If you are not humble, you are conceited or bragging. But there is a respectful, healthy position that people can express.

Another concept of extremes we were taught was that you are either selfless or selfish. You either give and give and give or you make sure that you get the most that you can, independent of the other person. Again, there is a healthy place in between: that of self-interest.

The difference between self-interest and selfishness is that self-interest is thinking, feeling and behaving in ways that promote the realization of your goals without *unnecessarily* interfering with another's freedom to make decisions. When you are acting in a self-interested way, as opposed to a selfish way, you also consider the feelings, wants and desires of the other person. If you don't, it stands to reason that the other person will not compromise with you and your life suddenly becomes more difficult.

Take intimate relationships for example: Why would your partner stay with someone who doesn't consider their feelings? If one of your goals was to share your life with your chosen mate, it is in your best interest to be considerate of the other person's feelings, though not at the expense of your own feelings.

Selfishness, on the other hand, is expecting everything to go your way without compromise, co-operation or consideration of another's feelings or wants. Selfish people are doomed to a life of achieving their goals the hard way, ultimately getting less out of life than their self-interested counterparts.

If you respond to the question "Why do you go to work?" by saying, "To pay bills," I suggest that you may be lacking self-interest. This response implies that you work to keep your creditors in business. A self-interested person might reply, "To maintain my standard of living." While both achieve the same results — getting the bills paid, each is approaching the question from a different philosophical stance.

In respect to relationships, the husband may send his wife a dozen roses. Self-interested? Definitely! If his goal is to have a strong bonding relationship, it is to his benefit to "give" in order to achieve his goal. This helps to develop a win/win situation, where his partner derives benefits as does he. Conversely, it is to his wife's benefit to encourage such loving actions with a response that will be pleasing to him.

Behaving with love and kindness with *part of your motivation* being rooted in self-interest is not selfish but a mature attitude toward life. I am speaking generally and referring to any consistent giving, not charity or helping someone in momentary distress. You wouldn't keep working if you weren't receiving a paycheck, and while you might stay late without pay to help a co-worker, you wouldn't do it daily for years. You wouldn't tell your daughter to get into a relationship and give up her goals so her partner can get more out of life. Besides, if you're not interested in your own goals in life, why should anyone else be interested in your life for you?

To achieve greater happiness and more of what you want out of life, learn how to act and react to people and situations in a way that will enhance your chances of achieving a happy, co-operative, fulfilling life. The trick is to learn *self-interest* without selfishness.

One avenue to healthy self-interest is first to trust in yourself, to believe in yourself. It's wise to assume that you are a person with good intent. To assume anything less than this is senseless and will achieve nothing of worth. Accept yourself for who you are with all your strengths and weaknesses. When so inclined, attempt to change that which you don't like about yourself and enhance those qualities that you do like. Remember that you have a right to be yourself and to like yourself.

True self-interest is being able to take care of one's self without causing another harm in the process. This requires that one's beliefs all be congruent which is a near impossibility without much reflection and focused consideration.

Throughout the 1970s, the "me generation" thrived. I think that the ultimate message was lost and got confused with selfishness. Many people attempted to become more self-interested by taking charge and making decisions for themselves. This is good, but many looked no further than *their* decisions and *their* lives. Many disregarded the feelings of others and the simple courtesies that so often make human interaction so pleasant. By standing behind the translucent wall of selfishness, proclaiming it to be self-interest, many disregarded the impact their decisions would have on another.

Striving to get more out of life is a responsibility each of us have. But I quarrel with those people who achieve by trampling on others. To achieve is good. But to achieve when it costs another *unnecessarily* is morally questionable. "Narcissism, like selfishness, is an overcompensation for the basic lack of self-love," says Erich Fromm in Escape from Freedom. It would then stand to reason that social interest is derived from self-love.

Self-love (and therefore self-interest) is fused with social interest. The reason you may choose not to drive drunk is two fold: 1) you have a love for yourself and don't wish to negatively interfere with your health or future and 2) you don't wish to harm others. In fact, all self-interest contains social interest in as far as it promotes your interests and beliefs.

You may choose not to litter, not because it doesn't look good but because it doesn't promote the type of culture you would like to live in or because it will eventually create higher taxes. You also might get fined or it would model a type of behavior that you don't want others to emulate. Self-interest, by definition, includes social interest. Selfishness does not. Self-interest looks at short-term goals *and* long term goals. Selfishness is narrow in scope and thus most often interferes with the achievement of one's main long-term goal: happiness.

Whether you adopt the philosophy of self-interest for benevolent reasons or simply to advantage yourself, this concept benefits both you and society. The chart below shows a comparative separation between self-interest and selfishness.

SELF-INTEREST	SELFISHNESS
- my **wants** as starting points	- my "needs" as the end and all important goal
- thoughtful process	-impulsive reaction
- balancing act between reality and personal goals	- distortion of reality and childish insistence
- movement towards personal and spiritual growth	- regression inward to infantile egocentrism
- fused with social interest	- disconnected from social interest

We know that the "give, give, give" philosophy doesn't work, nor does the "take, take, take" philosophy. It's important, if we wish to have ethical relationships with others and ourselves, to be socially interested, considerate, kind, warm and compassionate of another person's wants, desires and interests. It's important to consider how our decisions will affect our intimate partners, our friends, our acquaintances and our society. Like the pebble dropped into the pond, the ripples of the water flow outward from self-interest to social interest.

Some people have been almost entirely other-oriented and give all they have to give to others. Some people have been almost entirely self-reliant, not trusting or allowing others into their lives to help. Founder of the Humanistic movement of the 1970s, Abraham Maslow, believed that the ideal state was of interdependence: a mutual give and take, a sharing, a trust. This requires a strong sense of self, emotional stability and the desire to risk intimate involvement.

Chapter 4

Doing Good Things Creates Good Feelings

It's important to understand that when we think and behave in loving ways, it helps to increase our own good feelings of loving. Remember what Leo Tolstoy said in <u>War and Peace</u>, "We do not love people so much for the good they have done us, as for the good we have done them." When we do good things for other people it encourages us to get our heads into a good place. This helps us to feel good and to be happy. This attitude and behavior of loving and giving becomes a win for us and for our partner/others.

In 1957 Leon Festinger, a psychologist and researcher, expressed a theory that involved *effort justification*. He believed that the harder one works toward a particular goal, the more one values that goal. It would not make sense to believe that: "I worked hard for X" and "X is worthless." In fact, research suggests an extension to this: when we perform difficult tasks for difficult people, we are likely to justify our actions the most.

Effort justification would help to explain parts of the previously mentioned battered wife scenario and helps us understand a bit more about loving and how to acquire higher levels of self-love. A far too common situation most of us have either seen, experienced or know someone who has, is when the alcoholic husband mistreats his wife. She is asked, "Why don't you leave him?" She says, "But I love him."

Though there are a variety of complexities here, "effort justification" plays a significant role. If the wife, through her noble efforts, is compliant and puts energy into giving gifts, being romantic and generally, catering to him, this will not necessarily help to increase *his* loving of her. It will, though, help *her* to be more loving of him. The more effort she puts into the relationship, the more she justifies that effort and the more she desires her goal: him. His treatment of her will not match her belief that *he is wonderful*. She, then, is likely to defend and justify his behavior:

"He's tired." "He's stressed at work." "He didn't mean it."

As her husband mistreats her, he needs to justify his behavior within himself. He is less likely to fault himself because self-esteem is resistant to change. Instead, he faults his wife by saying, "She deserves it because she came in late," or "She doesn't care," or "She just doesn't understand me" or some other rationalization. As he becomes more critical of her and her behavior, his love for her decreases, as his effort in the relationship decreases. As his praise of her diminishes and his criticism increases, she extends more effort to please him. Her love or desire for him, then, may escalate as it would not make sense to display so much effort for a "jerk," so he really must be a good person deep down. In short, this becomes a negative, self-feeding cycle.

It's possible that when a man, for example, says, "I'm not romantic because I'm not in love," it may actually be false. The reverse may be true; the reason to be giving, caring and romantic is to remain in love. Effort justification is important to understand in this area and a practical application becomes evident. Putting energy into a relationship, remaining flexible to new ideas (which again requires effort) and minimizing criticism would be a formula, in part, to remaining in love. It would then follow that it is equally important to have your mate respond to you in *effortful* ways, so that your mate will also remain in love with you. Remember, we tend to value that which we work hardest for.

Now that you understand the concept of effort justification, you can apply this to yourself. One of our great failings in life is that we tend to put others first. The kids. Work. Household tasks. The bills. Your spouse. Your friends. And if there is time – and we know for almost certainty there will not be – then you can have time for yourself.

If you are an average person in this respect, you put virtually everyone and everything before you. If you put so much effort into others and so little for you, what's the inherent message? You aren't worth it. Effort justification kicks in and you end up valuing the other areas of your life more so than valuing you.

The message is clear. To increase your self-love and to value your own existence more, put more energy into you, your wants and your desires. Do wonderful things for you. Treat you as you would treat a very dear friend. Treat you like you would a partner you were head-over-heels in love with. Savor your time with yourself and truly enjoy every minute that you get to spend with this wonderful person: you!

You Are Important

There is an old saying, "Pay more attention to the eye than to the ear." Talk is cheap. Pay attention to what people do, not what they say. If you could watch how other people act toward themselves throughout any given year, you would almost have to conclude that they had little value for their own happiness, goals or desires. They put themselves at the bottom of the list. If we apply the most energy to those areas that are the most important to us, why are we last on the list?

I once asked a client who was very self-depreciating, "Why do you buy presents?" She responded by saying that she buys presents for people she values most and who have the most meaning to her. She wants them to feel good and wants to show appreciation for having them in her life. She also stated that she tends to put the most thought and money into the gifts for these people.

I asked her what she bought for her husband at Christmas time. She told me she bought him a very expensive hutterite down pillow. When I asked her what she got herself, she named a cheap bargain basement sale type pillow. The message was clear as crystal. Some people tend to think that this is trivial. It's not! There is a statement, subconsciously or indirectly, we make to ourselves every time we pass up the opportunity to treat ourselves wonderfully: "I'm not worth it."

Imagine that you have twins. It's their birthday and you buy one a new bike and many other presents. You buy the other a pair of socks. While you say that you love them both equally, will the one who received the socks *feel* like you love them both equally? No. Of course not. Our behavior speaks volumes.

From the position of an outside observer just watching your behavior, we can, with reasonable accuracy, determine who's most important in your life. Does your behavior undoubtedly scream: YOU? If not, then it's time you rethink your behavior toward yourself.

I encourage you to have a quiet love affair with yourself. You don't have to stop people on the street and tell them that you love you. I'm not suggesting bragging or boasting. I am suggesting that you treat yourself with the interest and passion as you would a lover.

You Come First

There is a general rule for you to follow. It requires some good common sense, but with a bit of thought it will serve you well: "Put yourself and your happiness first and those most important to you a close second."

If you were flying in a commercial airliner you would notice the flight attendants going through their pre-flight routine showing you how the oxygen masks work. If there are children on board it's common for the attendant to explain that in the case of a depressurization, you are to apply the mask to yourself first and then to your child. Why? Because if you are awake and safe, then you are able to protect your child. Obviously, if you attempt to apply the mask to your child and you pass out, your child is less likely to be able to help you.

So, by making sure that *you* are safe, happy and healthy — you are better able to help your child. By placing yourself first, you model for your child some very important lessons in life. If I asked you what you want for your child, you would say things like: I want my child to be happy and self-reliant. I want my child to be kind and compassionate while attempting to achieve his/her goals. I don't want my child to sacrifice his/her happiness just so others can be happy.

These are common desires of most parents. How will your child develop a healthy attitude if you do not model it for her by putting yourself first? If you come second to your child, you teach your child a very unhealthy lesson of self-depreciation and subservience.

Now I am not suggesting that you do not bend over backwards for your child on occasion or show an immense amount of love and caring. If you notice your child is going to play on the highway and your favorite show is about to start, your focus turns to your child. Keep things in perspective. Remember what's important. Your child and other people in your life need to know that you value *your* time, *your* desires and *your* goals. You want to let them know you will consider their interests as well as your own, and you would like them to do the same. Let them know that you will not *continually* put your life on hold for anyone else. If you are happy and healthy, then you will be an excellent model of emotional and spiritual health for others.

*"Be passionate about sharing
your love with others."*

"Your greatest benefits come from loving...not being loved."

Chapter 5

How to Get the Love You Want

What if you aren't used to actively loving yourself? What if it doesn't come naturally? What if the feelings of self-love just aren't there? Then what?

In one sense, the phrase "fake it until you make it" applies to aspects of self-loving. Behave like you are in love, speak the words of love and the feelings will tend to follow. If you wait to feel the emotions before you act on them, you'll be waiting a long time. It's like the person who says that when she overcomes her fear of elevators then she'll get into an elevator. It doesn't work that way. First you get into the elevator then the fear will go (see Sections IV and VII for the concepts and strategies that will help you to minimize fears).

There is an unbelievably strong influence of our thoughts over our emotions. Therefore, the first step is to think the thoughts you'd be having if you were deeply in love, and apply them to you. The next step is to act in accordance with those thoughts. Act towards yourself the way you would act towards a dear, wonderful, loving friend. When you act lovingly in harmony with loving thoughts, then the emotions are inclined to follow and you feel more loving towards yourself. The trick is to combine both the thinking and the behavior. Don't just do one or the other, but practice both in order for the feelings to change.

If treating yourself wonderfully feels odd or unnatural, it's because it's new and not because it's wrong. After you practice being actively loving towards yourself, it will feel more comfortable. It's a simple process but one that you want to practice on a daily ongoing basis for the rest of your life. Can you think of anything more personally impactful than to treat yourself with lots of love and consideration each day?

Here are some thoughts you can **THINK** to reaffirm your love for yourself:

I love me. I am a wonderful person and deserve to be happy.

I can enjoy myself, although I make mistakes.

I can continue to love myself, even if others don't.

I can handle any situation because I'm strong.

I know that no matter what, I can always love me.

I have a right to love me regardless of the mistakes of my past.

Here are some things you can **DO** to reaffirm your love for yourself:

Buy yourself a gift, flowers or other tokens of appreciation just for being you.

Splurge on yourself like you might a friend from out-of-town.

Take extra time just for you to enjoy doing what pleases you most.

Get a massage. Have a great meal. Read that book you've been wanting to read.

Push off tasks for one day and make this day a "special day" just for you.

Relax. Slow down. Take a mini-vacation on the next long weekend.

The Guarantee of Getting
All the Love that You Desire

Getting love is like going shopping. If you go to the store looking for something specific and they don't have what you want, you think "Oh, darn" and go to the next store. If the next store still doesn't have what you want, you don't get upset or stop looking, you just move on. This is the attitude you want to adopt with getting love and approval.

Unfortunately, many people just will not give you the love, the praise or the approval that you desire in just the way you want it, when you would like it. They may give you love when you are busy, pre-occupied and too distracted to really appreciate it and not show it at other times when you would like more of it. How do you solve this problem?

Simple — give it to yourself. You know yourself better than anyone. You know just how you like to be treated, how much love, the style and the kind of love you desire. Instead of leaving this up to others to figure out, take charge and be responsible for giving it to yourself.

At first, most people feel awkward about treating themselves in a truly loving fashion. They have never done it before and it's a new concept. "Acting in a loving manner towards myself? How do I do that?"

You would do that almost the same way you would do it for another. Let's say you are planning to spend time alone this coming weekend. Start a few days ahead and literally plan for a wonderful weekend. Think about spending time with yourself in loving and exciting ways. It feels awkward at first because you have never done that before but that's all. It wouldn't be difficult if you were thinking about spending this time with someone you were really "hot" over. Just put "you" in that special place instead, and think the same type of thoughts.

Plan. Get excited. And go through the motions — mentally and behaviorally — until it becomes second nature to think and to do these things. It only feels awkward because it's new. Practice and it'll feel comfortable very soon.

Think about how you would like to be treated, how you would treat a dear friend or how you might romance a potential partner. Now do some version of that for yourself. They say, "practice makes perfect." This is one area where you want to spend time practicing every day for the rest of your life to be perfect.

The Root of Emotional Entrapments

Emotional entrapments — being *apparently* unable to escape an unhealthy emotional state — can be attributed to the lack of self-love or appreciation either in a big way or small way. Throughout the rest of this book we will deal with the emotional entrapments of depression, anxiety, worry and anger and look at how to escape them. For now, let's look at the difference between a self-loving person and a person lacking self-love.

For this illustration, I am going to use an "alternate world" example: Let's say you live in a house that you CANNOT leave. It's a large house with all the amenities and newest gadgets. It has fresh running water, filled refrigerators and freezers. The large cupboards are stocked, and there is a greenhouse attached providing all the fresh fruit and vegetables you could want.

A friend of yours comes to visit and she has two big bags of groceries in her arms for you as a gift. You might feel appreciative and say something like, "Thank you so much. This was so unnecessary as my cupboards are full. I'll put these groceries here on the counter top. Thank you for such a wonderful present. Can I get you something to eat or drink?"

While you don't require any groceries, you are appreciative of the thoughtfulness of her gift, and you invite her to join you in sharing your food. If she came over and didn't bring any food, that too is fine with you. You would still be happy to share your food with her as you have plenty.

But what would happen if your fresh water had turned murky, the refrigerator and freezer were empty, the greenhouse was nothing but dry dirt and your cupboards were empty, except for one can of sardines? At your request to bring food, your friend came over. But as she walked toward your house you noticed she didn't have anything with her. For you, this is of great importance. Your cupboards are bare and you're starting to feel a bit desperate.

When you open the door for her, you are likely to have one of two responses: 1) You will be gracious and invite her in and maybe share your last can of sardines. You want to be courteous to her in hopes that if you are kind that she will bring groceries tomorrow. 2) You might get angry with her as you feel that by her not bringing groceries as asked that she has in an indirect way threatened your survival. Let's face it, you can't get food without her help. You're getting tense and uptight. So you get irritable, angry and demanding, or you acquiesce, give in and "make nice." Either way, you also feel anxious and worry about how you are going to acquire more food.

You might know where I'm going with this. What if the food was symbolic of love? If your cupboards are filled with love, you have all the love (really self-love) that you require. When someone comes over to give you more love, that's wonderful, but not necessary. You are very appreciative of her gift of love and thank her. But you do not require it as you have looked after your own garden, and there is an abundance of fresh love waiting for you each day. You tend to your garden daily to ensure its health and thus the bountifulness of produce.

What if there was little love (or self-love) in those cupboards, no fresh love growing in that house of yours and everything was either dead or dying? How would you feel if your friend came over without the love you think you required? You would tend to, again, acquiesce, be overly pleasant and make nice. You want her to like you. To love you. To give you the approval you think you so desperately *need*. You don't take a firm stand in your opinions. You won't express opposing views. You'll tend to offer a lot of those little white lies in an attempt to gain favor. You won't be yourself. You'll be feeling weak and manipulated by circumstances.

The other possibility is that you may get irritable with her for not bringing over the love that you think you need. You'll get annoyed, attempt to control her, belittle her or be more critical of her. You may become more demanding, controlling or abusive as you feel that by her withholding love she has in some way threatened you, your happiness or your existence.

While there are other possible emotional reactions, these are the two most common entrapments for people who are lacking a good supply of self-love. The solution to breaking free of these emotional entrapments is to provide yourself with sufficient amounts of self-love so that you are not dependent on others providing love for you. If you focus on getting love from others, you will tend to remain anxious, knowing that they could always restrict their loving at anytime.

Here's a rundown on how to provide yourself with more self-love — do as much of this as possible daily:

1. Start with an assumption that you are a person worthy of love, happiness and fulfillment.

2. Talk to yourself in loving ways — never debase yourself in anyway ever!

3. Actively treat yourself as you would treat a very dear friend or lover.

4. On the whole and with few exceptions, put your short and long-term interests first.

5. Be clear in your mind what treatment you will and will not accept from others, and then *only* accept the treatment that meets *your* standards.

6. Never let yourself be treated badly. Treat yourself wonderfully, being an example to others on how you expect to be treated.

7. Splurge on yourself simply to convey the message that you love and appreciate you.

8. Never do anything to *unnecessarily* risk you or your happiness.

9. Put the happiness of those most important to you a close second to your happiness.

10. Actively pursue interests, hobbies and passions that are unique and fulfilling to you.

11. Find activities that produce an outcome you can see; build, create or plant something.

12. Do things to encourage the happiness and well-being of others; e.g., volunteer at a hospital, be a Big Brother or Big Sister, help a neighbor or friend, engage in random acts of kindness, surprise a family member with something special or something that is unique to them.

13. Verbally and physically express more love and affection (as appropriate) to those you care about -- gesture, hug, touch, caress, embrace, cuddle, kiss; express to others the importance of what they mean to you in your life.

14. Learn by listening *and* doing; develop new skills and activities throughout the year.

15. Eat healthfully and get plenty of exercise — it conveys a message of valuing your body.

16. Mentally, physically, spiritually and philosophically be congruent in loving yourself.

17. Do not let anyone or anything "steal" today from you. Make today the best day of your life...and plan for it to be that way!

18. Make time each day or each week that is "alone time." This is time to just be with you and enjoying your own company without the distractions of others, TV, reading or completing tasks (see "A Self-Love Exercise" page 46).

*"Treat yourself as you would
a dear friend...or better."*

"What do I do?"

1. Visualize or imagine how you would like to be treated, spoken to or touched. Throughout each day, do this for yourself.
2. Set limits. Say "No" or deal directly with anyone treating you in ways that you don't like. Make the other person aware of your boundaries then enforce them. Speak up and act directly and confidently. You have the right to be treated the way you want and without explanation.
3. When feeling needy of another's love or attention, let that be a signal that you are not loving yourself sufficiently. Redirect your focus and attention on doing loving things that will comfort you.
4. To increase self-love, make a list of things you'd like to do for you, your pleasure, your benefit, and work on that list daily.
5. Make a list of self-loving statements unique to you. Rehearse these affirmations until they are natural and a part of you.
6. Make a list of *special* activities and do one a week or a day: read a book, listen to your music, go for a walk, take a mini long-weekend vacation, join a club, get a massage, take quiet time for yourself, etc.
7. Give to others in a way you find pleasing and satisfying.
8. Express more love and affection; give and accept compliments readily.

SECTION HIGHLIGHTS

➤ Develop *unconditional positive regard* for all people including yourself.

➤ Acceptance is the first step to change – before change will occur, you had better accept that what is, is just that way.

➤ Develop acceptance by accepting the facts and then actively attempting to change that with which you disagree.

➤ Mature love for others is conditional on having others treat you within your limits and respecting your boundaries.

➢ Emotionally healthy people love themselves regardless of their own abilities, mistakes and limitations.

➢ Although you may highly desire love and approval for emotional *and* practical reasons, you DO NOT NEED it.

➢ Selfishness is acting in a way that attempts to benefit primarily oneself at the expense of others.

➢ Self-interest is fused with social interest and is considerate of others as well as one's self.

➢ Behave in good ways and the resulting feelings tend to be positive and healthy.

➢ Treat yourself as you would treat a good friend or better.

➢ Put yourself first and those important to you a close second.

Section Appendix: A Self-Love Exercise

Daily, for the next week, sit in front of a large mirror for at least 5 minutes. Nothing is to interrupt this time.

You are to assume that the person you see in the mirror is a completely separate person from you but has had an identical life. Same parents, experiences, feelings, trials and tribulations. Everything identical.

Now your responsibility is to talk to this person out loud and get her (or him) to absolutely feel wonderful about herself. "Warm her over" as if you were talking to your dearest friend. Do your best to show her forgiveness and understanding. Tell her how important she is to you. Express caring and convey her value to you. Do this with love, tenderness, caring and patience.

Section II

The Unintentional Entrapment

═══════════════════════════════════════

Section Preface

What events do you tend to get most upset about?

❏ *Your child staying out past curfew?*
❏ *Someone treating you disrespectfully?*
❏ *Not being appreciated or acknowledged?*
❏ *Your spouse not calling when coming home late?*
❏ *Arguments? Disagreements? Stubbornness?*
❏ *Being caught doing something wrong?*
❏ *Performing poorly on the golf course or while playing another sport?*
❏ *The death of a close relative or friend?*
❏ *Being lied to?*
❏ *Child abuse?*

Think about those areas that you tend to be most sensitive about. Some people will take their car getting stolen in stride while getting very upset about finding a scratch on their favorite CD. Each person is unique. What are your "emotionally sensitive" areas?

═══════════════════════════════════════

Growing up, we never formally learned about emotional control. We learned how to read and write. We learned geography and that the earth rotates around the sun in 365 ¼ days each year. At home we each learned to turn out the lights when leaving a room or to chew with our mouth closed and to say, "Excuse me" after burping.

Out of all the very important things we formally learned, no one ever taught us how to control our emotions. Our parents never had a heart-to-heart with us to teach the dynamics of emotional control. It didn't happen at home or anywhere else for that matter. Emotional control was not taught because no one knew how emotions could be controlled. Emotional control was not even considered.

Growing up, you were expected to learn the fundamentals of reading, writing and math, but no one told you how to control your emotions. You were just expected to know how, without ever being taught. That is what this section is about.

For most of us, our parents were more shocked by our errors in etiquette than those in logic. We grew up in such a way that the desire for social approval motivated our conduct more than the consideration of principles. Instead of teaching us to think for ourselves, most were taught to repeat the right answer without thought.

More time is spent thinking about where to go on vacation than will ever be given to our thinking. Really, how many people spend 10 minutes a day or even a year thinking about their thinking? This ability to think about one's thinking is crucial in controlling our emotions and will be the focus of this section. It is time to travel inwardly and to become acutely aware of our thinking process.

Our thinking and our emotions are integrally intertwined. As you discover how emotions develop, teach this to others. This will have the effect of helping you learn the lessons herein…as we best teach that which we most "need" to learn. This will also have two other benefits: 1) you will become aware of any areas that you don't fully understand and will bring you back to review these pages for enhanced clarity and 2) you help to provide others with an education that was so lacking in their upbringing and that will benefit them greatly.

Chapter 6

Good Student — Bad Lesson

What makes you the most upset? Who makes you the most angry? What worries you the most? Does your spouse make you jealous? Does the weather, your job, your relationship, inflation or taxes get you down or depressed?

How did you answer these questions? Did you site something outside of yourself like job loss, having your car stolen, your kids talking back to you, lying, your child's poor school grades, your partner flirting with another or being late? The list is as individual as you are. But if you answered any of the questions by citing something outside of yourself, you have made a serious thinking error that I would like to explain.

If you ask the average person why she is feeling down, angry or worried — she responds by telling you that something outside of herself is the cause. While this is untrue, it is what we as a society have come to believe. We are the cause of our emotions, not things outside of ourselves, with one exception. I will explain that exception in a moment.

You were a very good student of human behavior growing up. You learned a language or two, how to socially interact, be polite, read, write and do math. You came to learn what happens when you touch something hot and how sharp a knife can be. You were taught the subtleties of human interaction and possibly how to even tell an occasional joke. These are no small feats for a child. You were a good student.

Unfortunately, as a child you largely, though not completely, believed what you were told. Most of the things children challenge are the most obvious rules. The vast majority of the subtle or implied or unspoken lessons likely went unchallenged. Tell a child that she is a "bad girl" when she does something wrong, and she will learn that making mistakes defines her worth. While she will never explain it this way, and it is not the intended message, this will be the unspoken lesson learned. Didn't most of us hear this growing up? Didn't most of us have difficulties with feeling good about ourselves? While there are exceptions, most kids struggle with liking and accepting themselves.

You were a great student because one of the things you almost certainly learned from your parents — not to mention society, religion, school and your friends — is that *things could upset you*. You heard it or saw it daily. Your mother saw a spider and screamed. Someone stole the lawnmower and your father was furious. Your brother had an exam to write and he was anxious. You learned that situations and things outside of yourself have the power to *make you* feel guilty, angry, worried or anxious. By the end of this chapter, I hope to convince you that none of this is true. Not even one iota.

This lesson — that other people or things could upset you — was assumed and believed by virtually everyone. It was just passed on to you unconsciously and unintentionally. Believing that others can upset you puts the power over your emotions in the hands of others. This is something you never want to do. It will put you into a position of powerlessness over your own emotions and how you will feel at any given time. This unintentional lesson, that others have the power to create emotions inside of you and the resulting consequence of powerlessness and being controlled, is the foundation to emotional entrapment.

How We Came to Know What We Now Know

During the second quarter of the 1900s a group of researchers went to a four square block area in New York City called "Hell's Kitchen." In a 10-year time frame, 11 of the FBI's most wanted criminals came from Hell's Kitchen. The question was "What was causing so many extreme criminals to come from such a small area?"

So a study was launched. The conclusions were basically this: The severity of conditions, such as poverty, violence and crime (the stimuli), were the *cause* of these individuals becoming criminals (the response). The theory that would be a model for decades to come was known as the Stimulus-Response Theory (or S-R Theory).

The **S-R** Theory stated that there was a Stimulus (the environment of Hell's Kitchen) that produced a particular Response (the criminal behavior). This seems, at face value, to be exactly the way things work. There is a stimulus: a snake, and there is a response: fear and a scream. The person was okay before seeing the snake and now the person is frightened. It seems to make sense that the snake caused the fear.

The problem is that it *seems* to make sense, but it doesn't in reality. It's an illusion based on inaccurate thinking and faulty perceptions. Here is how they found the mistake.

After the S-R Theory report came out, it was scrutinized as is typical in good scientific research. A few questions arose that lead to more questions and eventually a new research study. The researchers went back into Hell's Kitchen and discovered that other individuals lived in virtually the same environment as the "most wanted FBI criminals" but they turned out to be upstanding citizens. If the environment (stimulus) is the same, how could it produce a different result (response)?

The second study spawned the basic structure that is predominately used today. It is the **S-O-R** Theory. There is a given Stimulus and depending on how the Organism (the human organism in this case) thinks about this stimulus a particular Response is produced.

Two children are playing in the park. Both children notice a snake out of the corner of their eyes. One child screams and runs, while the other child might be startled but then moves toward the snake inquisitively. Why the difference? Each child thinks about the experience differently.

There have been numerous models emulating the basic concept of the S-O-R theory. One of the most usable has been Dr. Albert Ellis' A-B-C theory where A is the Activating Event, B is the Belief System and C is the Consequence. For more information on this outstanding therapeutic model — call the Albert Ellis Institute for their current catalogue at: (212) 535-0822.

Emotional Genesis

A myriad of things can create your emotions and then cause them to change. Your thoughts, beliefs, concepts, philosophies, and attitudes are all in one category, are all internal, and are *largely* in your control. Notice that I said "largely in your control." That is because as human beings we do not have complete and absolute control over our thoughts.

We *can* develop excellent control, but it is not flawless. Simply said, just too many factors influence our thinking to be able to develop our thinking skills to the point that they are without error.

One general category that impacts on our emotions is our thinking. The other category consists of that which impacts us physically.

Anyone who believes that our emotions are *only* created by our thinking was never thrown into an ice-cold river. If I take a stick and beat you, guaranteed — you *will* have an emotional change. If you are ill, drugged or injured — you will have an emotional change. If there is a hormonal imbalance, there will be an emotional change. We know that anxiety for some has a genetic component as there appears to be one for general happiness. Fortunately, genetics does not mean we have no control, it just may mean we had better apply more energy into making the desired change.

"Is 'emotional reasoning' an oxymoron?"

Chapter 7

Logical Thinking vs Emotional Reasoning

At a logical, rational level it almost becomes simple to see that how you think about something determines how you will feel about it. At an emotional level it is a whole other experience.

We *can* think logically about our emotions and who is responsible for them. If I asked you, "Who owns, creates and is responsible for your own emotions?" virtually all people will assume accountability. But if I ask the question in a more relaxed natural way, "Who *makes you* angry?" most will not attend to their thinking.

"I'm angry because I'm *demanding* that Joe treat me fairly, even though he didn't. While I do not like his unfairness, *insisting* that Joe be different from who he is will just distress me. It's better that I acknowledge this quality about Joe and deal with him in an effective manner that advantages me, to actively make changes when I can and to stop insisting that Joe or the world be different from the way he or it is."

This is a far more accurate and sensible approach when answering the question of why you are upset. But who speaks like that? Almost nobody. Why? Because almost no one was taught to take self-responsibility for their own emotions. We tend to reason emotionally. It is almost like the emotions override the logic and because we feel it emotionally, it must be true in reality.

We have all been taught to say things like...

"He makes me angry."

Instead of correctly saying...

"**I made myself angry** about what he did by childishly *insisting* that he act in the way I *require* assuming that he has *no right* to be who he is."

We have all been taught to say things like...

"That worries me."

Instead of correctly saying...

"**I unnecessarily worried myself** by focusing on a potential negative, treating it like a *disaster* and thinking that *I could not handle it* if it did occur."

Or:

"She makes me jealous."

Instead of correctly saying...

"**I foolishly made myself jealous** by thinking in *insistent* and *controlling* ways and by *not* trusting in myself as a person."

Or:

"Getting fired really has depressed me."

Instead of correctly saying...

"**When I got fired, I made myself depressed** by *whining* and *complaining* that things are not going my way. I am feeling *sorry* for myself and *blaming* others or myself for my situation instead of assuming I will have a positive future and then actively doing something to ensure that happens."

Do not be fooled into thinking that this is *just* semantics. How you think dramatically impacts on your emotions. Thoughts tend to have somewhat of a "domino effect" — one thought triggers others. When you say, "John makes me angry" you are outwardly stating and implying that: 1) John is the cause of your anger; 2) you are a passive victim having no option but to get angry because John controls your emotions, not you; and 3) John has to change for you to not be angry.

If it wasn't so sad, it would almost be humorous to hear the 6-foot-4-inch man say to the judge as he stands there in court completely believing in what he's saying: "But your honor, it's not my fault I hit my wife. *She made me angry* by lying to me."

It's not that it is just easier to say, "My wife *makes* me angry," as this is a literal, genuine belief. But this statement is inaccurate — a lie faulting another for one's own emotional states.

How do we know that the person actually believes his wife *made him* angry? Who does he attempt to change in order to feel better, 1) his wife who does *not* control his emotions or 2) himself? Almost invariably his focus will be on changing his wife in order to feel better.

When we say, "The snake *scared* me," it is as if it was the snake's fault and that the snake did the scaring. Nothing could be further from the truth.

We tend to trust our emotions in a way that often overrides our calm, rational thoughts. I was sitting there. I was peaceful and calm — and a snake slithers by. I see it and I jump. Thus, *it scared* me, right? Wrong!

Let's say that you were sitting there with your eyes closed. The snake could continue on by and you would never *know* any difference. The emphasis here is on the "knowing," which is a mental process, a thinking process. Depending on what this process is will result in whether or not you will fear snakes. This is true regardless of what the emotion may be. Your thinking determines your emotional response and not the event, stimulus or situation.

Some people argue that if the snake was not there in the first place, then you would not be thinking those thoughts and thus you would not be scared. Therefore, the snake scares you. But you choose your thoughts. It is not the snake's responsibility, it is yours. You do it to you.

While it is true that if the snake was not there, you would not be frightened, the exact same situation could occur, and if you were a snake lover, your thoughts would be very different. When the thoughts are different then so will be your response. Your thoughts are based on you and not the circumstance. Thus, your emotions are based on you and are your responsibility not anyone else's.

You Are In Control

It's very good that we are the creators of our own emotions. That way *we* are in control. Some years ago, I had a client that was telling me about how the events in her life were getting her down and depressed. I leaned towards her and gently pointed out, "Do you realize that you are the cause of your depression and your circumstances?" She said, "That's so depressing."

No. That's great! If we create our own emotional entrapments, such as depression, anger, anxiety and worry, then we have the power to free ourselves. We no longer need to rely on the whims of the world to change so we can feel better.

Do not misunderstand me. I am not saying that you *should not* feel depressed or angry. What I am saying is that *you are the cause* of these emotions. Before we can make a change it is important to acknowledge the reality first.

Some people believe that it's only *normal* or *natural* to get depressed, angry or anxious from time to time. Be careful of these two terms.

"Normal" simply means that it falls within the norm or the average. It is normal for people to catch a cold once every year or two. Some people fall outside the norm and get two or three colds a year while others go five or 10 years without a cold. Just because something is normal, does not make it healthy. It may be normal to get depressed when you lose your job, but it is neither healthy nor functional.

"Natural" refers to something that comes easily or is well practiced. A person may be a natural athlete — meaning she takes to athletics more readily than most. If you practice your serve in tennis enough, it may become natural to put a topspin on the ball. Natural in this case means almost reflexive. Saying that getting angry with your child for stealing is natural simply means that that particular emotional response is well practiced or reflexive and is no indication of appropriateness or emotional health.

Many people believe that it is "easier" to avoid change, emotional responsibility and personal growth. While this is clearly untrue, they attempt to convince themselves that change is impossible for them. Don't be one of these people. The overall cost is too high and the rewards are too grand to forfeit.

Be careful of using some very old rationalizations to stay the way you are and to convince yourself that emotional control is just outside your grasp:

You can't teach an old dog new tricks. (Even old dogs learn.)

A leopard can't change its spots. (You are not a leopard.)

That is my personality. (As if it can't be changed.)

I was born this way. (No you were not.)

I just can't help it. (Sure you can.)

That is the way I am. (You create each day who you are.)

I am too old to change. (Come on, who are you kidding?)

I have always been this way. (You are constantly changing.)

Old habits die hard. (Old habits can die out from lack of use.)

God made me this way. (Now it's up to you to change.)

It is my mother's/father's fault. (No it is NOT!)

But I came from a dysfunctional family. (So? Change now.)

I was abused as a child. (Then focus on today and tomorrow.)

It was meant to be. (Only by you, based on *your* thinking.)

All of these state outright or imply that change is impossible or an unrealistic expectation. It is a way of avoiding personal responsibility for one's emotions, while often faulting others.

So far, we are just assigning responsibility for who creates your emotions. Not good. Not bad. Just who is responsible. And the person responsible is YOU. Remember that I am referring to an adult and not a small child. Children do not have the capabilities to think with the same control or in the same way as an adult, and thus can have their emotions manipulated easily in a way that is outside of their control. As an adult, your thinking will be the primary source of your emotions. Besides, it is the area that you have the most control over, so why not focus on what you can control the most?

"Believe that life is worth living, and your belief will help create the fact."
William James, Psychologist

Chapter 8

How We Create Our Emotions

Now that you understand that *you are responsible for creating all of your own emotions*, let's look at a simplified explanation of the process of how these emotions are generated. I will refer to this 3-Stage Theory of Emotions explanation within future chapters, and as you will see, it is easy to understand and to apply.

Stage 1

Let us say that there occurs a significant event in your life. We will call this the "Trigger Event" because the event triggers or initiates a series of subsequent actions. It is NOT THE CAUSE of your emotions, but it may trigger a habitual, chronic or embedded belief system. The trigger event is substantial, at least to you. It is the event that you are emotional about. If the event was that your 15-year-old son kept tossing his sneakers into the middle of the living room instead of putting them away, this would be the trigger event.

Stage 2

The next stage is your "Belief System." The belief system encompasses your beliefs, values, morals, ethics, standards — your ideology. These are arranged, usually without conscious thought or consideration, in an order of strength and priority. You may believe that "it is better to give than to receive" and that "charity starts at home." These two seemingly contradictory beliefs will take a different priority depending on circumstance, as well as other relevant beliefs you may hold that relate to motivation.

The belief system is more than simple thoughts; it is what you *believe* to be true. I can *think* that the world will explode tomorrow; but you will not see my behavior or emotions change because I do not *believe* it is really going to happen. If I truly *believed* it was going to occur, then you would notice a reaction. There is a vast difference between superficially *thinking* something might be true and really deep down in your gut *believing* it to be true.

Self-limiting beliefs and beliefs that negatively impact are likely to be part of your belief system as are positive, healthy, self-enhancing beliefs. The unique combination and relative strength of your negative and positive beliefs will determine your level of emotional health.

THE 3-STAGE THEORY OF EMOTIONS

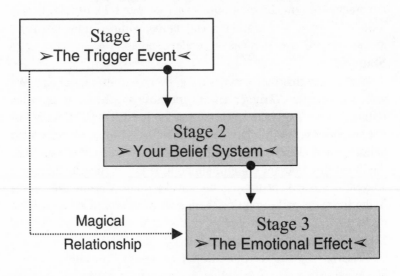

Stage 3

The "Emotional Effect" is the third step in this progression. As an example: When your teenager leaves his shoes out (the trigger event) you consult your belief system, and from there you start having certain thoughts. If your thoughts are reasonable, logical and rational, then you will experience an emotional effect that is appropriate and healthy. If your thoughts are extreme, demanding or irrational, then your emotions will be negative, excessive and unhealthy.

The vast majority of people still make a direct association between the trigger event and the emotional effect. Believing that the events in life are the *cause* of emotions creates an erroneous relationship that doesn't exist in reality and is a form of "magical thinking." This belief is developed because, on the surface, that's the way it looks.

When you were a child, you used a physical model of the world. If you fell down and scratched your knee, it hurt and you would say that cutting your knee hurt you. This is correct. If I took a knife and stuck it into your arm, you would say that I hurt you. This too is correct. This is the "trigger event" to "emotional effect" connection. It works in the physical world only.

Unfortunately, we use this physical model of the world and attempt to apply it to the emotional world, but it just will not fit. If I walk over to you and call you a string of vile names, you might get upset or you might just look at me as if I am crazy. Your response, irrespective of what it may be, will be determined by your attitudes, mind-set or belief system. People often believe that their distress is a direct cause of being called a name, or whatever the transgression may be. It's not! It is how you *think* about the transgression that creates your feelings.

It does not matter what the situation is; if it is not physical, then it is your thinking that creates your emotions. If you came home and found your wife in bed with another woman. You might think, "How awful" and you would be upset. Or, you might think, "Great! A fantasy come true." Depending on what your thoughts are, you could have very different emotional reactions.

If you experience a high state of emotional arousal, such as rage or a so-called anxiety attack, your ability to control your thoughts will diminish greatly at that point in time. Now the emotions are being driven by a physical reaction, such as adrenaline. When this happens taking medication or removing yourself from the situation and taking time to calm down is probably your best option. Then you will be able to think more clearly and further maintain better emotional control.

Appropriately Emotional — Not Unemotional

Emotional control does not mean unemotional. Emotions are the spice of your existence. They give variety and flavor to life. The last thing you want to do is become like Mr. Spock on Star Trek.

You do not want to "flat-line" your emotions, just keep them within a healthy range.

As there are three primary colors, there are three primary healthy negative emotional groupings:

Sadness

Concern

Frustration

The above healthy, but negative emotions can become unhealthy and be expressed as:

Depression

Worry / Anxiety

Anger / Rage

Some people have defended these unhealthy emotions, like anger, by saying, "But anger is good. It gets people to instigate change, to do things."

This is true. Anger can be motivating. It is definitely not boring. It gets the heart pounding. But here is the real issue: Anger is simply an exaggeration of frustration. Everything positive that anger gives you actually comes from the frustration. The intense frustration gets you off your chair to protest or to take charge or to write that letter or to voice your opinion or take a stand against injustice. Anger will also intimidate others or get them to war against you. Anger will get you to unnecessarily act aggressively, help to create an adversary, raise your blood pressure, aggravate ulcers and asthma, and give you an early coronary — all in one fell swoop.

Inflate sadness and you will get depression. Exaggerate concern and you will get worry or anxiety. Amplify the emotion of frustration and you will get anger or rage. The few positives that occasionally occur when emotions are intensified, comes from the underlying and embedded sadness, concern and frustration, and not from the depression, anxiety or anger. The unhealthy emotions tend to keep you stuck, rigid and thus emotionally entrapped.

Emotional control is about developing the ability to determine, with a good degree of certainty, how you will choose to feel. Healthy emotions promote psychological flexibility, better relationships, enhanced functionality, wiser decision making and greater creativity (your source of solving problems).

Unhealthy emotions help to keep you stuck in your own dysfunction, which will lead to more distress, less creativity, poor decisions and relationships that will help to reinforce and support your own special brand of craziness.

The Illusion of Emotional Control

It is guaranteed that you know people who *appear* to have great emotional control. They are calm, confident and *seem* usually happy regardless of the circumstances, or so they present themselves.

We all have presented ourselves in a certain way that is untrue or artificial for some practical or political reason. You're with a small child and appear calm when seeing that spider, while inside you want to scream. Or, you might be incensed at something your spouse said to you while at a party, but you continue to smile so as not to interfere with the flow of the event. This is not emotional control. This is emotionally hiding. It is a cover-up. It is a self-presentation lie put on for some particular reason.

There may be times that this ability to hide your emotions may be appropriate, such as at work. While the rule of thumb is to be emotionally honest — in other words, express yourself the way you feel — there are times when covering may be useful; but this is NOT emotional control!

Emotional control is one's ability to control, navigate or consciously decide on which particular emotions one will have. While I have never met anyone with perfect emotional control, all of us have varying degrees of some control.

We have all chosen, very consciously, not to think about certain things in order to maintain or alter our emotions. We made an attempt at focusing on the positive to change our feelings. These are examples of our attempts to gain emotional control. Now I am going to show you how it is really done.

"Intellect is lame without emotion.
Emotion is blind without intellect."

The Unintentional Entrapment

Chapter 9

How to Control Our Emotions

There are a series of steps that help us to develop the skill of controlling our emotions that were never taught to us as children. Come back to this chapter repeatedly to refresh your memory of these simple steps. Please do not confuse simplicity with ease. These steps are simple (not complicated), but they are not easy. It is not easy to change a lifetime of learning, beliefs and one's ideology in a single reading of one book. <u>This will take a lifetime of practice.</u>

1.   Become aware of your thinking.

If your thoughts are the primary cause of your emotions, and you are not aware of your thinking, how will you ever hope to gain control over your emotions? It is mandatory that you pay attention to your thoughts *if* you want to develop emotional control.

You will notice that you think in sentences. If you are angry that your spouse did not call when coming home late, what is causing your anger is the way you are thinking about that event. You are actually saying things to yourself inside your head and these things are in sentence form.

Make sure you are aware of the complete sentence and not just stating a thought in an abbreviated form such as:

"He didn't call again."

The complete thought really is:

"I really hate it when John doesn't call. That is so rude. He should be more considerate. I just cannot stand it when he treats me as if my time does not count. That is the 5th time this month. He is such a jerk sometimes, and I am a jerk for putting up with it. It's just appalling to sit here all by myself watching this food get cold."

The Unintentional Entrapment

When you expand on the abbreviated thought, it will be easier to find the areas of your thinking that are causing your distress. If you are not sure of your entire thought, take a guess at what it might be and see if it *feels* right. Your feelings or levels of distress will tend to match the words you use.

If someone was in a fit of rage and his/her thoughts were, "Oh, shucks. I really don't like that." This thought does not match with the degree of emotion expressed. If the thought was more extreme like, "That bastard shouldn't have done that. He knows better and is just a hateful son-of-a-bitch that deserves to roast in Hell." These thoughts would tend to bring on the emotion of rage, not "Oh, shucks."

If you pay close attention to your thinking, you will notice that there are usually two components to those thoughts that inflict emotional pain on you. One part is clearly rational, logical and makes complete sense. The logical side is usually that you do not like something, find something unpleasant, unjust or wrong. This may all be true, but it is not what gets you bouncing off walls emotionally.

The other element of your thinking will be illogical, irrational; it doesn't make sense and is basically a lie that is out of proportion and a distortion of the truth. It is this part of the sentence that is the root cause of your distress and will be covered in the next three sections.

When someone says: "I failed my exam, and that proves I'm a total failure," the first statement — that he failed — is true, but is not the *cause* of anger or depression. The first portion of the sentence might be the source of disappointment or sadness though. The second part is the irrational, "nutty" conclusion: "I'm a total failure." While it is true he failed, he took an unreasonable and untenable leap in logic: that failure at some task makes someone a failure as a person. The dynamics in this type of example are more fully covered in the section "Worth Entrapment." Suffice it to say that the part of the sentiment that distresses people is the one that will not make logical sense. See if you can find the irrational elements of your thinking before you get to the following sections where they will be fully explained.

The Unintentional Entrapment

2.   Learn what types of thinking get you upset.

The next three sections focus on the three types of irrational belief systems that ultimately get us into distress. Most areas of emotional entrapment utilize all three flawed belief systems. Rarely does a person get distressed and use one type exclusively. Rational Emotive Behavior Therapy along with other cognitive therapies identifies three types of irrational or unsound belief systems:

1. Insistence — believing that things *should* be the way we *want* them to be
2. Amplifying Negatives — taking a negative event and then exaggerating it
3. Assessment of Worth — believing that one's behaviors equal one's worth

Each type of irrational belief system will be examined and scrutinized in detail. I will show you exactly how and why subscribing to these types of beliefs will create your distress and can potentially keep you emotionally entrapped for a lifetime. Minimizing these three areas in your thinking will exponentially improve the quality of your emotional life.

3.   Dispute, argue and refuse to believe in irrational thinking.

Mindlessly repeating positive affirmations will not necessarily change a lifelong tradition of irrational beliefs. Simply acknowledging that a belief is irrational, nonsensical or foolish does not make it suddenly disappear.

Longstanding beliefs tend to be deeply rooted and intertwined with many core philosophies and understandings of ourselves and our world. Uprooting the nucleus of an irrational belief system requires, for most of us, consistent and deliberate effort until new, healthier replacement beliefs take hold.

Let's say that I have a half glass of sour milk, which represents our irrational beliefs and a half glass of fresh milk, our rational sensible beliefs. If I pour the fresh milk into the sour milk, would you then drink it? Probably not. Why? Because it would still taste sour.

If we placed the half glass of sour milk in the bottom of an empty swimming pool and filled the pool with fresh milk, would you drink from the pool of milk? "Probably." Why? Because the large amount of fresh milk will sufficiently dilute the sour milk to the extent that it will still taste fresh.

But by the next day, that pool of fresh milk will have started to go sour. Why so quickly? Because it had been "infected" with sour milk. This is also true of our thoughts and beliefs.

Simple affirmations do not work well all by themselves, as long as there are still active irrational beliefs operating. If you flood your mind with positive affirmations, they will *appear* to work for a short time, but then the irrational beliefs will "infect" these affirmations, and they soon become ineffective.

Debating, arguing against and discarding these irrational belief systems is the key to long-term escape from emotional entrapments.

4.   Adopt more realistic and healthier rational beliefs.

When dismantling irrational beliefs or assumptions, it is equally important to fill the void with beliefs that are functional, valuable, sensible, and help to promote the healthy emotions you desire. The next three sections will provide you with rational replacement beliefs for the irrational ones.

Practicing these new beliefs until they become reflexive, natural and automatic is important, especially in times of stress. When stressed, hurried or pressured, we tend to lean on those beliefs that are most readily available or accessible to us. Unfortunately, these beliefs are often the older, deeply ingrained irrational beliefs. This is why it is so important to place concerted attention on the development of the newer, healthier beliefs, so when problems occur you will naturally and effortlessly utilize them without conscious thought.

5.   Behave in accordance with these new rational beliefs.

Changing thoughts alone tends to be a lame approach in escaping emotional entrapments. The goal is to challenge, disrupt and discard the old belief and replace it with a new, healthier belief while acting in the way that you would ideally like to be.

If a person was afraid of getting into an elevator, it would be important for him to challenge those beliefs that are causing his fears, replace them with more appropriate beliefs *and* make attempts at getting into the elevator.

When the thinking and the behavior match — then the feelings change. Buddha stated this 2,500 years ago. He basically said that if you want to make a change, think in the way you would be thinking if you had already made that change; behave in the manner that you would be behaving if you had already made that change; and focus on those feelings that you would have if you had already made that change. When the thoughts, behavior and feelings have changed, you will be the person you want to be.

6.   Practice with duration, intensity and frequency.

To empower yourself to make emotional change, it is important to practice being the way you would like to be as often and as consistently as possible. When you challenge an irrational belief system or attempt to behave in new ways, do this for increasingly long periods of time, putting emphasis and focus on this new way and then do it frequently.

There is not much benefit in attempting to make a change if 1) the attempt only lasts one minute at a time. Little progress will occur if 2) you just pay "lip service" in your attempts to make a change. And, if 3) you only attempt to make a change one day a month, progress is likely to be non-existent.

Therefore, the three qualities to creating change are:

1) Duration: length of time focused on making a change
2) Intensity: the degree and completeness of focus of attention on making a change
3) Frequency: how often you focus on making a change

Duration, intensity and frequency will help you to determine your degree of progress in controlling your emotions. If, when you get angry, you only stay angry for 10 minutes instead of two hours, then you know you have made progress — the duration is less. If you yell instead of beating someone to a pulp, it looks like you are progressing — the intensity has lessened. If you only get angry once a month instead of three times a day, you are doing better — the frequency has lessened.

These six steps above on "how to change our emotions" are the foundation to making long-lasting or permanent change. They will be emphasized in the chapters that follow. Practice discarding old, ineffective belief systems in favor of newer, healthier beliefs, and then act accordingly. It will not be long until you will escape the emotional entrapments that have bound you.

> *"He who learns to fly must first*
> *learn to stand and walk;*
> *one cannot fly to fly."*
> Friedrich Wilhelm Nietzsche

Chapter 10

The First Step to Change

The first step in the process of escaping emotional entrapments (outlined in the previous chapter) is to become acutely aware of your thinking. In doing so you can also learn to accept responsibility for who is making you upset.

Attempt to notice what you are thinking generally throughout the day. Attempt to think back to what your thoughts were *right before* you became aware of your distress. These thoughts are likely the cause of your distress. Notice your thoughts *at the time* you are feeling some form of emotional distress. If something bad happens to you during the day and you find yourself getting down, angry or worried, notice the thoughts you use. Be specific. What were you specifically thinking — word for word?

As I mentioned earlier, if your thoughts largely create your emotions, and you are unaware of your thoughts, how are you ever going to gain emotional control? So, place a lot of emphasis on your thinking and you'll soon notice that you do talk to yourself — silently — in your head *and* in sentence form. Being aware of these thoughts/sentences will help you apply and make use of the information in the following chapters.

Remember that by altering your thinking, you can gain better emotional control and as such, you will tend to make better decisions. There is this domino effect. Stronger, happier people tend to make better decisions than distressed people. As psychologist William James said in the early 1900s:

"Man can alter his life by altering his thinking."

If you said, "John really ticked me off," change it to "I really ticked myself off when John did that." Attempt to speak the truth. Take responsibility for your emotions. Practice being accountable verbally. This will be awkward at first but keep it up until it becomes natural.

Comments that express that
I'm <u>NOT</u> responsible for my emotions...

He made me angry.

When she stays out late, it worries me.

The weather is so depressing.

Mom makes me feel so guilty.

Exams always make me anxious.

He hurt my feelings by lying.

Driving at night scares me.

She makes me jealous when she flirts.

Snakes and spiders scare me.

Comments that express that
I AM responsible for my emotions...

I made myself angry.

I worry myself when she stays out late.

I make myself depressed with this weather.

I make myself so guilty when Mom says...

I make myself anxious during exam time.

When he lied, I got myself all hurt over that.

I make myself scared when I drive at night.

When she flirts, I make myself jealous.

I scare myself when I see snakes and spiders.

The Unintentional Entrapment

At the start, it may feel awkward to change your speech. It may feel unnatural. This feeling will disappear quickly as you develop this new habit of speaking in an emotionally responsible manner. It only feels awkward because it is new to you. So practice until it becomes natural and reflexive. Make it almost a game. Have fun with it. Catch yourself then correct yourself right away — on the spot! As an example:

"Mary really got me angry when she…well…umm, I guess…I really got myself angry when she stood me up."

Catch yourself midstream if you have to, like in the above example, but catch yourself as soon as possible. The apparent hesitation in your speech will disappear, and it will become one unbroken flowing, *truthful* sentence.

Many people in an attempt to speak truthfully will say: "I let John upset me." It is a good try but you cannot "let" John upset you because John does not have the power to upset you in the first place. You upset you. Now, you may not like what John did, and that is fair and true. But no matter what he did, he doesn't have the power to alter your brain chemistry and create a neuronal path way in your brain resulting in what we call emotions. He doesn't have that power. Only you do. So, you didn't *let* him upset you…you *made* it happen.

Also, be careful of saying, "I let myself get upset." While this may be true (you did let yourself get upset) it's a passive style of expressing yourself. Take charge and be responsible using first person active language: "I MADE myself angry about what John did!" If you speak as though you *let it* happen, it is as though you were passively sitting there and took no action to stop it.

The development of your emotions is not a passive state. You, consciously or unconsciously, actively create your emotions. This is an active process, not a passive one, so speak confidently and assertively stating the truth of who causes your emotions.

You may notice that in the beginning it is difficult to be aware of your thoughts. You'll say, "My lack of finances is really getting me down" and not realize until much later that you faulted your financial situation as the cause of your depressed emotions. When this happens and you become aware of it, correct yourself immediately. Give yourself a firm talking to:

> "I told Chris this morning that my finances are getting me down, but that's not true. My finances do not have power over my emotions, I do! I am getting myself frustrated and depressed over my finances. The responsibility rests on my shoulders for my emotions. While I do not like being financially strapped, my emotions are created by my thinking and not by my bank account. I am making myself down by how I think about my finances and as I learn to think differently, I will feel differently."

When you correct yourself in this manner, you tend to apply 1) duration — you correct yourself and really *take the time* to think it through; and 2) intensity — you emphasize and focus on making that correction in your thinking so it is less likely to occur next time. Then practice, practice, and practice, which is 3) frequency.

Correct yourself immediately whenever you can and soon you won't be catching yourself after-the-fact. Within a short time, your speech will begin to flow more naturally and fluidly. So, when someone asks you how your day was, you can honestly take responsibility for your emotions: "I had a good day over all but *I got myself really angry* when I came out of the store and noticed that someone had sideswiped my car." If you diligently apply the information within this book, if someone sideswipes your car — while you will not like it — you can remain emotionally healthy feeling the frustration but not the anger *and* still have a good day.

Serious Consequences for Our Children

Speaking in a manner which expresses that *you* are the cause of your emotions is not only healthy, good and true for you emotionally, but also has many other benefits. When you speak in terms of you creating your own emotions, others tend not to get defensive, which allows them to listen better, communicate more effectively and be more empathetic to *your* feelings and situation.

There are a number of reasons it is so difficult to change our speech to emotional self-responsibility.

1) We are usually unaware of our thinking process. We do not think out a sentence and then speak it. Our speech is developed automatically at a subconscious level based on our experiences and learning.
2) Simple habit. We have always spoken like that.
3) We were unaware that we weren't taking responsibility for our emotions, so we never attempted to change.
4) We are reinforced to speak that way because everyone else does. We simply emulate what others do.

This last point is very problematic for our children. If you speak to your child saying, "*You* MADE ME angry," then the child will believe what you are telling him/her — in essence: "*You* have caused the anger in me, and the emotions that I experience are caused by you and are your fault and your responsibility. For me not to feel bad in the future, you must behave differently. It is your job as a five year old to take care of my emotions."

This, of course, sounds absurd to the adult, but think about what the adult actually says to the child... and now take the five-year old's point of view. What does she hear? That she is responsible for her parents' emotions. Most of us heard it and to various degrees believed it. That's why we blame and fault others when we are upset and abdicate personal responsibility for our own emotions.

When speaking to others, children or adults, speak in a way that reflects self-responsibility for your own emotions. Here is an example of an emotionally responsible but angry parent talking to his or her child:

"You know that I love you no matter what you do, but I am really displeased with you for playing with that ball in the living-room and breaking that lamp after being told not to play there. You can see that I am angry with this but that is something for me to deal with. Right now I am having a hard time not making myself angry over this, but I will get myself to calm down in a few minutes. As a result of not following the rules you don't get to play with your ball for two days (or whatever the appropriate consequence is for the age of the child)."

The essence of a reprimand of this nature, delivered in a very firm tone, can be very effective if the child is used to hearing the parent speak like this. But (most) parents just don't speak like that. A child would likely feel confused and not understand if his or her father suddenly spoke in such a manner. But if a child is raised with this philosophy and understanding, then it doesn't sound out of place and the message is received.

You can show displeasure and apply a consequence to the child's behavior while reinforcing the idea that your anger is *your* responsibility and does not interfere with your love for your child. Wouldn't it be great if we all had parents who spoke to us that way? In this way, we do not propagate the notion that your children or others have the power to upset us. Thus, you also teach your children to be self-responsible for their emotions and that you are not responsible for their upsetness, such as when applying consequences to their behavior. In essence, you do not perpetuate the myth that others have the power to cause *your* anger, depression, worry, etc. You also teach that you do not have the power to create *their* emotions.

Practice speaking to your children, your partner, your colleagues, your friends and family in a way that promotes self-responsibility and your own self-awareness of who is the creator of your emotions. It is the first step to emotional control and growth.

"What do I do?"

1. Teach the 3-Stage Theory of Emotions to three people this week. The goal is to help *you* clarify your own thinking.
2. Notice your internal self-talk, expanding on all your thoughts so as to express them fully.
3. Express your healthy emotions (i.e., happiness, joy, excitement, sadness, remorse, sorrow, concern, etc.) and become a more three-dimensional person.
4. When distressed, express the healthy emotional equivalent:
   depression: sadness, concern, self-love and taking action now!
   anxiety: concern while being proactive
   anger: frustration and assertiveness
5. Speak in 1st person singular. For example: "*I made myself* unnecessarily upset." Practice the "I made myself..." until it's natural for you to speak in this emotionally accountable way. Remember that it is you who also makes you happy.
6. When expressing displeasure to others, clearly state and take responsibility for your emotions and assert what you want changed in the future.

Section Highlights

➢ You learned well as a child, but unfortunately many of the lessons were ineffective, impractical or simply the wrong ones.

➢ You can gain excellent, though not perfect, control over your emotions.

➢ Biology can dramatically impact on your emotions.

➢ If it's NOT physical or biological, what causes your emotions is your thinking.

➤ **S-O-R** means that when a **S**timulus is experienced the human **O**rganism's thinking determines the **R**esponse.

➤ No matter how it *seems*, you DO have tremendous control over your emotions.

➤ No matter how old you are, you can learn to improve your skills at controlling or altering your emotions.

➤ 3-Stage Theory of Emotions: when a trigger event occurs, you think about it (based on your belief system) and it's those thoughts that cause your feelings (emotional effect).

➤ Depression, anxiety and anger are unhealthy exaggerations of the healthy negative emotions of sadness, concern and frustration.

➤ Emotional control doesn't mean suppressing or holding in your emotions, but deciding on how you will feel.

➤ Become aware of your thinking.

➤ Learn what types of thinking make you upset.

➤ Challenge and refuse to believe in irrational thinking.

➤ Adopt more realistic and healthier rational beliefs.

➤ Behave in accordance with these new rational beliefs.

➤ Practice with duration, intensity and frequency.

➤ Attempt to speak in first person singular, such as:
   "I MADE myself upset."

➤ Assume personal responsibility for your own feelings and for who is making you upset: YOU!

The Unintentional Entrapment

Section III

Insistence Entrapment

Section Preface

Psychologically speaking, it is a good idea never to break your own moral code. Doing so can bring on much emotional distress. There is a difference between what is a moral and that which is a societal standard/personal preference.

What is the difference between the two for you? Attempt to answer this question as you read this section.

Maxim: It is the person with a solid conviction that can afford to be open minded.

As mentioned in the introduction — "It's About You" — we have three primary irrational concepts: Insistence, Amplifying Negatives and Assessments of Self-Worth.

This section will deal with insistence. The emotional entrapments caused by insistence can inflict some of the most intense emotional pain. For some people, it can be the most difficult to fully understand and to overcome. It would be virtually impossible to sustain any serious emotional distress without utilizing this concept of insistence. It is the foundation of emotional entrapments.

Some emotional entrapments employ insistence more than others. Anger, for example, is dominated by insistence. Look at people who are angry or enraged. Aren't they insisting that others or their environment be different — the way *they* want?

Usually angry people feel that they are justified in their anger and the abuse they bestow upon others; thus anger is almost always self-righteous. One might think that "anger management classes" would be full with the number of angry people in our society, but they are not. That is because angry people think, "If only *you* would behave correctly, then *I* wouldn't have to be angry" making *their* anger the other person's responsibility. So if you find yourself with a tendency to get irritated or angered easily, pay special attention to this section.

While anger is the most outwardly destructive emotion we have, guilt is the most internally destructive. Anger and guilt are the two cutting edges of the same sword. Freud said that depression is anger turned inward. To a large degree he was right, because much of the time, guilt is the culprit causing depression. If you find yourself getting down, blue, melancholy or "emotionally blah," then this section may be *just what the doctor ordered*. While guilt, like anger, has more components than just insistence — insistence remains the primary villain of depression.

As you read the chapters in this section, attempt to apply the information directly to your life. Keep in mind the times when you have been most angry or depressed. Once in mind, filter everything you read through this image, these thoughts or that memory. In this way, you 1) tend to undo the past that may sometimes haunt you, 2) you help yourself to feel stronger presently and 3) you provide yourself with a shield of armor for the future.

Remember that nothing happens without effort...consistently applied effort. Implement the lessons that follow and you will largely eradicate critical anger and depression from your life.

Chapter 11

Insistence Is Omnipresent

Think for a moment, and seriously answer this question: "In my life, what are some of the things I think I should do?"

Such as, I should...

...be respectful and courteous.

...be kind and thoughtful.

...treat my children well.

...work hard.

...keep my word.

...not harm others.

...not steal.

These are very common answers, and by the end of this section I will attempt to convince you that none of them are correct. It is not that you "should" steal, it is just that it's erroneous to believe that you "shouldn't," rather than it's "better" not to steal. Stealing is illegal and often considered immoral and if you do so, you may get yourself into trouble, and thus it is *better* that you do not steal. Believing that something isn't good and believing that it shouldn't exist are two different things. While it is advisable generally not to steal, each person has an inalienable right to make a personal choice as to whether or not to steal...or to do anything else for that matter.

The simple difference is between thinking that you *should not* or *must not* do something and thinking that it is *unwise* to do it. The first way blindly utilizes a rule, usually chiseled in stone, and the latter requires reason and thinking to determine the validity of that action (i.e., stealing). The traditional linguistic rules governing the use of *should* are largely ignored in modern North American practice and typically imply insistence or obligation.

Insistence is fundamentally the belief that a certain thing or situation must or must not exist or that such things as success and approval are necessary. Insistence implies an absolute.

"I *have to* (or should) be on time" is implying there are no other options.

"I *prefer* (or want) to be on time" suggests a personal desire but not a necessity.

Human beings seem to have a propensity to think both...

logically/rationally/preferentially

and

illogically/irrationally/insistently.

We can see the beginnings of emotional entrapment from the earliest years of childhood. Children can easily insist, demand and scream, whine and complain about some minor transgression. It is also amazing to see how children can also think very logically and rationally, cutting through the *adult-made* complexities of life at other times. This is what the phrase "out of the mouth of babes" refers to.

When we insist that our world be different from the way it actually is, we tend to get ourselves distressed. Simply insisting that today be Saturday when it's Monday is wasted time, energy and is an effort in futility. This is also true regardless of the situation. Insisting that your world be different from the way it is simply does not make sense. It is exactly the way it is until it changes — regardless of the amount of insisting. Not liking something and insisting that it not exist are two completely different attitudes that are often irrationally combined in one thought: "I don't like it so therefore it shouldn't happen."

If your daughter comes in late far past her curfew, insisting that she be in on time does not change anything. The reality: she was late. Nothing in the real world changes. No amount of insistence alters that reality. The next time, either she will or will not come home on time. All we tend to do is to get ourselves upset over the way things already are. Since we cannot change the past, getting upset and distressed over it is truly wasted energy. One of the few noted female psychologists of the first half of the 20th century, Karen Horney, aptly referred to the concept of insistence as the "Tyranny of the Shoulds." Dr. Albert Ellis commonly refers to this insistent attitude as demandingness, shoulding and to create emphasis, humorously coined the term *must*urbation.

To relinquish the attitude that you must get what you want *and* to abolish the demand that particular frustrations not exist, it is advisable for you to stop taking yourself and your world so seriously. It is a simple process of accepting reality exactly the way it is and then making attempts to change that which you do not like. The essence of this is expressed in Reinhold Niebuhr's serenity prayer:

God grant me the serenity to accept
the things I cannot change,
The courage to change the things I can,
And the wisdom to know the difference.

If we could live by this philosophy, emotional distress would largely go the way of the dodo bird. We tend to philosophically accept many things in our environment — both good and bad. There are though, many things we choose to get ourselves bent out of shape over. It is a very personal decision that varies widely from individual to individual. The famed psychologist Abraham Maslow in his book "Motivation and Personality" looked at acceptance this way:

"One does not complain about water because it is wet, or about rocks because they are hard, or about trees because they are green. As the child looks out upon the world with wide, uncritical eyes, simply noting and observing what is the case, without either arguing the matter or demanding that it be otherwise, so does the self-actualizing person tend to look upon human nature in himself and in others."

Do not confuse acceptance with agreement, complacency, compliance or sanctioning. I accept the fact that there is starvation in Ethiopia. I can take action against it by donating to charities to abolish starvation. While strongly disagreeing with and protesting the many government policies that allow it to continue, I do not distress myself over this abhorrent situation. Insisting that starvation not exist, thinking that it *shouldn't* exist changes nothing and potentially continues a rhetoric discourse that may actually delay action and distract governments from taking real action to change the circumstance.

Insistence is the cornerstone of emotional entrapments, indeed, *all sustained* emotional distress (barring biochemical or organic influences). It is virtually impossible to *remain* distressed, regardless of what that distress is, without some sense of insistence going on in your thinking.

You can spot insistence in your thought patterns by the words you use to express your thoughts. The most common words we use when insisting are:

Should

Have to

Got to

Must

Need to

Ought to

Supposed to

Insistence Entrapment

"I *should* go now." "I *have to* go now." "I've *got to* go now." "I *must* go now." They all express the same concept, but are just used differently depending on the context of the conversation. Remember that it is not the words themselves that are the problem, but the rigid insistent philosophy that they represent.

When a should is not a *should*

"Does a 'should' or a 'have to' always imply insistence?"

No. We often use the word *should* as a preference. The *have to* is not literal, although the person almost acts as if it is. When someone at a luncheon says, "I *have to* go now," she does not usually mean that she has to go or she will die. She means that it is time for her to go as she has other things to do. "I *should* get milk on my way home tonight" most likely implies that it is a good idea. This is what I refer to as a "soft should." This *should* is used as a want or possibly a strong preference. Unfortunately, soft shoulds tend to very quickly turn into "hard shoulds" — those that imply insistence.

The *should* can be used in language in a way that is predictive: "The bus *should* be here in 10 minutes." You can also use it in an advisory manner: "You've *got to* try the crab dip." A frequent use of the should is in the conditional sense. It is applied in the context of "if-then": "If I want to vacuum, then I'll *have to* get it repaired."

Soft shoulds are used with great frequency as are the insistent or hard shoulds. How can we tell the difference? The decisive test is: Would you get upset or stressed out if things do not work out as you want or expect? If so, it is a hard should. The shoulds I will be referring to from now on will be the "insistent shoulds."

The hard should is often a moral imperative: "He *should* treat me fairly" or "You *must not* drink and drive" or "They *have to* tell the truth." While all are desirable, none are absolute as the individual literally can be unfair, drink and drive as well as lie. There are reasons to act morally or justly but accurately speaking, you do not have to.

"Aren't we just splitting hairs? Isn't this just semantics?"

Well, yes and no. It is not *just* splitting hairs because *what* we think strongly influences *how* we feel. If we are feeling lousy then it is definitely time to really look at our thoughts in a more fine-tuned way. And, yes, it is semantics but it's not "just" semantics.

If a man turns to his wife and says "Hey, bitch, will ya get me a cup of coffee?" this will evoke a very different response than if he said, "Hey, honey, will ya get me a cup of coffee?" If it was *just* semantics then the woman's response would be the same. But we know it will not be the same. Words have meaning, and as such, evoke various emotional and behavioral responses.

It would be a good idea in general to eliminate the *shoulds* and *have to's* from your vocabulary, and more importantly, from your thinking. You could stop using this demanding style of speaking and utilize a calmer, warmer and definitely saner style of language…one of PREFERENCES.

Instead of "I *have to* go" you could say, "I think it's a good idea that I go." Instead of saying, "I've *got to* get to the meeting on time" you could say, "I want to get to the meeting on time."

Behind every *should* there is a *"want."* It is not that "I have to clean the house" but that I *want* a clean house. It is not that "I need to get to work on time" but that I do not *want* to get fired for coming in late. It is not that "You should lose weight" but that it's healthier, feels better and is generally a good idea to lose weight. It is not that "Others ought to treat you fairly" but that it is more desirable for others to be fair so you can work together more effectively. It is a good idea to express the truth — *what we want* — instead of expressing our desires in an insistent, demanding, dictatorial manner.

Here are some of the words that state, imply or suggest preference:

Want	Like	Prefer	Desire
Hope	Wish	Better	Yearn

Remember that this is not about changing our language. This is about changing the way we think. Our language is a reflection of our beliefs and philosophies. If a person slams his hand down on the table yelling that he *wants* something, he may say "want," but he is acting (and you can bet, thinking) in an insistent, demanding way.

What do you *want* to do?

Since our earliest days our parents or society taught us that we *should* study hard at school. We *should* go onto higher education or get a job. We *should* climb the ladder of success, save for retirement, get married, have 2.4 children, buy a house with a white picket fence, and so on.

I am not devaluing any of these goals. They are noble and help to make life work. What I am addressing is the idea that we *should* aspire to achieve these goals. While all of this may make you function effectively, by definition you can not feel fulfilled by doing something you think you *should* do. You derive satisfaction from doing the things you *want* to do.

Think about it. The things that are usually most satisfying and fulfilling are the things you do because you *want* to do them. Sometimes that means breaking the rules and at other times you comply with the rules. Either way it comes from the position that it is you who *wants* to do it, independent of the rules. It's the time you spend too much money while on vacation, come in late, take the day off from work, splurge on your new living room suite — this is when you feel fulfilled or satisfied or are simply having fun.

I am not suggesting that we abandon rational thought or live without guidelines or a structure. I am suggesting that we actually each use our respective 1000 grams of gray matter and think for ourselves instead of following some "other imposed" should. You might actually ask yourself, "What do I *want* to do," instead of "What *should* I do." A good rule of thumb would be to think through your situations from the perspective of: What is *good* for me to do? What do I *want* to do?

Others may think you should, ought to or need to behave in a certain way, but it will always remain untrue. That kind of thinking will tend to cause an emotional entrapment. You get to act in anyway that you choose. You also get to receive the results of the choices you make. Fair enough?

In a song sung by Whitney Houston, "The Greatest Love of All" she sings:

> "I decided long ago never to walk in anyone's shadow,
> If I fail, if I succeed, at least I live as I believe.
> No matter what they take from me,
> They can't take away my dignity."

If you live your life in a certain way or do things because you think you should — based of course on other people's or society's shoulds — you will not feel fulfilled. Even if you succeed, there really is little satisfaction, and you may feel let down or resentful for not having done it your way.

If you do it your way and you fail, you tend to learn more and will derive satisfaction because you learned from your own errors and grew as a person. If you succeed, then there is a double bonus of succeeding *and* doing it your way.

It would be irrational to do something your way *just* for the sake of doing it your way. I am suggesting that you trust yourself and ask yourself what makes sense to you, what is logical or what is practical *as well as* considering how you feel. What do you *want* to do? What is *better* for you to do? What would you *like* to do? These questions are too often lost in favor of what we think we *should* do.

Have you ever been in a quandary, stuck between two decisions? "Should I take this job or that job?" "Should I go here or there for my vacation?" "Should I get married or not?" The list can be endless. The problem when we are feeling stuck between two alternatives is that we are asking ourselves a faulty question: "What *should* I do?" Well, there is nothing you *should* do! The question is: "What do I *want* to do?" or "What is *better* for me to do?" or "Where will I be happiest?" or "What will be most fulfilling for me?"

Insistence Entrapment

When you ask yourself "What should I do?" it is like asking yourself "What color is the number 3?" It is a nonsensical question. It does not make sense and therefore is unanswerable. It is *not* what you *should do*, but what is good for you to do or what do you want or desire. Frequently there is a compromise or a balance in choosing what you want to do and that which is good for you to do. This you can work out and decide what is better. "What *should* I do?" you need not ask because there is no answer to it.

"Conscious choice provides for a mature, directed life, unlike those who simply re-act or blindly follow the rules of others."

"Flexibility and the ability to adapt is the key to a happy life."

Insistence Entrapment

Chapter 12

The Tendency to Resist

We may want to do certain things, but in the blink of an eye we can resist that very thing we first wanted to do simply because of the *should*. As free and autonomous human beings we resist being controlled. This has been true throughout history — slavery, repression of women or the imposing of a curfew on an adolescent.

This idea of resisting being controlled is researched in social psychology and referred to as "reactants." That is, we re-act to being controlled. Numerous replicable experiments and real life situations illustrate our resistance to being controlled. Here is one situation that most of us can relate to:

> People are driving down the highway at 60 miles/hour and come upon a construction zone with a sign that asks them to drive at 40 miles/hour for the next two miles. At the end of the zone, drivers are asked to resume to their original speed, but they do not. Drivers, on average, go faster than their original speed and continue for a long period of time — suggesting that it is not simply an attempt at regaining lost time.

When we are held back for any reason, there is a natural tendency to push forward and plus a little bit more in an attempt to exert our own sense of individuality and freedom. We can see this demonstration of self-determination in virtually all areas of our lives. No one likes to have his or her autonomy usurped or overruled. Let's face it, we do not like being told what to do even when it's something we want to do.

As an example, lets say that a 22 year old very virile guy is excited all day at work knowing that he will be going to his girlfriend's place that evening for a night of sexual passion. He walks through the front door of her place and she's standing there with nothing on but a towel. She's gorgeous. As he walks toward her, she turns to him and says, "You *have to* make love to me right now. You *should* as it is your duty to do so." The first or second time, he may be thinking that she is being assertive, but in short order he will back off thinking "I'll make love to you when I *want to*, not when you tell me that I *should*."

Isn't that interesting. Something that he was looking forward to all day, suddenly got turned around simply because of the *should*. We want to be sexual because it is fun and desirable, not because it is a duty or a should. Simply spoken — we resist that which we think we *should* do.

Many people have heard of "reverse psychology" but don't really know what it is. Reverse psychology is based significantly on the shoulds. Tell a child that he *should not* open the cupboard door and then leave him alone in the room. We know what he is likely to do. Hell, we know what most adults would do — open the cupboard door! Telling someone what she should or should not do is very often going to get her to do exactly the opposite.

While reverse psychology can't be applied to all situations — telling a child he shouldn't do the dishes isn't suddenly going to get him to do them — its operating principle is the "should." And speaking of children, parents often ask, "If I don't use the word should, what do I say?"

Reason Over Insanity

Many parents attempt to guide their children and keep them out of harm's way by telling them what they should do, must do, need to do or have to do. "You *have to* stay in the backyard" is a typical statement that a parent might say. The child, of course, immediately sees through the bravado and craziness of that statement and thinks, "No I don't! I don't *have to* stay in here, I can leave if I *want to*." And he's right. He doesn't have to. It is only the *preference* of the parent. As soon as the parent's back is turned, the child hops the fence and out he goes.

How does a parent handle this situation? Kids aren't stupid.

Sometimes they may act that way and we shake our heads over their antics, but they actually have a very good reason for acting out. But staying with the situation at hand, the parent can turn to the child and say something along these lines: "I *want* you to stay in the backyard. (The parent can also give a logical reason.) And if you leave the backyard (whatever the appropriate consequence is for the child) will occur."

Now the child understands *what* you want. He understands *why* you want it. And he understands what *will happen* if he goes against your wishes. This is a good form of sanely relaying your wishes to a child instead of using the insanity of insistence. It helps him to reason, to think and to understand. You will also notice that the parent does not play the "heavy" or the bad guy. There is an action and a reaction: touch the stove and you get burned. Cause and effect. Stay in the yard and play or leave and get an unpleasant consequence. It is as simple as that. The child gets to assume responsibility for his or her actions.

Some parents gripe that telling a child, or anyone for that matter, what they *want* or *desire* is not strong enough. Telling a child what he *must* do, have to do or need to do is displaying greater authority. And it is. It displays an authority over the child (or any other person for that matter) as *if* the child is a non-thinking piece of chattel.

Think about it. If your firmness in expressing your *desire* to have the child stay in the backyard — and you can be very firm in your expression — and the potential negative consequence if the child disobeys doesn't get the child to comply, nothing will.

Expressing your *desires* and applying consequences and allowing the child to make up her own mind and receive the outcome of *her* choice is far more effective. In this way the child learns from thinking and doing and not just blindly following a command. So it appears that *telling* a child what to do encourages the reverse response (back to the topic of reverse psychology), while being respectful in expressing your desires and the consequences of the child's various choices will encourage not only a better choice but also help in developing a thinking child.

While this example uses a child, it is equally true regarding adults regardless of whether or not they are our friends, co-workers, family members or spouses. People do not like being told what they *have to* do. Besides, anytime you tell yourself or someone else what they should, have to or ought to do — you have just lied. It is untrue. False! Why? Because there is nothing you literally have to do. Well there is one thing.

There is One Thing You Have to Do

People say that the two inescapable things in life are death and taxes. But we know that taxes are escapable. We could skip the country, move up north in the wilderness where we won't be found or we could shoot ourselves. All are not normally considered very good options, but options they are nonetheless. If there is an option to paying taxes then it is not something we *have to* do. It is a choice! "Have to," means there are no alternatives, no other choices.

Think about it. What do you *have to* do in life? "Eat?" No. How absurd. Imagine turning to starving children in Ethiopia and you say to them "You *have to* eat. I know there's no food, but you have to eat anyway." They would look at you like your porch light was flickering — not all there. "Well, you have to breathe don't you?" Nope! My father died in '85. He didn't have to breathe. He just died. And there is the answer to this conundrum: The only thing that is inescapable that you have to do where there are no choices is to die.

You *have to* die. I have to die. But you do not have to go to work, pay taxes, get married or get out of bed in the morning. These are all choices.

I've had clients turn to me and say, "Come on Dan, I know what you're saying, but realistically I have to pay taxes. I'm not going to shoot myself or skip the country so I *have to* pay taxes." My response is, "Come on. Let's be honest. You really do not *have to* pay taxes. Paying taxes or doing anything is a choice. It really is! You may make the choice to pay your taxes because it makes sense to you — so you don't go to jail or get fined, but it still *remains a choice*."

Insistence Entrapment

You see, both you and I will pay our hydro bill every month like clockwork. Realistically, very few people choose to live without electricity. So you and I are going to write a check each month to the power company to keep our lights on. If you think about paying your bill in terms of "I have to," you are already behind the 8-ball. You put yourself in an unhealthy psychological position. First off, you just lied to yourself — this is the foundation of emotional entrapment, and you will never do better in life lying to yourself than being honest with yourself. You do not "have to" pay your bill, it is a choice! Secondly, you will have a tendency to resent paying your bill or you may resist paying it by procrastinating. Either way, you will end up feeling controlled and manipulated by the system of living life, or you will simply resist putting out money each month to the power company.

On the other hand, if you asked me if *I have to* pay my bills, I would answer "Of course not. I choose to pay my bills because I like to maintain my standard of living and this includes having electricity." In this way I focus on the benefits of paying my bills and of the benefits electricity provides me, thus I pay my bills. It is my choice. Its called reciprocity. They give me electricity and I reciprocate by giving them money. It is a fair and mature philosophy to life. Thinking that I *have to* pay my bills is more like a little boy whining about something that he does not like.

Inherent Freedom

What I have been talking about is actually all about freedom: the freedom to choose. In reality you choose life over death, eating over starvation, to go to work over being unemployed, to remain married over being single and the list is endless.

We, in North America, say that we live in a free country. Meaning that there are few restrictions on what we can do. We all agree — at least in theory — to abide by the laws of the country. We are of course free to break those laws. The essence of freedom is the right or the ability to do that which is wrong or illegal. If you break a law, you may be incurring a consequence thought to encourage future compliance, such as a fine. If the infraction was serious enough, society might attempt to restrict your freedom by placing you in jail where it is more difficult for you to do wrong.

Remember that as a free citizen, any day of the week you are free to take a knife and stab someone. While this is morally reprehensible, the law does not tell you you cannot do that; it just tells you what will happen if you do. The law does not state that you can't drink and drive. That would be silly and untrue. Of course you can drink and drive. But if you do and get caught at it, the law will provide you with certain consequences. It is always a choice.

A friend of mine who is a biblical scholar offered me this interpretation of "God created man in His image." The image isn't a literal one of two arms and two legs, but that of the freedom to choose. God is free to choose and so are we. All other animals — as far as we know to date — are driven mostly by instinct and reaction to their environment. It is the human being that is free to choose in a manner unlike all other animals.

Regardless of the religious connotations, the truth remains that we *can* choose. And choice equals freedom, and freedom is the antidote to all forms of emotional entrapment.

Isn't freedom defined as the right or the ability to do that which is wrong? If you have to do the right thing, then you do not have freedom. You always have an option to do the wrong thing, but hopefully choose not to. You have the freedom to choose, and with that choice you will receive a natural consequence. Choose wisely and you receive a good outcome. Choose poorly and your consequence may be far less than desirable.

In World War II when the Nazi Storm Troopers were rounding up the Jews and said, "Come with me or die," the option of course was always to not go and to die. And some did. Not a good choice either way, but always a choice.

Dr. Viktor Frankl wrote shortly after his stay in a German POW camp that the Nazi's could take away everything he owned. They could take his land and his possessions. They could even take his life. But the one thing they could not take away was his freedom to choose how he would respond to their treatment of him.

Insistence Entrapment

Whether it be a life and death matter or simply day-to-day living, what you do and to a great extent how you feel is in *your* control. When you think in terms of what you *should* do, you act as if there is some overriding entity that forces you to behave in a certain way as if you were a mindless piece of machinery or an automaton. You are not. You are a thinking human being with the ability to make choices.

"Freedom is the ability to choose freely, without emotional coercion from yourself or others."

Insistence Entrapment

*"Your first priority is
to take care of yourself.
It's not that you should,
but think of the alternative
if you don't."*

Chapter 13

But I Didn't Use the Word "Should"

There are many hidden demands in our language. Remember when Mom looked at you in her "special" way and used *that* tone of voice and then asked you politely if you wouldn't mind performing some task for her? As a child, you knew that it was not a question as much as a command. The demand or *should* was hidden in the tone of voice and the look. You can imply insistence without ever using a demanding word, and the response will be as emotion-filled *and* as negative as if you did.

Sometimes questions can be an honest attempt to obtain information. Other times they are conveying a message as to how wrong the other person thinks you are or to disapprove of your behavior. Rhetorical questions can be used to tell you what others think you should or should not do.

QUESTION...	MEANING...
How can that be?	It *should* not be that way!
How could you do that?	You *should* not have done that.
Why did you get home so late?	You *should have* come home earlier.
Are you ever going to cut the grass?	You *should have* cut the grass by now.
Isn't it time you started your homework?	You *should* do your homework now!
When are you ever going to listen?	You *should* listen to me and *should* do what I say.

Insistence Entrapment

Short sentences that do not use demanding words can often be skillfully used to convey a message of insistence and are a powerful way of disguising the *should*. Incomplete sentences can be used to express an unspoken should — just falling short of using the word. While unspoken, the demand and the *should* remain very apparent.

He didn't fix the car...
> ...*as he should have.*

You're late again...
> ...*and you shouldn't be.*

I didn't even get an apology...
> ...*and I should get one.*

The dishes still aren't washed...
> ...*and you should have washed them by now.*

The lights in the basement are still on...
> ...*and you should have turned them off.*

There are a few words that stick out in our language as implied shoulds or have hidden shoulds so closely aligned to them as to be *guilty by association*. Here are the main culprits:

Implied/Hidden Should: Responsibility
"It's your *responsibility*."
"I'm a *responsible* person!"

And you *should* be responsible, right? Wrong! Most of the time and with only a few exceptions, if you are irresponsible you only hurt or inconvenience yourself. Don't go to work on time? You get fired. Don't call when you are late for a date? You will have relationship problems. Don't write or call to say thank you to someone who's treated you well? They will just stop being so nice to you.

Your lack of responsibility may at times have an impact on others temporarily, but it will be *their* choice as to whether or not to remain in some sort of relationship with you. You do not *have to* act responsibly. People so often treat responsibility as a moral issue. It's not. It is just *usually* wiser to act responsibly. If being responsible is the right and correct way of behaving, you still have the *right to be wrong*. You just probably will not like the outcome, and that's a good reason to be responsible all by itself, not simply because you were raised to believe that you *should* be responsible. On the other hand, as Winston Churchill said, "Perhaps it is better to be irresponsible and right than to be responsible and wrong."

Implied/Hidden Should: Supposed to
"You were *supposed to* be here by now."
"You were *supposed to* pick up that parcel by noon."

"Supposed to's" are usually implied shoulds. They are spoken usually as if there was a contract or some other type of agreement to adhere to. Supposed to's are usually used just short of a slap on the face. Or at least that's the way it's felt. It's simply pointing out to you that you were wrong and did not do as you were expected...like you *should have*!

If you were late because you were stuck in traffic behind an accident, where are you *supposed to* be? My guess: in your car, stuck in traffic behind the accident. Why? Because that is where you were. Are you supposed to be some place different from where you actually exist?

Now, you may be late because you agreed to be some place else at a given time. True. You may not be following through on what you said. True. Are you *supposed to*? (Catch the implied *should* in there?) It would be nice if you did as you said, but it still remains a choice.

Here is another twist on "supposed to." Let's say I ask a deliveryman to put the footstool in the living room, but he puts it in kitchen instead. Where is the footstool supposed to be? (Be careful now.) If you said, "in the kitchen" you are one of the few; but you are so right.

Shouldn't the footstool be exactly and precisely where he put it? (*Notice the correct use of the should?*) There is no reason why the footstool *should* be some place other than where it exists. Wouldn't it be odd if the deliveryman put the footstool in the kitchen and it magically appeared in the living room?

While he was asked to put the stool in the living room, that is not what he did. If he put the stool in the kitchen, then that is where it *should* be, whether or not we like it. Thinking that it should be, ought to be or is supposed to be some place else does not make sense. Thinking that "I wanted it in the living room but it's not" is conforming with reality and expressing your desire.

Implied/Hidden Should: Too
"You're eating *too* much."
"You're spending *too* much money."

These hidden shoulds are disguised in this little word "too." When someone reflects, "My dad says I'm *too* outspoken" the *too* suggests that one *should not* be so outspoken. Often times, in some crazy social fashion in an attempt to be humble, we will hear people say, "Oh, you are just *too* nice to me" ...as if you should not be *that* nice. "That's *too* expensive a gift for me," meaning that the person shouldn't spend *that* much on conveying a "thank you."

Implied/Hidden Should: Deserve
"I *deserve* more money."
"He *deserves* better treatment."

Deserve is something that only humans think about. "It is or it is not" is the way all animals seem to behave, but not we humans. A dog in an alleyway knocks over garbage cans looking for food. After 10 minutes of searching and not finding anything, it does not sit there, pout and think "I'm a good dog, I *deserve* to find food." It knows that either it continues to knock over garbage cans to find food or it goes hungry. That's reality. The *deserve concept* attaches to the *should* as: "I should get what I deserve." This hidden should is especially pernicious, causing anger and hurt feelings and often times combining with a self-righteous sense of superiority. Much of this concept can contribute to such things as physical abuse and homicide.

Implied/Hidden Should: Obligation
"I'm *obliged* to help him paint his kitchen."
"It's an *obligation* to return the favor."

Obligation or the feeling of obligation is one of the more glaring *shoulds*. Parents, siblings, friends or coworkers will sometimes use this particularly offensive concept. It is an assumption that "because I did something for you, you damn well *should* do something for me and it *should* be what I say it *should* be." Almost always, it's NOT because of some spoken or agreed upon contract or understanding, but is used to emotionally "arm-twist" the other person.

I ask a friend to help me paint the garage on Saturday. Two weeks later he asks me for a favor. Am I obliged to do it? No. A favor is a present and does not *have to* be returned. If it *has to* be returned, then it is a business contract — I do this for you and I get "X" in return. Now you may *want* to return the favor to advantage your desires of maintaining a good relationship, to encourage your friend to continue being of help to you or just out of simple kindness, but you are not obliged to help him.

Imagine a parent telling a child "I carried you for nine months...." or "I worked two jobs for twenty years to put you through medical school...." This type of statement creates guilt, and controls and obliges the other person to act "appropriately." In other words, to give in and do it his or her oppressor's way. This behavior is coercive to the individual and corrosive to their relationship. You have a right to choose which favors you wish to return, if any, and without obligation. No one put a gun to his or her head to help you out and just because he or she did help you does not mean you *have to* reciprocate, although you may *wish to* do so for any one of many reasons.

Implied/Hidden Should: Promise
"Do you *promise* to help me?"

When someone asks you to promise, she is asking you not to change your mind even if changing your mind is a wiser decision. She is in essence saying, "You are not allowed to change your mind now that you have promised, even in light of new information. You are required to help me even though it may turn out to be disadvantageous to do so."

Children or people with a childish attitude more often use the "promise." It is rather insulting to most people to be asked to promise something as if their word is not good enough. Also for most adults, it's automatically understood that people can and do change their minds over time given a change in circumstance and new information. The promise is akin to obligation and usually implemented as a form of coercion if you do not do what you said, "But you promised!" Simply put, the *promise* is just another disguised *should*.

Chapter 14

Insisting On Others

When you *insist* on others, you simply encourage their distress or their resistance towards you and what you are asking of them.

Turning to your secretary and saying "This document *must* be in the mail by 5 p.m. today" is absurd for two reasons. One, there is no reason that conforms with reality as to why it *must* be in the mail. There are excellent reasons and many benefits for why you *want* it to be in the mail by 5 p.m., but there is no reason why it *must* be in the mail or that you *must* receive the benefits. Two, telling your secretary what she must do is disrespectful. If you encourage her to think in terms of what she "must" do, her stress levels will go up as might her resentment for being treated in such a demanding fashion. The result might be an overall drop in her level of performance. This is exactly the opposite of what you would want to occur. Simply emphasizing the importance of getting a document in the mail will be sufficient for any adequately functioning secretary. If it isn't then it's time to seriously think about replacing him or her. *Shoulding* will only worsen the situation.

The shoulds will only give you a neutral to negative response. Let's say a friend turns to you and says, "I'm having a party this Friday evening, you really *should* come." You're not going to run away from your friend screaming "He shoulded me! He shoulded me!" You got the message — the invitation. But this feels warmer: "I'm having a party Friday evening and it would be really nice if you could come."

In the first invitation, the *should* implies obligation or duty, ever so slightly. Thus, there is greater resistance to it, while the other version is a more welcoming invitation. It is a style difference that can make the difference. Whether you are talking to yourself or with others, it is important to minimize the style of conversation that creates resistance and enhance the style that encourages acceptance.

Master/Slave Mentality

When you *should* on yourself, you tend to be your own slave driver. Let's face it, aren't we usually our own worst critic? We often insist and demand of ourselves things that we would easily forgive in others. We *have got to* be responsible, *supposed to* get to work on time, *must* do the shopping, *should* save for retirement, *ought to* help out my neighbor, *need to* hand in my report by its due date — and if we don't do the things we think we *should* do, we psychologically and emotionally crucify ourselves, beating ourselves mercilessly.

Let me illustrate metaphorically how the vast majority of people tend to treat themselves when *insisting* that they conform to some societal, moral, ethical or arbitrary standard.

Suppose this is Nazi Germany and you were being sent to a prisoner of war camp that has just been completed and is now ready to accept prisoners. But there was a clerical error and all prisoners were diverted to another POW camp except for one: you. So you are the only prisoner in this one camp. The guards are rather bored so they pick on you to paint this, move that, peel potatoes, dig a ditch…that sort of thing. Well, you aren't going to be writing home telling everyone that you're having fun and wishing they were there with you. You will likely be feeling rather stressed. Let's face it, this is serious stuff. The guards would be just as happy to shoot you as to look at you. Your life is in constant peril and you will feel the tension inside of you.

You are in as close to a "have to" situation as possible. You still do not have to conform to the guards' wishes, but they will kill you if you don't. So, while you do not literally *have to* comply, you will be feeling like it.

Well, what you may not realize is that in everyday life when you are *shoulding* on yourself, you are not only the prisoner, you are also the guard. You act as if there is a Storm Trooper with a machine gun behind you telling you what you *must* do…or else. But the reality is that there are no guards, there are only prisoners. The gates are wide open. All you need to do is to walk through them. Once you leave the compound of the prison and the shoulds behind, you get to decide moment to moment, day to day what you *want* to do and what makes sense *for you* to do.

Every time you *should* on yourself, you don your guard's uniform, point the gun and demand that you behave accordingly. This creates tension. Walking free without the *shoulds* is a feeling that is uplifting, energizing, creative, loving and will help you to remain at peace with yourself.

Shoulding ourselves is primarily the root of emotional entrapments like depression, conceit, performance anxiety, jealousy and perfectionism. Virtually all emotional problems contain at least some self-shoulding. Minimize shoulding on yourself and you will have a very difficult time remaining distressed for any extended period.

One of the reasons that it's difficult to stay in emotional distress without self-shoulding is because you will tend to be more creative, and creativity is important in finding solutions to your problems. When there is an absence of shoulding, you tend to experience the healthy range of negative emotions when things go wrong such as: sadness, annoyance, loss/grief, concern, dislike or distaste. With the *should*, these healthy but negative emotions get amplified to a degree where they become destructive, stagnating, distressing and self-abusive.

While you may want something, prefer this to that or desire that the world treat you in a certain way, there is no reason why it *should*. It would definitely be nice if it did. How wonderful for you to get your way *all* of the time. Wouldn't it be a pleasure if everyone you considered important in your life treated you with courtesy and respect, and if no one ever lied to you or stole from you? Only if life were truly fair, life would truly be grand. But life at times *is* unfair and people will *not always* treat you the way you would ideally like to be treated.

The hard lesson in life is that life *is* tough. It is important to learn to live with reality and roll with the punches. Adapt. Or be devoured by the ever-changing complexities of life. While your world may be an obnoxious place to live at any given moment, you may not approve of other people's behavior as well as your own from time to time, if you don't learn to flex and bend and keep smiling for the most part, you'll go the way of the dinosaur — emotionally speaking. You'll get mired in some negative, unhealthy emotional entrapment like anger, depression or anxiety and there you will stay until you *do* change your attitude. Change is a way of life. Inflexibility is the way to death. In ultimate terms, it *is* death.

The whale and the sea lion inhabit the same waters. The sea lion can withstand two degrees warmer water and two degrees colder water than the whale. The sea lion can give birth on land or in the sea. The sea lion is thriving while the whale is dying off. It's not just because of poaching but because of environmental changes and changes in feeding territories. The ability to adapt is a key ingredient to survival, to happiness *and* an emotionally healthy life.

Imagine that the hostess, just before her guests arrive for the evening's party, starts thinking: "For me to have a good time, three women must be wearing dresses. And for me to enjoy myself, at least 8 out of the 10 couples have to come. All couples ought to bring some token gift or bottle of wine for me to consider this party successful." As you can see, the greater the number of requirements she has, the greater the likelihood that her requirements will not get fulfilled and she will be disappointed and in distress. Learning to be psychologically flexible and living *with* the world around us is greatly preferable to fighting it.

Now don't get me wrong. If there is something you can do to proactively make changes to your world, definitely take action. Fight injustice. Take a stand against prejudice. Give to your favorite charity. Vote. Involve yourself in community affairs. Volunteer at the hospital. Be interested and attempt to make a difference. Just don't believe that the world *should* be different from the way it is. Sanely *want* situations to be different. *Prefer* them to be different. *Wish* they were different and then *do something* that makes a difference!

Insistence Entrapment

"Life has no other discipline to impose, if we would but realize it, than to accept life unquestioningly. Everything we shut our eyes to, everything we run away from, everything we deny, denigrate or despise, serves to defeat us in the end. What seems nasty, painful, evil, can become a source of beauty, joy and strength, if faced with an open mind. Every moment is a golden one for him who has the vision to recognize it as such."

Henry Miller (1891-1980)
The World of Sex, 1940

*"To insist unrelentingly that
the world be different
from the way it is,
creates a foundation
that breeds distress."*

Chapter 15

How to Stop Insisting

You will never completely eliminate insistence because you are born with the propensity to think irrationally. While it makes no sense to *insist* that the world, others or ourselves act in a desirable way, human beings still insist on using that "*should*."

Change the way you express yourself. To minimize this pernicious concept of insistence, it is important that you recognize when you are thinking in insisting ways. Look for that should; seek out that need; hunt for that must. TRY THIS FOR ONE DAY TO START WITH: do not use any word that implies insistence.

Change from...		to...
I have to go now.	⇨	I think it is a *good idea* that I go now.
You should be on time.	⇨	It's *beneficial* to all if you are on time.
He ought to tell the truth.	⇨	He would be *wiser* to tell the truth.
They shouldn't be racist.	⇨	It would be *better* and saner not to be racist.
She has got to apologize.	⇨	I would *like* her to apologize.
He has to study harder.	⇨	I *want* him to study harder.

I shouldn't have screwed up.	⇨	I *wish* I had not screwed up.
I need to lose weight.	⇨	I don't like being over weight and *prefer* to lose weight.

Most people find watching the "shoulds" in their speech surprisingly difficult to do, partly because they just aren't aware that they use the "shoulds" as frequently as they do and partly because it's simply a habit to think in such ways.

It's not uncommon that after an hour-long discussion with a client about not using demanding phrases, he or she will say: "I will *have to* work hard at this." Of course, you might have to work hard *to* achieve results (notice the appropriate *conditional* use of "have to") but you don't *have to* do the work or to achieve the results. Others often ask: "So, I *shouldn't* use the word should?" And, it's not that you *shouldn't* use the word should, it's just *preferable* or more beneficial that you don't.

Practice restructuring your speech. At first, this will seem awkward, unnatural or uncomfortable. Remember that it's not that it's wrong, but that it's new. If you have not danced in 10 years, dancing will feel awkward, but after a short while you can boogie to your heart's delight. Here is an example of how to restructure your speech *and* how using shoulds weakens you:

If you were to say to the hostess at a party "I *have to* go now because I *have to* get home by 11 p.m. to relieve the babysitter" — you have just lied. Of course, you don't have to! You choose to. This style of speech portrays you as weak and not in control. This is the long-winded version of what was just said...

> "I have got to leave now because I have no choice. I am not in control of my life or my schedule. It is not my fault. It's my babysitter's fault. I take no responsibility for my behavior. Poor me."

Insistence Entrapment

If you say to the hostess "I *want to* leave your party now" she might feel offended. So, how might you handle this?

> "Thank you so much for inviting me to this wonderful party. I have enjoyed myself so much. Unfortunately, I have a babysitter at home who can only stay until 11 p.m., so I told her that I'd be home by then. I do not want to lose her as a babysitter, so I think it's *better* that I head out now."

Here you have explained your reason for leaving early and why it is in *your* best interest to do so. You were courteous and gracious in your approach so no feelings would be hurt.

You can correct yourself after the fact. If you were having lunch with a friend and you told her that you *had to* go now, you could correct yourself later when you realize what you had really said.

> "I told Lidia that I *had to* go. That's not true. I could have stayed and been late for my appointment, but I chose not to. Next time I will correctly express myself in a stronger fashion by telling her that it's *better* that I go, so I won't be late for my appointment."

Confront your "insistence" philosophy. Remember that it is *not* about simply removing all insistent or demanding words from your speech and replacing them with words that imply preference. This would only be palliative or superficial and produce temporary results at the very best. The idea is to eradicate the philosophy from your thinking, your ideology, your belief system.

When you use a *should*, ask yourself questions such as:

"Why should I?"

"Who said he must?"

"While it would be better, does it have to be better?"

"Do others really have to do as I would like?"

"Are there other possibilities?"

Then, seriously try to answer them. Some of your answers may appear to validate the should, such as, "Because it would be better." But just because it's better does not mean that you should. It would be better for me if you give me a thousand dollars, therefore you should? Of course not. Any answer that appears to give credence to the *should* is a logical error by definition as the should is illogical. Ask yourself, "Are there other possibilities?" If there are, then you DO NOT *have to*, but you choose to; maybe because it is the best of the available choices. But no matter how you look at it, it always remains a choice.

You want to correct yourself *every time* you use an insistent or demanding phrase verbally or in your self-talk or thinking. Correct yourself with a sense of firmness and passion. Do not just pay lip service during this process.

Religions of the world tell us that things will not always go our way, but to have faith. Religious and colloquial statements throughout the ages remind us to be patient; to continue working hard.

> "In this world ye shall have tribulation:
> but be of good cheer…"
> John 16:33

> "In your patience,
> you shall possess your souls."
> Luke 21:19

Listen to when others use "insistence." Do not accept it when other people "should on you." Correct them silently to yourself. If your employer were to say to you: *"You have to* get this report finished by tomorrow noon." Make sure you do not reinforce such nonsense with any self-shoulding like: "He's right. I have *got to* get this report done on time."

It is also a good idea to re-word your employer's statement, such as: "He seems to have a very strong preference that I get this report done by noon tomorrow. I know it literally doesn't have to be done, but I do want to keep in good standing with him. I also would like to get it done on time, but I know it doesn't *have to* be."

Practice anti-insisting in every area of your life. You can apply "anti-insisting" to the smallest areas of your life to practice being aware of the freedom of choice that you truly have, but may not always be aware of. Here's an example: You are currently reading this chapter. When you finish, what are you going to *choose* to do? Not, "what do you *have to* do or *should* you do" but what are you going to CHOOSE to do?

After that, then what will you *choose* to do? Keep the idea of *choice* in mind as much as possible on an ongoing basis, especially at the start when your are first developing your anti-shoulding awareness. Listen for insistence or demanding phrases in *other people's language*, on TV and on the radio or in anything you read. Each time you become aware of insistence, challenge it and then change it in your mind.

Learn by teaching. Teach what you have learned in this chapter to others and help them become aware of their insistence as well. Spreading *the word* is good for you because we learn best that which we teach. Teach the concept of the shoulds and anti-shoulding, and you will get very good at minimizing the shoulds in your own life.

> *"The stone and the water*
> *are in a struggle.*
> *In time, the water wins."*

Insistence Entrapment

"What do I do?"

1. For the next three days, train yourself and do not use any insisting or demanding words or phrases: should, must, need, have to, got to, ought to, supposed to, etc.
2. Think and speak using preference words and phrases: like, wish, hope, desire, prefer, had better, etc.
3. Before you decide to do your next activity, ask yourself, "What do I *want* to do?" or "Is this in my long-term best interest?"
4. Express requests to others in terms of: what you want, what's good or what's beneficial.
5. Avoid hidden or implied "shoulds" by expressing your thoughts fully in terms of desires.
6. Listen to the "shoulds" in other people's speech and silently correct them understanding their message in terms of what they want or desire.
7. Explain the concept of insistence to others.

SECTION HIGHLIGHTS

➢ All humans think logically (using preferences) and illogically (using insistence).

➢ Just because you dislike something doesn't mean it shouldn't exist.

➢ "Insisting" is involved with all emotional distress — look for the shoulds, musts, and needs.

➢ Wanting something to be different and accepting that it's not ISN'T equal to complacency.

➢ Real prolonged emotional change occurs when the philosophy of insistence changes and not just the words.

➢ "Should" can be used as a strong preference, but often turns into insistence.

➤ Shoulds can be used predictively, as an advisory or conditionally (if-then).

➤ The test for the should: if you are upset or in distress…you are shoulding! Look diligently for the "shoulds" in your thinking and speech.

➤ When distressed, fine-tune your thinking by being clearer in your thinking — use preferences.

➤ Think in terms of what you want to do, like to do, or what's better — NOT what you *should* do.

➤ We tend to resist that which we think we should do — don't should on others or yourself.

➤ There's only one thing you literally have to do and that is to die — everything else is a choice.

➤ Choice is the epitome of freedom. Shoulds and insistence restrict freedom of choice.

➤ Invitations using shoulds are not warm and friendly as they imply duty or obligation.

➤ Hidden or implied insisting words include: responsibility, too, supposed to, deserve, obligation and promise.

➤ Adapt. Change. Roll with the punches. Grin and bear it or do something constructive about it.

➤ Flexibility is the key to survival and happiness.

➤ Be aware of your spoken and internal use of the shoulds and immediately challenge them.

➤ Thinking in "preferences" and "choosing" keeps you in charge — "shoulds" weaken you.

Section IV

Awful Entrapment

Section Preface

Think back to when you were a child:

1) What specific thing frightened you? What did you say to yourself (or think that you said to yourself) at that moment?

2) What were you afraid of doing? What thoughts entered your mind?

3) What is your biggest fear today? What do you dread most? How about "rejection"? Or "failure"? Now, what are you telling yourself about these fears? Notice that what you are saying to yourself today has a similar "flavor" as to what you said to yourself when you were frightened as a child. Keep these fears in mind and see if they lessen as you read this chapter.

For *Some* people, life seems to be a never-ending series of hassles and problems with an occasional tragedy thrown in. It's a constant struggle to remain even somewhat positive. Each day seems to contain a myriad of frustrations, things to worry about and a little anxiety of what tomorrow holds.

Other people seem to find most of life a joy. It is not that these people do not have problems; some have very serious ones at that. These *Other* people might live next door to *Some* people. Same neighborhood, same government, similar income. These *Other* people have deaths in the family, kids that get into trouble at school, lost jobs or acquire serious illnesses, but these *Other* people seem to take life in stride. Why such a different reaction to very similar situations?

Some people seem to swim against the current of life or at least tread water as the current drags them downstream. *Other* people swim with the current and in doing so, pick a destination and then reach it with a lot less effort than Some people.

This section is for *Some* people who want to become the *Other* people. It's a chapter for those who want to understand how to take life as it comes, to roll with the punches and to make the most out of life, even when things get really rough. This section is about the second of three irrational belief systems that cause emotional entrapment: amplifying negatives.

Virtually all distress contains, to various degrees, an amplification or exaggeration of a negative. If it isn't all that bad and you will handle it and survive it, then why get so distressed? Amplifying negatives is the basis for all fears, anxieties and self-pity, which is really the hidden truth behind all anger and many depressions. As you might be aware of by now, different emotions are linked together in sometimes subtle and not-so-obvious ways.

Chapter 16

What's Awful?

We have all had bad things happen to us. Some are everyday minor-type of occurrences, like breaking a nail or spilling food onto the kitchen floor, for instance. Other negatives that occur can be life altering. What are some negative things that have happened to you or that you would consider extremely bad?

What do *you* think of as truly awful? How about: getting cancer, losing a leg, having your house burn down without having insurance, the death of a child or spouse or losing your job? The list could be endless and will vary greatly from one individual to another.

By the end of this chapter I hope to convince you that not only is nothing *literally* awful, horrible or terrible but that you'll be stronger, more confident-assertive and have more freedom and control by minimizing this style of thinking in your life. This chapter is really about *minimizing negatives*.

Losing a leg, being stuck in an elevator, getting fired or receiving disapproval may be bad, inconvenient, frustrating or unpleasant, but what makes these things awful, horrible or terrible? For many, this question seems absurd as it almost appears self-evident as to why these things are awful. But I'd still like for you to pause right now and think about it: What makes losing a leg or getting trapped on an elevator awful?

You can substitute another illustration in that query, but the question remains the same. What makes *anything* awful? Hold onto your answer and let's see if I can persuade you to alter your thinking about what you define as awful over the next few pages.

The Language of Emotional Entrapment

Throughout history, language has been used to express our thoughts, philosophies, loves, disappointments and desires. We use language creatively in song and in poetry. Language can be used to illustrate, entice, evoke or jar emotions and to demonstrate originality and variety.

When we are happy and content, we *tend* to use words loosely, almost in a poetic or generalized sense to illustrate or demonstrate our intended meaning. When we are in distress, this loose language and the utilization of non-specific and irrational thinking that forms much of the foundation of our language *is* our culprit. Here, our physical health can be compared to our emotional health:

Many people can eat a variety of foods. Their health remains generally good. But if they develop food allergies, how might they discover which specific food is causing the problem?

It's time to go on a strict diet eating only those foods they *know* are good for them. They can introduce other foods one by one to find which food is their nemesis. When our emotional health suffers and emotional entrapments occur and we are fearful, anxious or are in any kind of distress, it is important to clarify our thinking and avoid irrational or nonsensical thinking. As with the "shoulds," the awfuls are not the problem; it is the philosophy they represent: the *amplification* of a negative. Before we delve into the awfuls, i.e., the amplification of a negative, it is important that we both have the same understanding of a variety of concepts presented here.

Let's first define *rational*: that which makes sense, is logical, practical, functional, is scientifically provable or benefits us and is in accordance with our goals. Something does not have to be scientifically provable to be rational, but if it *is* provable then it *is* rational. If you wanted to lose weight and you ordered two cream puffs, this would be considered an irrational thing to do. *Irrational* then would be the opposite of rational: that which does not make sense, is not practical or functional, is not scientifically provable or disadvantages us. Rain may be at times a disadvantage, but it *is not* irrational, while driving faster when it rains would most likely be an irrational thing to do.

"*Good*" could be defined as: that which advantages our goals, helps us to live long, happy lives or adds quality to our existence. Then "*bad*" is something that hinders our achievements, minimizes happiness and longevity or diminishes the quality of our lives. Receiving a university degree would generally be considered good while losing a leg would generally be considered bad. Good and bad are thought of as provable based on what *I* consider good and bad specifically *for me.* While a warm sunny day is factually *good for me,* a warm sunny day *itself* is neither good nor bad — it just is.

Fact vs. opinion. Another area of confusion is the differentiation between fact and opinion. This is sometimes trickier than it looks. If I were to hold up an expensive gold Cross™ pen and say to you, "This is the most beautiful pen in the world." Is this a fact or an opinion?

"Opinion." Good. It is only my opinion that it's the most beautiful pen in the world. *You* may think differently.

"Earth is the third planet from the sun." Fact or opinion? "Fact." Good. This is non-disputable.

"It's a beautiful day today." Fact or opinion? "Opinion." Right! You may not like the weather today, and consequently, have a different opinion.

"We have to pay taxes." Fact or opinion? "Fact." Wrong! This is an opinion. We don't *have to* pay taxes; it is an option. We could skip the country or shoot ourselves.

How about… "I like Disneyland." Fact or opinion? "Opinion." Bzzz! Wrong! It is a fact (assuming it is true). I do like Disneyland.

Sometimes separating fact from opinion can be tricky, but it is important to do if you are in distress. Believing that something is an irrefutable fact when it is actually an opinion can be very troublesome and is the root of emotional entrapments like worry, depression or anger. One defining characteristic of emotional entrapments is:

"Emotional entrapments exist because you devoutly believe something to be true when it's actually false."

It would be like believing "I *have to* and *must* get to my appointment on time or the world will explode." It is *not* true. Your response will be much more severe based on the extremity of your belief when such a reaction is completely unnecessary.

Awful Entrapment

It is common for people to say things like, "It is a nice day out today." Or, "He is handsome." We use "is" — the verb "to be" — as if it *is* a fact that he *is* handsome, instead of the truth — *I* find him handsome. We so often treat something as a fact when it is actually an opinion. Here is an example:

Let's say you and I go to a world exposition. There are pavilions from many far off countries there. Many of the pavilions have restaurants serving foods indigenous to that country. We go to the serving counter and notice that the specialty of the house is buffalo brains. You look at them (the trigger event) and knowing your own culinary tastes you think (your beliefs and attitudes) "Buffalo brains? Yuck!" Then you feel (your emotional effect)…Yucky! Unappetized. Turned off. (Reminder: S-O-R Theory, page 51 and the 3-Stage Theory of Emotions, page 59.)

But someone from that country might go to the counter, look at the buffalo brains (the exact same trigger event) and think (the beliefs unique to this person) "Buffalo brains? Mmmm. Yummy!" Then the feelings occur (the emotional effect that corresponds to this person's belief system). Excited! His mouth waters with anticipation.

It is the same food, but two different thoughts about the food give two very different reactions. We often think that the taste of the food is inherent to the food itself, as opposed to: it just *is* and everything else is my opinion about it. It is the difference between "The movie *is* enjoyable" to "*I found* this movie to be enjoyable." The former states that the enjoyability is in the movie itself and the latter states an opinion, and thus the onus is on the individual to find the movie enjoyable.

The Illusion of Awful: To be or not to be?

When we use the words awful, horrible, terrible, horrendous and atrocious in a merely descriptive way and remain emotionally calm, there is no problem. If you said, "It's a horrible day outside today" we all understand that you are using horrible in a descriptive sense to emphasize how much you dislike the weather today.

Others might say, "The way the government wastes money is an atrocity." Again, we understand their intended meaning. But if you are in distress and upset about the situation, then we had better talk.

I asked you earlier, "What makes anything awful?" This is a bit of a trick question. Any answer to that question implies that awfulness resides in the object or event. Losing a leg is not awful; it would only be *your opinion* that it is awful. What if you had a diseased leg that was causing you excruciating pain and was paralyzed? Losing the leg might seem like a Godsend. Even if everyone agrees with you that it *is* awful, it remains an opinion.

But what makes it awful? By definition it may be bad as it does not advantage, but hinders you in achieving your goals. It may be unpleasant, inconvenient and frustrating. This is all true. But what makes it awful, horrible or terrible? There is no horror or terror in having only one leg, although it may remain highly objectionable for an entire lifetime.

When we say something like "This *is* an apple" — using "is," the verb "to be" — we suggest that it was an apple yesterday, it is today and will be tomorrow, unless we destroy it in someway like pouring acid on it. When we say, "Losing a leg *is* awful" we suggest that it *was* awful, *is* awful and forever *will be* awful. But this is not true. It is an exaggeration with no basis in fact. It is an opinion that is treated like a fact and that is from whence the emotional entrapment develops — believing something to be true when it is actually false.

I had a client some years ago with only one leg. I asked him about when and how he lost his leg. At the time of the amputation he thought it was awful, horrible and terrible. He wanted to die. He thought he would never, could never be happy. As understandable as it is, he was making huge, unfounded exaggerations. You and I might do the same, but nonetheless these exaggerations would be the basis of the *extreme* distress felt. Sadness, grief and sorrow would be a natural emotional expression to loss. *Awfuls* intensify these emotions to an extreme, potentially to a life-threatening extreme.

Awful Entrapment

My client continued to tell me that he finally accepted the loss of his leg and that he no longer thought of his loss in such extreme ways. He said that some mornings he goes to jump out of bed and almost falls over because he's forgotten about only having one leg. He has become comfortable with the fact. Acceptance is the place most people arrive at, eventually, when dealing with dramatic, life-altering circumstances.

The fact is that losing a leg *is* inconvenient, frustrating or unpleasant. It is an opinion that it's awful, horrible or terrible. Losing a leg *is* bad (by definition of his wants and desires it does not advantage him, and thus it is bad). If losing a leg *is* awful then it would always remain awful. But that is not true. Most people after a period of adjustment rethink their situation and redefine the loss of a leg as inconvenient, a hassle, a royal pain in the rump. When the attitude changes, so does the emotional response. That is the whole point of this example!

Tragic vs Sad

Not getting something you want is sad or unfortunate. It is not tragic, horrific or catastrophic. The natural expression of not getting something you want is disappointment, frustration or sadness.

If I go to a store and ask for a package of mints and they don't have any, I think "Oh, too bad" and go to the next store. At the next outlet I ask for mints and they don't have any, again I feel frustrated and think "Oh, guess not" and move onto the next confectionery. What I *do not* think is: "This store not having mints is *awful* and *tragic*, and the next place *must* have them or that would be *terrible*." Unfortunately, this attitude is expressed as anxiety, depression or anger in far too many people in our culture. Not getting something we want, whether that be mints, a specific mate, a particular job, good health, you name it, is not tragic or terrible, but may be sad, frustrating and unfortunate to varying degrees.

When negatives occur or might potentially occur, if you exaggerate your thoughts from inconvenient to awful, you *will* increase your distress, and move from frustration to anger, from sadness to depression and from concern to fear or anxiety. Awful is merely an unrealistic extreme of bad or unpleasant.

Some people think that saying "Losing a leg is bad (or inconvenient or unpleasant)" is understating the enormity of the situation. Well, we could say that it is *very* bad, *very* inconvenient or *very* unpleasant. This is not understating the situation; it is an expression of truth. And that is all it will ever get to be. Calling it awful, horrible or terrible would be *over*stating the problem *and* is untrue. "Awfulizing" is another term coined by Dr. Albert Ellis, who a half century ago spearheaded the idea that exaggeration of negatives is a cognitive structure that increases emotional distress.

Overstating a problem has, unfortunately, become the accepted norm. Discussing problems accurately and realistically is considered understating or minimizing the problem.

Feelings Prove Only that You Feel

"But it feels awful!" This sentiment is often used to prove the validity that something really is awful.

The fact that it *feels* awful only proves that you feel; it does not prove that the situation *is* awful. If I hop around my living room and tell you I *feel* like a bunny rabbit, that does not make me a bunny rabbit. If I *feel* like a millionaire, it does not make me a millionaire. Feelings only validate that you feel; they do not validate reality.

Now if your friend has just lost a leg and was telling you about how *horrible* it is, I would not suggest you correct him. That would be insensitive. This method of *realistic, rational* thinking is to help the motivated understand the dynamics of their own distress *and* help them to gain better emotional control. It is not to be used as a weapon against others or as a tool in "one-upmanship." We can rise above provoking others with our display of rationality while providing them with the support they desire or require. We can be sympathetic to our neighbor's sensitivities while learning to keep ourselves excited about life, emotionally calm and centered.

When we use the awfuls, we suggest a number of things. 1) We suggest that some situation or potential situation is bad. This may be true. 2) Then we imply that it is more than bad, that it is more than completely, fully and entirely bad. More than inconvenient or unfortunate. This *is* untrue, as how can anything be more than 100 percent bad? 3) We imply that because of this bad thing occurring, we cannot be happy. This *is* also untrue.

Not only is it impossible for something to be 101 percent bad, happiness is virtually always found sooner or later after the dreaded event has occurred. Even to say that something is 100 percent bad suggests that it *could not* get any worse; but that is not true. It could always be worse — more pain over a longer period of time, greater impact on your life, etc.

"The universe is change: our life is what our thoughts make it."
Marcus Aurelius
121 — 180 A.D.

Chapter 17

Keeping Perspective

Thinking in terms of "if this or that were to happen that would be sad, unfortunate, unpleasant, disadvantageous" is not only realistic, but also far more functional. It helps you to keep calm and handle things more efficiently and effectively. Being angry, worried, scared or anxious is not a state you want to remain in when it is imperative that you handle something that is of great importance.

I saw a bumper sticker once that said, "If you're remaining calm when all others are running around in a panic, you don't understand the problem." I laughed at the absurdity. It is almost a given that the opposite is true. The more you understand the problem and appreciate its significance (or lack thereof) within the scheme of life, the calmer you will likely be. The more you understand the seriousness of a problem, the more you understand the importance of remaining calm and thinking clearly.

Have you ever taken an exam that was of great importance to you and there was a question on it that you knew the answer to, but at that moment just could not remember? As soon as you handed in the exam and walked out of the room, the answer came rushing into your head. Why? Your anxiety dropped and the memory block vanished. Anxiety and worry interfere with performance. This is the essence of many game shows.

"For $500,000 name three flowers in 5 seconds." "A rose...uh, uh, uh. A daisy...uh, uh..." Bzzz! Too late. You can do it under normal circumstances, but apply a little pressure and your anxiety goes up and just like that, performance goes down.

Others may not perceive you as caring if you do not get distressed when bad things happen. "Don't you care?" has been a question I have been asked many times in the light of a possible serious negative event because I do not tend to get anxious. How silly. Of course the non-anxious people of the world care. They just do not get anxious or worried.

Years ago my partner and I were flying to Hawaii and about two hours into a five-hour flight she asked me if I could remember if we had turned off the stove. I couldn't remember, but it was my guess that we had. She got very anxious about not knowing and wondering if our house was at that very moment on fire. When I showed little emotional response to her posing this scenario, she asked, "Don't you care that we might be losing everything this very minute?" Of course I cared. My thinking was simplistically clear: "At this moment we can't do anything about it, so let's enjoy the rest of the flight. When we land we will call our neighbors and have them check the stove for us. That is, if the house is still standing and not smoldering in a pile of ashes." When nothing more can be done, what is the value in getting upset? It is important to take in stride that over which we have no control. It's equally important to act when action is warranted. It is even more important to be able to distinguish between the two.

The absurdity of connecting the amount of emotional distress with the amount of caring can be shown in this example: Jane and John are walking their dog. The dog gets away from them and is hit and killed by a passing car. Jane holds the dog and cries. John goes over to the driver, beats him up, breaking his legs and arms, blinding him and thrashing him to within an inch of his life. Thus, John cared more for the dog than Jane because he was more visibly upset? Nonsense! Of course not. John just got himself all crazy over it, that's all. In fact, he need not have loved the dog at all. Maybe he was upset because his property (the dog) was damaged.

As you can see, there need not be a strong correlation or even a connection between loving and distress. Calmness does not imply less concern or lack of assertive action. It is more likely that the calm, centered person will take *appropriate* action instead of flailing around in a panic. It is a truer sense of real caring.

Other people sometimes have a hard time appreciating the value of emotional calmness during a crisis because they themselves would be so self-consumed with their own emotional distress. Let's say you had a young daughter who was involved in a serious car accident. You went to the hospital and by the time you got there, she had already been sedated and was going to sleep through the night. The surgeon tells you that depending on her condition in the morning there are three possible surgeries — each with its own risks — that can be performed and that you, as the parent, will have to decide which surgery and thus the type of risk you want your daughter to undergo. You are advised to get a good night's sleep as there will be some very serious decisions to make in the morning.

The next morning you are making coffee just before you rush off to the hospital and your next door neighbor rushes in saying, "I just heard about your daughter! I am so sorry. I bet you didn't sleep a wink last night." And you respond with, "Thank you, but I slept very well."

In all likelihood, you would be perceived as callous and uncaring. But let's face it, your daughter's well-being is at stake. You cannot afford to be so self-indulgent as to distress yourself all night and be an emotional wreck when making an important decision about your daughter's life. How selfish! It is time to think about your daughter and what is best for her. And what is best for her, is for you to get a good night's sleep so you can be alert and clear thinking as to what decisions to make. While the neighbor may see you as uncaring, true caring is behaving in a way that is most beneficial to your daughter.

This approach, for most people, is extraordinarily difficult. Emotional control was not taught as we were growing up, and it is often assumed that our emotions are simply a reaction to our situation. Real caring is about doing what is most beneficial to those concerned. Caring is also sidestepping the social rebuff that one may incur when behaving calmly in a situation that most people would be upset over in order to do what's right, not what's popular or politically correct.

The Self-Evident Negative

As was mentioned earlier, "awful" is used in the colloquial sense as "more than extremely bad." In its original sense, awful meant "full of awe or wonderment." Today it implies the worst possible outcome, a true exaggeration of a negative.

It makes sense to be concerned over negatives. In fact, evolutionarily speaking, focusing on negatives would have a big pay-off. Hearing a twig snap in the brush 100,000 years ago and reacting to it strongly might alert you to an animal who was intent on having you for dinner. A *heightened* sensitivity to negatives might have saved your life, thus allowing you to pass on your genes. This reaction today is just not necessary. Society, however, has evolved much more quickly than human genetics, and thus we are "stuck" with this ancient tendency to focus on negatives.

Negatives also have the very distinctive quality of bringing themselves to our awareness automatically. Even when we try to ignore them, they jump up and slap us across the face to grab our attention. Don't pay your phone bill and they cut off your phone. Hard to ignore that. Fail an exam and you do not pass the course. It sure stands out when you do not graduate. Drop a crystal vase onto the floor — difficult to disregard. Negatives usually become instantly self-evident.

If you for any reason were not aware of the negative, you can bet someone else would bring it to your attention. Ever notice how people are ready to point out the negatives in your behavior *as if* you were unaware of them? Back into another car in a parking lot and the person in the other car jumps out and screams at you "You idiot! You ran into my car." As if you were unaware of this fact.

So let's take it for granted that negatives abound. That we have a natural tendency to be aware of them. Negatives are something to be concerned with for our own good and for the good of others. Negatives are usually best handled in a calm, assertive fashion minimizing anxiety as much as possible. Given these truisms, why is there so much emotional distress over the negatives in our lives?

Negativity Training

Some people erroneously believe that we require negatives to help us appreciate the positives in life and without them the positives would have no meaning. First off, we have all had at least some negative experiences early on in life; no one escapes this fact.

We do not require more to let us know how good life can be. When was the last time you heard someone who was having a great time at a party say, "Boy, I can't wait to have something bad happen so I can appreciate the good times even more"? Imagine saying, "I wish I would have had something bad happen yesterday so I could *really* enjoy today." How preposterous. We do not require more negatives to show us how good life is or can be. Positives can stand alone and be appreciated for what they are, like being captivated by the awesome beauty of a South Seas sunset.

Secondly, there seems to be a pervasive attitude of "If I can abolish all the negatives from my life, then I can be happy." Let's be honest. Nobody gets rid of all the negatives in life. Frequently, the difference between happy people and those who are not, is not the amount of negatives in their lives, but how they have learned to think about and then deal with those negatives. Happy people have all the same problems as unhappy people. They just don't make a big thing over negatives; they change them when possible, grin and bear it when they can't change them and then focus on the positives and what can be done to improve their respective lives.

One of the primary reasons for distressing ourselves over negatives is because, as human beings who share a characteristic inclination to think illogically and irrationally, we drive our thinking from the reasonable to the extreme. Think of the consummate firefighter. Imagine if he amplified his thinking to the point that he developed anxiety or panic. His ability to function would be greatly impaired. Panic would be a more common reaction for the untrained individual. Panic would also likely be fatal. Extreme thinking tends to produce extreme consequences.

While we have a natural tendency to think in exaggerated negatives, our family, friends and society tend to help us along. From our earliest days, the child is exposed to people who show extreme reactions to everyday situations. The mother screams at the sight of a spider. The father is enraged when a driver cuts in front of him on the highway. The brother is pacing the night before an important exam. The neighbor almost has a conniption when she finds out a pesky raccoon got into her tomato patch.

When children observe adults getting upset over rather small issues, as important as the issues are, children tend to escalate their thinking, believing what has happened is a catastrophe. Many bad things that happen are personally very disappointing, discouraging, frustrating and sad. But that's all they get to be. It is unfortunate that very bad things happen to some really wonderful people, but they do. When we get ourselves twisted into knots over our negative past (if it happened a minute ago, it is the past) we model for children that distress is the appropriate emotional response when things occur that we dislike. The same is true for the future, which is something we cannot control though we try with futile persistence.

There is a propensity for people to accentuate the negative and minimize the positive. This is exactly the opposite response to living a happy and emotionally healthy life. Here is an example:

I walk into a restaurant where I am meeting you for lunch. When I get to the table, you notice that I am angry. I tell you that someone just stole my wallet and it contained not only my money and credit cards but the *only* photo of my deceased father. You would understand why I was so upset. In fact, others at tables near by would be cheering me on (along with my distress) silently thinking, "You bet you're upset. I know what that feels like. That *is* just *awful*. I hope they catch the creep who stole your wallet."

Now what would happen if we were ordering lunch and I ordered chocolate milk and the server said that they had just got some in fresh that morning. Well, I seldom have chocolate milk and rarely do restaurants have it so it is a real treat for me when they do. So I get all excited and start saying in a slightly louder voice, "I'm getting chocolate milk. I can't wait. I just love chocolate milk. This is so exciting. Mmmm, this is going to be just wonderful."

Others around me would twirl their forefinger by their temple and think, "When did they let him out? This guy isn't all there." In essence, they would be thinking that I am *too* happy *just* for chocolate milk. That I am making *too* big a deal about chocolate milk. Now if I had won a million dollars, then they would understand, but not for chocolate milk.

Awful Entrapment

Can you see what is happening? They will downplay my happiness as if I *should not* be so happy, especially for something as simple as chocolate milk. But in the case of having my wallet stolen, something that I can no longer change, they will join the cause and encourage me to be upset. While the wallet being stolen is very important to me, *in the scheme of life*, it is rather minor. Overall people tend to minimize positives and accentuate negatives. For a happy, functional life and to curtail emotional entrapments, just the opposite is what is required: exaggerate positives and minimize negatives.

Attempt to see things as they are and to *consciously* accentuate the positive to enhance your positive feelings. Regarding mental and emotional health, it is far better to think that something is *wonderful* over *good* than to think that something is *catastrophic* when it is really just a *hassle*. It is better to amplify positives than negatives. Do not get me wrong. It would be a Pollyanna mentality and a denial of reality to ignore the negatives or to try to think that a negative is really a positive.

If you lose a leg, it *is* bad for you. To try to ignore that and simply focus on the positives would be unrealistic for most people. It is a negative, and it is better to deal with that up front. Are there positives? Definitely. But the few positives at the start are likely going to be strongly outweighed by the significant number of severe negatives. There is no comparison.

The main point is that although negatives exist, do not amplify the term "negative" into awful, horrible, terrible, atrocious or catastrophic. Even if you could prove that awful wasn't just an opinion but an irrefutable fact and you could register awfuls on your "Negativity Meter," I would tell you to lie to yourself, disregard it and think in terms of bad, unfortunate or hassle. This more moderate way of thinking will help you to be happier *and* more functional. Isn't that what life is all about?

Style: Be Unfashionable

Many people don't think about it much, they just simply tend to find a lot of negatives and awfuls in life. These people are the first to point out that tiny little scratch on your brand new car. When you hear them talk, they are more often than not saying that this or that is awful, that this horrible thing happened and that some terrible person is looking at them the wrong way. *Terribles* and *awfuls* consume their existence, and they likely don't even know it. Amplifying negatives is a pervasive and common style of thinking. So be unfashionable and think positively. And, amplify those positives.

As times change, the phrases may change. "It's the pits" or "gag me with a spoon" have been used in years past to convey awfuls. Every few years different phrases arise in popular culture with the same *awful* meaning and with the same detrimental results. Remember it is the meaning that is the offender and not simply the statement.

This style of thinking or expressing yourself is a style that will weaken you over time. Are you more likely to feel stronger if you think that something is horrible, terrible and catastrophic or will you feel stronger thinking in terms of unfortunate, unpleasant and just too bad? The latter will obviously help you to feel like you can handle the situation more effectively than the former style of thinking.

TRY SAYING IT OUT LOUD RIGHT NOW: "It's too bad." "That's unfortunate." "I don't like it." Now try: "That's awful." "How terrible." "I can't believe it, that's horrible." Which set of phrases helps you to feel stronger and more able to affect a change? Now go with that.

Chapter 18

There Are No Tragedies

During the first few weeks of 1986 there was an accident that setback the space program almost a decade. It has become known as the Shuttle Tragedy. During this time I was teaching a course on how to eliminate emotional entrapments. We had just completed the class where we discussed that there are no awfuls or tragedies when the next day the space shuttle Challenger exploded and seven lives were sadly lost. People in the United States were in mourning.

While to this day this event remains sad, I have yet to appreciate why it is a tragedy.

"Because it's bad?"

No. Badness does not equate to tragedy. There are many bad things happening in people's lives, but we would not normally classify them *all* as tragedies (I personally would not classify any of them as tragedies regardless of what they were). So *badness* does not equal tragedy.

"Because there were seven lives lost needlessly?"

That's sad. That's unfortunate, but hardly a tragedy. Around the world, forty thousand children under the age of five die each day from starvation and dysentery, both which are readily preventable. This would be much closer to the definition of a tragedy than seven people who died in an accident while doing something they loved. Stalin said, "A single death is a tragedy, a million deaths is a statistic." Why? Because we cannot know a million people but that one person who dies has become personal to us. While it may *feel* like it is a tragedy, it does not make it a tragedy. It *feels* that way because we *think* of it that way. Remember that feelings only prove that you feel. Nothing more. Be mindful that it is your *thinking* that determines your *feelings*.

Such a number of children dying is extremely sad, unfortunate, and unconscionable when it is so easily preventable, but what makes it a tragedy as opposed to sad and unfortunate? What makes the shuttle mishap a tragedy? Did we expect the astronauts to live forever? They had to die sometime. It is too bad they died so young. Turn to a 95-year-old man in good health and you will find he is in no hurry to die just because he has lived longer than most. No matter at what age we pass on, it may *seem* like a tragedy to that person or his family, but the truth is it's a fact of life and, at most, is sad and unfortunate.

Is it a tragedy that the astronauts got to do what they loved? Got paid well for it? Had millions of people envy their achievements? Didn't succeed? Died doing something they loved? Where's the tragedy? I cannot find it.

If you think you can find what is so tragic, ask yourself if "it" is sad or unfortunate. You will undoubtedly say "Yes." Then *it is* sad or unfortunate, but what makes *it* tragic? When we say something is a tragedy or is catastrophic we, again, are amplifying a negative from bad to terrible.

Again, some may argue that sad and unfortunate does not convey the depth of the problem. We can preface these expressions with "very" or "extremely," but what is the value in exaggerating negative experiences into catastrophes? We know they are bad. Very bad. Extremely bad. But why make them worse than they really are? What is the value in thinking in tragic ways? If you feel the way you think, then thinking in exaggerated negative ways will only increase your discomfort and decrease your ability to function effectively.

You see, I believe that as a culture we made a huge mistake by calling the shuttle mishap a tragedy. Virtually every school kid in America watched this explosion. Instead of conveying the idea that it was sad that seven people died doing something so courageous and adventurous, it was conveyed that seven people died a horrible tragic death doing something that was dangerous. There were shows in the following days about how dangerous space travel is, that astronauts are putting their lives on the line riding upon millions of tons of explosive fuel. What is the message that was being conveyed? Why not instead celebrate the creative, adventurous, dynamic and risk-taking human spirit?

Awful Entrapment

It would not surprise me that we, as a culture, have not yet seen the real effects of the shuttle mishap. We quite literally taught our children to think of death as a tragedy and that taking risks is something to be avoided. Not taking risks, and thus, not living the life that you have would be so very sad. Unfortunately, it is true for so many people.

If we could define catastrophe or tragedy, it would have to be the occurrence of the worst possible event. Maybe the nuclear annihilation of earth? The slow eradication of the human being because of germ warfare? You get to decide if there are tragedies and what defines one. Your definition will help to define you and your degree of emotional entrapments you may experience in life.

Self-Weakening Beliefs

There is a "disease" that has infected vast numbers of people across many continents. It tends to make people feel weak, nervous, agitated and anxious. Some find themselves feeling irritable and short-tempered or possibly feeling down with little energy and motivation. It is frequently passed on to others, especially children.

The name of this disease is: "I-can't-stand-it-itis" (itis: pronounced I-tis). There is an institute dedicated to helping people with this disease, it's called the Albert Ellis Institute for Rational Emotive Behavior Therapy (REBT). Call for their current catalogue at: (212) 535-0822

There are styles of thinking that inherently strengthen you or weaken you. It is important that you believe, really know that you can handle anything that comes your way in life.

"I-can't-stand-it-itis" a term coined by Dr. Albert Ellis to playfully but powerfully emphasize the invasive and destructive nature of this type of thinking. Thinking that you can't stand something can become a style of thinking that is like a disease that spreads throughout your psyche, like cancer through the body. When you think and then actually start to believe self-weakening thoughts, like you really can't stand something, you are in psychological trouble. While you can virtually stand anything, thinking that you can't is like a virus to a healthy psychological system.

Most of us have used these types of phrases:

"I can't bear this hot, muggy weather."

"I can't abide being lied to."

"I can't handle it when other people are late."

"I can't tolerate it when people are rude."

"I can't take it when we fight."

"I can't stand it when…"

The list can be as infinite as the human imagination. The reason this way of thinking is so destructive is because it's untrue and weakens us at our very core. It is a direct statement to ourselves that we are weak and incapable of handling something. This is simply not true, even in the most extreme situations.

"I can't tolerate it." You know that in reality you can and will stand it, tolerate it, endure it and live through it to see another day. Remember that it is not *just* an expression. It is a thought pattern with meaning. It is an expression that is corrupting to your emotional well-being, and over time it will erode the strongest of characters. Like the endless drip, drip, drip of water that will eventually cut granite, nurturing self-limiting beliefs will eventually cut a healthy self-image in two.

We also know that it is not just an expression. There is a strong correlation between strong and confident individuals who seldom use this type of thinking to the anxious, depressed and emotionally entrapped individuals who have this motto as their credo. Confident, self-assured people just do not use this type of expression. They also DO NOT use other types of put downs and self-limiting statements that they don't believe, like: "I'm stupid." "I'm hopeless." I can't do anything right." "I'm ugly."

If you continually tell a child or your spouse that he or she is stupid they will, over time, tend to believe it. This is even truer if you tell yourself such nonsensical absurdities. The point being, don't treat this one lightly as if it's *just* an expression — it's an expression of a developing belief that you are inadequate and impotent in the handling of the challenges you face in life. This is blatantly untrue!

The fact is: You *can* handle anything. You *can* stand anything. You *can* endure, cope, strive and grow beyond any problem or difficulty...or you die. It is that simple. You stand it and live, or you do not stand it and thus you die. Period!

If you were being tortured by having your skin peeled off with a dull knife, you could stand it. Now, you're not expected to like it. You'll do a lot of crying and screaming, but you will stand it right up until the moment you die. Then you stop standing it. Fortunately, most of us will never be pushed to such incomprehensible limits, but the fact remains: You can stand anything or you die. As philosopher Friedrich Wilhelm Nietzsche once said, "Anything that doesn't kill me, strengthens me."

Assuming you don't die, and thus by definition you *can* stand it, will telling yourself a thousand times — "I can't stand it" — help you to stand it? Help you to cope? Help you to feel strong? Help you to be happy? Not in the least!

Telling yourself an untruth — a negative, self-weakening, self-depreciating statement — will never give you anything of worth. Never! Like other self-limiting philosophies, "I can't stand it" can be expressed as "I can't bear it," "I can't cope," "I can't deal with this." Sometimes self-weakening beliefs are expressed in an exclamatory statement: "Oh my God!" "You did what!?" "Oh, no!" All of these exclamations can be followed with "That's awful." Both the "I can't stand it" and the "awful" are amplifications of a negative and thus unhealthy.

The Chain-link Theory of Thinking

You may have heard of the term "free-association." It comes from Freudian theory and works basically this way:

I say...	then you respond with your first thought...
Knife	Fork
Boy	Girl
Salt	Pepper
High	Low

The theory is that your dominant or most reflexive well-used thoughts will be the most immediate or spontaneous replies. Look at the last example for instance. Instead of answering "low," a marijuana smoker might have said, "Pot" or "Grass." This word association of how one word triggers another related word is a natural expression in a healthy mind. It also gives the therapist clues as to how the client is thinking.

If I were to start talking about my last trip to Hawaii, you would undoubtedly begin thinking about vacations, sun-tanning, romantic sunset beaches, Polynesian dancers and the like. We tend to link thoughts and ideas together, as in free-association, like links on a chain.

Wouldn't it be odd if I said, "This awful thing happened to me today and I'm having a lot of fun"? If I said, "I just received the most tragic news and I'm so happy," you would be confused. The first part of the sentence does not fit with the last half. But if I said, "This awful thing happened to me today and I can't stand it," that fits together nicely. Or, "I just received the most tragic news and I can't bear it," then it would seem congruent.

Imagine the links of a chain. As one link is pulled up, the next link follows. As that link is pulled up the one after that follows.

This is how we make strings of thoughts, form sentences and paragraphs. When I say, "Something horrible just happened and I'm having a great day," it just does not seem to make sense.

"Awful" and "I can't stand it" are integrally linked. When you pull up the awful link, the next link on the chain that pulls up is, I can't stand it. They just seem to fit. But there is an unasked or silent question every time you use the phrase: I can't stand it. "Why not? Everyone else stands it. Why not you?" And the only answer is: "Because I'm weak (or some variation on that theme)."

This is how the exaggeration of negatives produces an overall sense of weakness in one's character or personality!

First link...	Second link...	Why not?	Third link...
That's awful	I can't stand it	...	Because I'm weak!
How horrible	I can't bear it	...	Because I'm weak!
It's terrible	I can't handle it	...	Because I'm weak!
That's horrid	I can't take it	...	Because I'm weak!
How dreadful	I can't tolerate it	...	Because I'm weak!

No matter how you slice it, you get the small piece. You end up feeling weaker and more prone to emotional entrapments like anxiety, worry, guilt, depression and anger. It is time for a change.

"There is nothing either good or bad, but thinking makes it so."

Hamlet, act II, scene ii
William Shakespeare

Chapter 19

Shredding Self-Weakening Beliefs

There are three links in developing self-weakening beliefs: 1) Amplify a negative into something that is awful, horrible, dreadful, etc., 2) tell yourself that you are not capable of coping, such as: I can't stand it, and 3) then conclude with an explanation for your inability to cope with "because I'm weak." To eliminate self-weakening beliefs you question, argue, rip-apart all three segments until you come to a new self-strengthening philosophical belief.

There is a dramatic difference between understanding or thinking something to be true and really believing something to be true. You can give the person who is afraid of flying a volume of statistical facts on how and why flying is safer than driving. But the person who is terrified of flying still will not get onto the plane. She knows it is safer. She is aware that planes rarely crash. But this one particular flight, the one she is on, *will* crash (a perfect example of emotional entrapment). Thinking it will not crash and truly believing it will not crash are two different things.

Challenge the first part: This is awful.

Many therapies fail in the most significant part of the therapy process: teaching clients to challenge their self-limiting, irrational beliefs. Ellis' Rational Emotive Behavior Therapy pioneered the use and advancement of the process they refer to as "disputing." Ellis states the most common reason for lack of progress is a result of insufficient or ineffective disputing.

Do not hurry through challenging, but rather take your time. You can do a challenge in 10 seconds, but several minutes will be dramatically better. Do not just say, "It's not awful" and then move on. Stay the duration and do not let go. Really challenge your concept of awful — over and over. Ask yourself:

Why is *this* awful?
("*This*" can represent anything that you consider awful.)

Where's the proof of awfulness?

How is it awful and not just bad or unfortunate?

Is it true?

Why is "awful" a useful term to use?

Is this an overgeneralization?

Why is it more than bad and frustrating? (Explain specifically).

Let's assume the worst, could I handle that?

Will thinking of it as awful help me to handle it or be happier?

Could I still find happiness eventually?

If I do not get what I want, can I still be happy?

What is the realistic probability of it happening?

How would it be the end of the world if it happened?

As long as I continue to believe in awfuls, how will I feel?

Will focusing on a negative help me to feel better?

If I tell myself a thousand times that it is awful, will it help me?

Would I suggest to my best friend to think this way?

Awful Entrapment

Sometimes self-weakening beliefs are not obvious in your thinking: you might not notice yourself feeling anxious or worried specifically, but it shows up in your behavior. If you find yourself pacing, unable to sit still or doing things for no apparent reason, such as chain-smoking, over-eating or obsessing on things like cleaning, shopping or work, then the culprit is often the "awful." Assume there is an awful operating — that you are amplifying some negative in your life — dig it out and then rip it to shreds.

When you challenge the idea that something is awful, even though it doesn't readily appear in your thinking, do not let it go. Press yourself, assume that you are thinking *something* is awful and sure enough an implied awful will raise its ugly head.

Ask yourself, "What's awful?" and see what comes to mind. Your first thought is likely the area causing you the problem. If nothing comes to mind, look at the areas of dissatisfaction in your life and make a statement like:

"It's *awful* that…(state your dissatisfaction)."

Does that statement *feel fundamentally* true? If so, then you found your hidden "awful." If not, try another dissatisfaction and another until you have located what you believe to be awful.

The above method of challenging and questioning flawed ideas or concepts can be a very powerful way of uprooting them from your self-weakening belief system. Challenging can be done with self-talk, but produces better results when written. Written challenges help you focus; they force clarity, and you can add to it or review the challenge at a latter time.

Make sure that when you end your challenge you finish on a positive:

"So I guess this really isn't awful. There is nothing terrible about things not going the way I want. I can handle anything and will take assertive action when I can, and other than that, I will choose to *make myself happy* and enjoy the present moment the best I can. Nothing in the past or future is so important as to make *now* miserable."

Awful Entrapment

When you challenge "This *is* awful," really challenge it vigorously. Take your time whenever possible and then repeat it, again and again until you see a change in your moods and in your behavior.

Challenge the second and third parts together: I can't stand it because I'm weak.

In the same vein as when challenging the awfuls, challenge the "I can't stand it because I'm weak." Here are some possible questions and comments you could verbalize to yourself:

Why can't I stand it? Everyone else stands it. Am I going to die?

I have stood every bad event in my life until now. Is there any reason to believe that I will not stand this one?

There is nothing new coming my way, and I have stood everything else before now so I can stand this! I really am strong!

I remember the time I overcame "X" and I again found happiness. I can do it again this time.

I am a capable person, able to handle any situation. I am a wonderful person and strong and very able.

Remember that when you challenge any irrational, nonsensical thought, there are three qualities of the challenge that make it more effective.

Frequency. If you challenge the awfuls once in a month, the chance of eradicating them from your thinking is slim to none. Challenge irrational ideas often. Challenge them whenever they arise, if possible.

Duration. You can challenge the awfuls 20 times a day, but if it is a maximum of 15 seconds at a time, you are NOT likely going to see much progress. Take at least several minutes and the longer, the better. A 15-second challenge is better than none at all, so do it when that's all you can do. To ensure significant change, make sure most of your challenges are more than brief "thought snippets."

Intensity. No matter how often you challenge the awfuls in your life or for how long you challenge them, if you are only paying lip service to the challenge it will not prove fruitful. If it's like rhyming off the alphabet without a single thought then you might as well not waste your time. Focus intensely and concentrate about what you are saying when challenging any amplified negative.

Change the way you express yourself.

Another strategy for undoing self-weakening beliefs is to make a very conscious attempt to change your "awful" language. Speak using moderate, more realistic phrases like:

That's too bad.

How unfortunate.

That is so sad.

It is really bad when things like that happen.

What an unpleasant situation. It must have been very uncomfortable.

As difficult as that was, I bet you handled it well.

I know you are strong enough to deal with such unfortunate situations.

Anytime you catch yourself utilizing amplified negatives, 1) change them immediately into a moderate and realistic negative, 2) reframe them into a positive when it is appropriate or

3) challenge their validity outright. Eagerly attempt to speak to others leaving out amplified negatives or the awfuls entirely. This may be difficult at first but will get increasingly easier. As you practice, watch your confidence increase and your stress or anxiety decrease.

The bible assures us that we are strong and can handle anything.

Religion is a major source of strength for many. Religion reinforces the belief that we are hearty enough to withstand any adversity.

> "Take therefore no thought for the morrow: for the morrow shall take thought for the things of itself."
> Mathew 6:34

> "So far you have faced no trial beyond what man can bear. God keeps faith and will not allow you to be tested above your powers, but when the test comes he will at the same time provide a way by enabling you to sustain it."
> 1st Corinthians 10:13

Be careful of emotional reasoning.

Remember that feelings are just that. It would be equally unwise to ignore feelings or to make decisions *solely* based on feelings. Consider as much as reasonably feasible when making decisions and include feelings. Also attempt to separate your thoughts from your feelings. People often say things like:

> "I *feel* you are not telling me the truth."

This is not a feeling, but a thought. The feeling may be one of trepidation or fear, but you cannot *feel* that someone is not telling you the truth. That is a thought.

> "I *think* you are not telling me the truth and
> I *feel* uneasy about that."

Similarly, people often say: "I *felt* rejected." Rejected is *not* a feeling. It may be a fact, an assumption, a perception or thought, and the feeling that follows might be hurt or disappointment, but rejection is not a feeling. Separate the feeling and the thought: "I *feel* hurt that you rejected me." Make sure you separate thoughts from feelings.

Learn by teaching.

Many people who attempt to teach this concept that nothing is awful, frequently encounter fierce opposition. Some people are so rigid in their thinking and so entrenched into believing that there is some objective reality that contains the quality of awful in it, that they will fight to the death believing in awfuls.

Remember that when you attempt to teach others, while they may benefit, your task is to learn by teaching. You will find out just how well you understand this concept as soon as you are challenged on any area of the awfuls. If you don't know your stuff, you will stumble through it. This just means that it is a good idea for you to reread this section until you can answer any question that comes your way.

You are not required to convince your audience of anything. You are just sharing what you have learned and are answering their questions to the best of your abilities. If you walk away feeling like you did a good job, and if they are still believing in awfuls, so be it. They have that right. As a skilled therapist for over two decades, not everyone has left my office convinced that awfuls do not truly exist. Some minds are not only closed, but rusted shut.

"There are no benefits to exaggerating negatives."

"What do I do?"

1. Be aware that thinking that something is awful will tend to create the corresponding "awful" feeling. Change your attitudes and you change your feelings. The goal is to be less distressed and deal with the problem effectively.
2. Negatives are self-evident. Deal with them, but focus on the positive.
3. For the next three days do not use any amplified negatives (e.g., awful, horrible, terrible, etc.), and use the more realistic language of: sad, bad, unfortunate, unpleasant, regretful, etc.
4. Practice amplifying positives — make it a habit.
5. Remind yourself daily or when faced with a difficulty or disappointment that you *can* stand anything and that you *are* strong.
6. Practice reframing a negative into a positive (find the positive hidden in the negative — there is one, big or small, guaranteed).
7. Explain the problematic nature of amplifying negatives to others.

SECTION HIGHLIGHTS

➢ All humans amplify negatives and positives — amplifying negatives is more common.

➢ When in distress, be very specific and clear in your thinking to locate irrational, unrealistic or nonsensical thoughts.

➢ Facts express reality — opinions express individuality: separate facts from opinions.

➢ Awfuls are opinions of reality and are not facts about reality.

➢ Awfuls are unrealistic amplifications of negatives and thus, will intensify negative emotions.

➢ Myth: Negative events *can be* awful, horrible, terrible, tragic, or catastrophic.

➢ Fact: Negative events may be extremely bad, inconvenient, frustrating, or unpleasant, but are <u>NEVER</u> awful.

➢ "Awful feelings" do not prove awfulness, but only that you feel.

➢ Not getting what you want (regardless of what that is) isn't tragic. It is sad or unfortunate and even given this fact, you can still make your life meaningful and fulfilled.

➢ Amplification of negatives underscore virtually all emotional entrapments.

➢ Amplification of negatives drive worry, anxiety, panic, rage, depression and jealousy.

➢ Remaining calm in order to handle problems effectively is a truer sign of caring than is panic.

➢ The amount of distress does not reflect the amount of caring, but rather the lack of emotional control.

➢ Negatives are self-evident; it requires energy to find and focus on positives.

➢ Fewer negatives will not guarantee a happier life; happy people also have negatives.

➢ Amplify and focus on positives; minimize and actively address negatives or ignore them.

➢ "I can't stand it" weakens you; "I *can* stand anything" strengthens you.

➢ Practice shredding self-weakening statements frequently, with duration and forcefulness.

Section V

Worth Entrapment

Section Preface

When reading this section, keep in mind the thing that you are or have been most angry with yourself for doing or not doing. This could be something from when you were a child...or last month. Maybe you were caught cheating on a test in grade three. Maybe you were angry with yourself for not fighting back harder when you were sexually attacked as a teenager. Whether it seems trivial or significant to others, if it was a big issue for you, keep this in mind now.

Filter everything we will talk about in this section through this memory of what you did and the anger, disappointment and sadness you had or still have towards yourself regarding this situation.

The Worth Entrapment section looks at the unsupported concept that resides behind guilt and all forms of punishment (as differentiated from discipline), retribution, vengeance, homicide and genocide. We are a culture that almost seems obsessed with evaluating, appraising or rating others and ourselves. While it is a good idea to monitor our progress at various tasks, this monitoring often goes beyond evaluating behavior and translates into evaluating our "selves."

If you've ever felt guilt — and who hasn't? — then you are acutely aware that you put yourself down based on something you did or didn't do. You weren't just saddened by the choices you made, you were attacking your "self" based on those choices or their outcomes. Guilt, plainly put, is anger at oneself. It is a poor attempt at paying penance for a mistake made and a poor attempt, at best, of correcting the problem or ensuring that it isn't repeated.

Guilt is self-destructive and will weaken you until you begin to become depressed and self-pitying. Like anger, guilt is a look into the past, which causes distress in the present.

While guilt is the most *internally* destructive emotion we have, anger — at others or the world — is the most *externally* destructive. Anger — at ourselves, the world or others — is a childish, immature emotion basic to our character as humans. To many people's surprise anger can be readily controlled.

During the 1960s people were told that is was good to let out their anger — by hitting pillows or beating a tree with a big stick. But, if anger is so good, why is it that no one ever suggested that it is healthy to express anger towards oneself? Why then, was anger okay to express to others? Well, it's not healthy in either case.

Unfortunately, it wasn't realized until much later that the more people practice something the better they get at it, and this was also true of anger. So, thousands of people were just getting more comfortable with and better at expressing their anger. This approach did not seem to be minimizing people's anger, but was actually exacerbating or promoting it.

Authorities agree that it's healthier to express anger than to hold it in and fume. It wasn't until the mid-1970s that self-help books suggested that anger *did not have to* be an issue in the first place. It had not occurred to anyone that maybe, just maybe, a person DID NOT HAVE TO get angry over any particular event. There were and are different emotional choices for any given situation, i.e., different people display different emotional reactions to the exact same set of circumstances. (Remember the S-O-R Theory, page 51 and the 3-Stage Theory of Emotions, page 59?)

Regardless, of whether your anger is directed at others, the world around you or yourself, the fundamental problem is the erroneous assumption that one's behavior and one's value, worth or intrinsic significance are somehow connected. Throughout the following section, you will come to understand how to escape the emotional entrapments (i.e., anger and guilt) caused by appraising a person's worth.

Worth Entrapment

Chapter 20

The Value of a Human Being

Evaluation of human worth: the belief that value or intrinsic worth as a human being increases or decreases based on one's decisions or actions.

How could this be? While behavior may be valuable, inconsequential or destructive, how can the inherent worth of an individual go up or down based on that behavior? Our life *is* about our existence and *not* the evaluation of our intrinsic worth based on some arbitrary rating system. When we focus on contemplating our worth, this leads us down the wrong path.

So, let's take a moment and look at why the question of "human worth" is faulty.

It makes sense to evaluate a person's behavior. If you were hiring a keyboard operator, you'd want to know his typing speed. If you were hiring a limousine driver, you'd want to know her driving record. You might want to rate your own skills as a parent, and if your skills rate poorly, then you can take action to improve them. You can rate your behavior as a chef, a public speaker, electrician, father or taxi driver. In fact, it's often a good idea to rate your skills just to see if you are progressing toward your goals or not. But how would we/could we evaluate *your* worth?

Although it is common practice, it doesn't make sense to evaluate your worth based on your behavior for a variety of reasons. To clarify this issue, I dug out my notes from a college philosophy class. Stan Persky, a brilliant man who taught the course, always had a lot wisdom to share. Here is a partial summary of the main points:

1. We would have to evaluate all of your behaviors from the heroic to the mundane. You exhibit a truly countless number of behaviors in your lifetime. We would have to

evaluate them all to get a global value of who you are. It would be unfair to give you a rating on only one or two of your most significant behaviors and ignore the rest.

2. Even if we could list all of your behaviors, we would have to determine a rating scale that would be universal throughout all countries, societies and nationalities as to avoid an ethnocentric bias or racism. The rating for each behavior would have to be a global standard, whether you were a pygmy in Africa or a débutante in Paris, France.

3. It would also be important to rate both genders equally in *all* areas so as not to be sexist.

4. Then we would also need to rate qualities such as consideration, compassion, tolerance, forgiveness and appreciation. Does forgiveness rate more highly or less highly than empathy?

5. One's motivation would also have to play a part in accurately evaluating a person. If you give to charity to lower your income tax bracket, that's very different than giving to charity because you care for those less fortunate.

6. Who would be assigned to do this rating? There must be no room for personal bias or preference in order to rate fairly. Could an entirely objective scale ever be designed?

7. Even if all this *were* possible, it leaves out one crucial point: You are an ever-changing, dynamic person with qualities that are in constant flux. How could we apply a rating of the whole person using only a slice of time? We would need to rate you only after all the available information had been tabulated. That would be after your death, and then of what value to you is that?

Even if it were possible to evaluate your worth today, what value would that have to you? So you received an overall GPR (Global-Personhood Rating) of: "B+." So? How does that help? What good is it unless your goal is to deify or demonize yourself or others in someway, unless you want to prove for some misguided reason that you have a greater or lesser intrinsic value than someone else.

Opposite Sides of the Insanity Coin

Pride and shame. Pride has the *appearance* of being positive, and shame is generally considered a negative. I say that pride has the "appearance" of being positive because this is only an illusion. Both concepts are really based on the same flawed concept: My value is determined by the value of my behavior.

Pride:　because my performance was good or superior
　　　　　I am therefore a good or superior person

Shame:　because my performance was poor or flawed
　　　　　I am therefore a poor or flawed person

People tend not to want to give up pride because pride feels good, at least momentarily. The problem is that the same concept produces shame, and this not only feels bad, but can produce emotional entrapments that can cripple a person's sense of self-acceptance.

Pride versus shame is a game of one-upmanship or one-downmanship. "I am so proud of you for receiving your degree" the parents say to their child. Would they feel no pride for their child or feel shame if the child did not get her degree? Stepping into this concept is like stepping into quicksand; you just get stuck, struggle and get pulled down.

"I'm proud of what I've accomplished": in other words, I feel better about who I am because of what I did. This concept is not a problem as long as you are an extremely high achiever who rarely makes mistakes and virtually always meets your own established goals. Can you think of one person alive who fits that definition? If so, ask her and she will likely tell you that she is frequently falling short of her own expectations.

Pride feels good because it raises you up: gives you a *sense* of strength or superiority. But this is an illusion. Not only is it false because it is simply a lie (you are not a better person for behaving well) but because eventually you will trip, stumble and fall. Fail badly and you will unmercifully flog yourself by feeling ashamed, feeling like you *are* flawed and unworthy or *are* a failure because you have not succeeded in some activity or have acted badly.

When you buy into this concept, you buy into a dangerous irrationality. This concept will rip apart any sense of self-acceptance and positive self-regard. It will keep you from what is really important: leading a happy and experientially productive life. Both pride and shame are based on this faulty idea: how I behave indicates my worth.

When you were a kid your parents, your teacher, neighbor or someone of influence may have said to you when you did something wrong, "You're a bad boy for doing that!" Or, you may have been thoughtful or did something right and you heard, "You're so thoughtful, you're such a good boy." Both of these statements relate your behavior to who you are, your sense of "self" — and that is the problem.

You are not a bad person for behaving badly, and you are not a good person for doing a good deed. The concept of being or not being a "good person" was taught to you. It is not in your genetic makeup. In fact, there are societies that do not promote a sense of "self." Separateness, uniqueness and individuality exist, but not the concept of "I." Traditionally, Canada's First Nations people, the Modoc, speak in terms of "we" and don't use "I."

Unless you are an anthropologist, it is hard for most people to imagine what life would be like without a attitude of self. Imagine...no self-love or self-hate. No self-esteem or self-acceptance because the ideology of *self* does not exist. Almost from birth, we have been taught the concept of self (and it's counterpart, ego) and it has been problematic ever since.

Most likely your parents encouraged you after your first successful attempts at walking by saying, "That's a good girl" or something similar. You were just formulating language — the concepts that will follow you through life, and the most fundamental concepts you learned are: Do good and you are good. Do bad and you are bad.

It's back to this black and white thinking. There were many subtle or indirect messages throughout childhood. You watched TV when you were growing up. TV taught you to be self-critical. Use this hair coloring or buy these jeans to be accepted, to be okay, to be part of the group. If you don't, and you express your individuality differently, that makes you a bad person and you will be rejected. Most commercials attempt to get you to feel like you require their products in order to be a good, complete and whole person. This is claptrap at its worst.

*"Serenity is accepting all of who you are,
abandoning both pride and shame."*

"To be proud of virtue is to poison yourself with the antidote."
Benjamin Franklin

Chapter 21

The Human Collage

It almost seems intuitive that if a person behaves badly then he or she is a bad person. But we know this is faulty reasoning when we look at children. Let's say that a child of three knocks over your favorite lamp after you told him not to play in the living room. He behaved badly (the parent usually says, "Bad boy";) therefore, he is a bad human being. Right? Wrong!

But what about when this concept is taken to the extreme? Let's give it the acid test and see if the concept holds up. Ted Bundy murdered a number of women in cold blood. This is one of the most atrocious, abhorrent acts we can think of. Bad behavior? To the extreme. Therefore, was he a bad person?

Well, if we say "yes" then we run into all kinds of difficulties. You might agree that he is a bad person because he behaved badly but, he also behaved kindly, caringly and considerately at other times. These are all good behaviors. If we stay with the consensus that good behavior makes good people and bad behavior makes bad people, *then* we would *have to* conclude that when Bundy was doing good things — he was a good person. Doesn't feel right, huh?

The reason that calling Bundy a good person is erroneous is the same reason why calling him a bad person is erroneous. Bundy has done many good things from giving to charity to stopping at stop signs when driving to patting a dog on the head. He has also done some contemptible things. In pure numbers, he has done more good than bad things. This is true for all humans. But we all would agree that there is no comparing the goodness of patting a dog on the head to the badness of the cold-blooded murder of women. The badness of murder strongly outweighs the goodness of giving to charity or patting a dog on the head. This is without dispute.

Can you see what has now happened? The argument is about comparing the two acts, the two behaviors: kindness to a dog and the murder of women. Bundy himself has been removed from the discussion, and we are now, rightly, discussing his behavior.

This does not mean that we may not want to take Bundy and throw him in jail for the rest of his life or place him on the electric chair (which is what happened). We may want to take immediate and severe action, but let us keep focused on the issue at hand: evaluating his behavior.

When a police officer stops you for running a red light and gives you a ticket, is he ticketing you as a person or your behavior as a driver? Right. Your behavior as a driver. Hopefully he does not come over to your car, kick the door and tell you what a schlemiel you've been. Unfortunately, this sometimes happens when the crimes are more severe — there is an evaluation of the worth of the suspect by some police officers as opposed to dealing strictly with the person's offensive behavior.

A person's behavior is a compilation of both good and bad. Thus, to say a person is good or bad based on her behavior is a gross overgeneralization. We are too often focused on the personhood instead of the behavior. When a child does well, we can say, "How wonderful! I love you so much." When a child does poorly, we *can* say, "That's wrong because (whatever the reason is), *and* I love you no matter what." In this way, the child will easily learn not to associate her value to you or her sense of self-acceptance or positive self-regard to her own behavior. In other words, children can enjoy themselves and learn from life without ever having to evaluate their "self."

<u>Power of Myth</u> author Joseph Campbell believed that when people were focused on proving themselves or focused on attempting to understand the meaning of life, they were sidetracked. Campbell said:

> "It's not the agony of the quest but the rapture of
> the revelation. Life is not a problem to be solved
> but a mystery to be lived."

This concept of individual worth detracts us from living and enjoying life. While intellectually we may be able to understand it, undoing a lifetime of learning to evaluate ourselves and others is a struggle that can carry us over many years. The rewards, though, are well worth the effort.

Who's to Blame?

Figuring out "who's to blame" seems to be a popular pastime in cultures around the world. We seem to want to blame and denigrate someone or something. It's the individual. It's society. It's the tobacco or gun companies. It's genetics. It's their upbringing. It's you. It's me. It's the full moon or the bogeyman.

A marriage ends. Who's to blame? A 12-year-old child starts doing drugs. Who is to blame?

A paroled 17-year-old goes on a shooting spree in a school. An estranged man commits a murder-suicide in Hollywood. A 9-year-old is convicted of armed robbery in the ghetto. You and your spouse leave for vacation and forget that the stove is on, and your house burns down. Who is to blame?

The question of who is to blame is misguided and at best: a poor attempt to understand what happened. In an ever increasingly complex and dynamic world, there is no one single cause of society's worst ailments. But most people keep hoping that if the alcoholic will just stop drinking that evil whiskey, then he would become a loving, thoughtful, caring father and husband. If we could only get those wicked drugs out of the schools, then we would have happy, eager-to-learn children.

We are looking for that *one thing* to blame, to play the bad guy. Have you ever heard of a scapegoat? In many ancient cultures, a goat was fed rotting scraps of food and then killed to symbolize ridding the village of disease and to ensure a bountiful harvest. At one time, the Hebrews for the Day of Atonement, called upon the high priest to bestow the sins of the township upon a goat and then it was taken to the wilderness and allowed to escape.

While the ritual has changed, the overly simplistic belief still exists today. Just place *all* the problems of society in *one* area, then eliminate that area. The scapegoat is the guy wearing black in the

Westerns. He is the punk on the street. The person selling drugs to our kids. It is the alcohol or the cocaine. We want to find one person or thing and focus all our ills on "the bad guy." He is bad. It is bad. They are bad. Now isn't this the basis for prejudice?

It seems to me, however, that the world and the people in it are a blend of colors from Mother Nature's palette. A rainbow: with a mixture of colors that blend, and with no absolute, definable characteristic of what makes you, you or me, me.

Here is a very old Judeo-Christian ethic: There is a heaven and a hell. Good people go to heaven. Bad people go to hell. This is the informal, popular version — biblical scholars of course would take exception to this — though most of society agrees with this in the generalized sense.

This popular model of good vs. bad was taught to us from our earliest days: We heard fairy tales then watched Westerns and police crime shows on television and Hollywood mega-hits all with this completely good/totally bad theme in it. You are either my friend or my enemy. You are either for me or against me. It seems important to take sides. It is not uncommon that mutual friends of a divorcing couple are pulled to make a decision on who they are going to side with, instead of supporting both parties equally. You are expected to be on one side or the other. You are in one box or the other. You are either white or you are black.

Not all cultures have ideologies with this black and white perspective. A popular Asian symbol is the Yin-Yang.

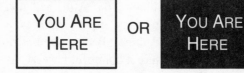

This symbol is thousands of years old and embodies a better-balanced perspective of the human being. Instead of there being a bad guy and a good guy, the yin-yang symbol suggests that in the white there is also some black. In the black there is also some

Worth Entrapment

white. In the symbol itself, black and white are intertwined. And that's what this chapter is about: the whole you. The black in you. The white in you. No blame. No condemnation. No denigration. Just an open honest look at you, our sample human being.

The question at the start of this section was "Who's to blame?" I am going to try to convince you that not only is the concept of blame misguided, it is dangerous to our physical and emotional health. It is the original source of punishment (not discipline, which is something else entirely). It is the single most common denominator in depression and all forms of anger and violence.

Responsibility vs Blame

When things go wrong, don't we have to blame and denigrate somebody? Isn't somebody at fault?

These are two very different questions. "Who's at fault?" and "Who's responsible?" are valid. "Who's to blame?" is erroneous with no valid answer because the question is founded on a flawed and unreasonable assumption: that blame is a logical, sensible concept. It's not! Let me explain the difference between responsibility and blame:

Let's say that two or three months go by and you still have not paid your phone bill. The phone company cuts off your phone, which means you get to go to the corner and drop quarters into the pay phone there. You are RESPONSIBLE for that. True.

But on the other hand, let us say that two or three months go by and you have not paid your phone bill. The phone company cuts off your phone which means you get to go to the corner and drop quarters into the pay phone there...AND somehow you become a crumb, a louse, a bum for having made that decision. False! Untrue!

There is a major difference between making a decision, even a poor one, and who you are. You are who you are, independent of whether you make a good decision or whether you make a bad decision. This is a tough concept for most people to really wrap their arms around. Almost everything we have been taught says the opposite. Make a bad decision, mess up, screw up and you *are* a screw-up. Essentially, blame is responsibility plus schmuckhood.

"Label things...not people."

Chapter 22

You Aren't What You Do

I would really like you to consider the falsity of combining what you do with who you are. As a society we are entrenched in this notion that my behavior some how defines me as a person. It looks good at face value, but becomes increasingly problematic the second a glitch arises.

We have all heard of athletes who become extremely depressed because of an injury that permanently took them out of the game. Nevertheless, they can lead very normal lives. They just cannot compete at a professional level anymore. People who equate what they do with who they are, are making the same critical mistake. If you are what you do, then who are you when you don't?

Labels are used with great abandon. "*I am* a financial analyst." "*I am* an artist." "*I am* a football player." Every time we use the verb "to be" — *I am* — we over-generalize. The truth of the matter is that "I act some of the time as a therapist," but that is not who I am. It is what I do.

Typically, we use labels to simplify our language. If I say that "I am a consultant" — everyone understands what I mean by that; it is my vocation. That is not the problem. It becomes a significant problem when a person identifies so closely with her behavior that her identity has become infused with that behavior.

If I asked you, "Who are you?" What would you say?

The answer to this question has kept philosophers busy for five thousand years. If you complete this sentence, "I am…," then you have over-generalized. All you can say is, "I am." You were born an "am" and you will die an "am." That's it. Everything else is your behavior, your thoughts or your feelings. Who you are seems to be an indefinable quality. If scholars have been unsuccessful in five thousand years in solving the "I am" quandary, I will not attempt it now.

What I do want to make you aware of is, to be certain that you do not use the labels "I am..." to define who you are or your existence. You have existence, and hopefully you will continue to maintain your existence and attempt to achieve your goals and to be maximally happy with a minimum of pain.

Where people often get into trouble is when they cross a line that they have drawn for themselves and then label themselves as bad. No matter how often you act a certain way, it does not make you that way. If during Halloween I got dressed up like an elephant, walked like an elephant, made sounds like an elephant, tried to think like an elephant, wouldn't it be odd if in the morning I thought: "Yesterday, I looked, acted and sounded like an elephant; therefore, I must be an elephant. Today I'll pick up everything with my nose." How bizarre. You would be calling the men in the white coats to take me away.

Look for these types of phrases in your speech and attempt to alter them to something more realistic:

Over-generalization/label...	More accurate...
I am a teacher.	I work (*some of the time*) as a teacher.
He's a jerk for cutting me off.	I do not like him cutting me off.
I'm a jackass for forgetting my appointment.	I wish I did not forget my appointment.
I'm an idiot for making that mistake.	Making a mistake is human and I'm just practicing my fallibility.
He is a genius.	He has genius-like qualities.

Chapter 23

Verbal Violence

"Sticks and stones will break my bones, but names will never hurt me" has been said by many a school child. This is basically true only if the person calling you names is not you!

It is important that you do not slip into the habit of degrading or castigating yourself by calling yourself names (or in any other manner for that matter). Sometimes we say things like, "Boy, wasn't I stupid?" or "Just call me an idiot" or "I'm a real jerk for having done that." It sometimes starts with raised eyebrows, a smile and a light tone in the voice. We are trying to be light-hearted about a goof-up that we made while acknowledging that we are responsible. Here's the problem: We are calling ourselves names and putting ourselves down. We would not stand for anyone else doing that to us and even if it is in fun, we do not tend to like it. It is not respectful.

What starts as an occasional "funny" putdown can turn into a "cute" routine when admitting mistakes. Over time that style of thinking slowly eats away at one's self-image. For some people, it really is just a style of self-denigration. That style though is usually there because of what is operating underneath: a continually weakening self-image.

Isn't it interesting that someone would even make such a statement? There are an endless number of ways of amusingly admitting a mistake without a self-putdown, but some people do this automatically. This habit may be unconscious, but it's there because the individual believes it to some degree. Even with the best-case scenario, self-denigration will never produce a positive, and chances are the product will be a significant negative.

If you had a child, and he spoke to one of your friends by calling her stupid, even in fun, you would probably find that disrespectful. It does not matter how you slice it, name-calling *is* disrespectful. So, do not ever put yourself down. It is unnecessary and potentially harmful, even jokingly.

Calling other people names is no different. Like a self-putdown, name-calling is a form of blame and condemnation. The message is that you *are* a jerk for acting jerkily, and of course, this is not true. I would like you to think about name-calling for what it really is: verbal violence. If unnecessary violence is immoral or unethical, then this is also true of verbal violence.

If there is anger erupting in the emotions, then the violence becomes instantly apparent. When a parent reprimands by calling her child stupid — the child starts to associate her behavior with who she is. "If I behave stupidly, then I am stupid" is the child's erroneous conclusion. The child will also tend to adopt this newfound philosophy, and the next time she behaves badly, she will act verbally violently toward herself and berate herself. Did you have a critical parent or other significantly critical people in your life? In all likelihood, you learned to be self-critical from them.

Another important issue that is sometimes overlooked: When a parent berates a child, the child feels bad and will come to associate feeling bad with the parent. Not good! If substantial criticism happens between two people of similar social status, a fight of some sort — direct or indirect, verbal, emotional or physical — is often impending.

If a parent calls the driver of another car a name, while the other driver may be oblivious to the name-calling, the child in your car is not, and again will tend to adopt a blaming attitude: behave badly and *you* are bad. No matter how you look at it, name-calling acts as a poor model for others to follow; it's a form of unethical violence and tends to create negative feelings and a weaker self-image in others or ourselves.

Try not to make things personal. Leave one's personhood out of it. Instead of saying, "He's a jerk for cutting me off" try saying "I don't like the way that guy is driving." One is an attack on the person and the other is a statement about another's behavior. The first is illogical and abusive, the second is an opinion or fact without the personal attack.

What the World *Doesn't* Need More Of

There is a substantial difference between a critique and criticism. A critique is an evaluation of something, providing the strengths and the weaknesses. Criticism is your basic faultfinding. The former is often helpful for positive changes to occur. The latter tends to be negative with few, if any, positives associated with it.

Who wants to be criticized? Try standing up in a group sometime and ask that question: "Who here would like me to come over and criticize you for 10 minutes?" My guess is you will not get many takers. If criticism was a positive then you would get a whole slew of people raising their hands.

What about "helpful or positive criticism"? I do not think people want criticism of any kind, positive or otherwise. I think that people would like praise on their attempt at a task and then, *possibly*, information on how to improve. This is the best case scenario. Notice I said "possibly"? Not all people want or appreciate unsolicited advice on how to improve.

People seem to be very generous when it comes to dishing out criticism. Remember when you did something wrong in grade school? Usually, a dozen kids were there to point it out to you — and kept mentioning it for days on end — as if you didn't realize it. Dent your parent's car as a teenager and the criticism that was forthcoming was usually abundant, as if causing the dent was your intention so as to invite more criticism in life. People in general are all too willing to criticize and far more hesitant to praise.

It would seem as if our philosophy is to err on the side of criticism. We would not want to accidentally praise when it was unwarranted, unsolicited or unexpected, now would we? That really would be a tragedy, huh? I'm clearly being facetious to make a point that our obsession with criticism is asinine and that it is better to err on the side of praise.

Criticism is inherent in blame. Criticism itself does not constitute blame, but the criticized individual will very often denigrate herself and feel like she is somehow less worthy as a person. Criticism is something that the world just does not require more of. If you think of it, there really isn't a shortage of criticism. In fact, we tend to stock pile it — remembering every little thing gone wrong. God forbid that we forget when we or someone else made an error. If we keep count, then we can tally up the score the next time a mistake is made and really get into some heavy-duty name-calling and blame.

While I am poking fun at our societal tendency to criticize, it is anything but funny. Criticism keeps us focused on the problem, instead of the solution and helps us develop feelings that will keep us blocked from finding solutions and encourages others to be critical in return.

If you believe providing a critique is appropriate or it is important to voice your displeasure, here are a couple of points to keep in mind:

1. Rarely criticize; praise in abundance.

2. Focus on the behavior only and not the person.

3. Praise a person's attempt, his/her effort or positive intent.

4. Explain why you are voicing your thoughts.

5. Provide ideas on how to achieve better results next time.

6. Praise and show appreciation for the individual.

The Conceited Fascist

Some years ago, I had a client who had spent a good chunk of her session adamantly expressing what a no-good crumb she was. She expressed, in an almost prideful way, what a screw-up she was as a parent, wife and employee. At times she got visually angry with herself. Then I stepped in with a comment that she truly was not expecting.

I said very softly but with firm emphasis, "You know, I don't think I have ever met anyone as conceited as you are." Her face went blank. She didn't know what to say. She had just finished telling me what a screw-up she believed herself to be. How could I think that she was conceited?

I asked her if she would be angry with me and degrade and berate me if I told her that I had made a mistake at something. She said, "Absolutely not." Why not? Because lowly, undeserving, fallible peasants like me are *expected* to screw up, but not worldly, saintly, people like her.

Every time you give yourself a tongue-lashing or denigrate yourself for making errors, regardless of what the error is, you act as if you are somehow privileged on this planet and *should not* make mistakes. As if you are better than everyone else because, after all, others are allowed to and in fact, expected to make mistakes. If we are all humans and as humans none of us are perfect, then by definition we are supposed to make mistakes as we travel through life. It is inevitable. It's a given. Fait accompli.

So as an imperfect, error-making, blundering human being, why *shouldn't* you make mistakes? There is, of course, no reason why you *shouldn't* make mistakes. It is desirable and beneficial not to make mistakes, but as a human, you will.

"But I know better."

This retort usually comes from a person arguing for why he/she really is a no-good-nick. What would make anyone think that just because one knows better he/she will not repeat the same error over and over and over? Just because we know better does not mean that we will not forget, not pay attention or not simply fail to learn from our errors and then repeat them. That's what people do. Again and again and again! Somehow, because it is a good idea to learn from our mistakes, we think that we absolutely should.

"But there is no excuse for not learning from our mistakes."

I wish we would consistently learn from our mistakes and never repeat them, but that is not the case. Sometimes we do and then we progress. Sometimes we don't, and repeat the same mistakes until we learn from them. Either way, belittling yourself will not help you.

When you denigrate yourself, you are acting like a little Hitler. A fascist. Something is wrong and you are going to have a temper tantrum and beat up on yourself. Doesn't the fascist take the stance that there are good, deserving, superior people and there are bad, undeserving, flawed people? The good people — the Aryans, and the bad people — the Jews. The good people — the whites, and the bad people — the blacks. This highly pernicious, destructive and dangerously flawed thinking is the essence behind all forms of blame: There are good people who do things correctly and are deserving and there are bad people who screw up and warrant condemnation.

When someone errs in life, there are usually natural consequences or man-made consequences. I am not suggesting in any way that consequences should not be applied to mistakes. In fact, negative consequences help people learn from their mistakes. Buddha believed, as is supported by current psychological research, that it is unwise to intervene between a person's behavior and the consequences of his/her behavior. This is a good rule of thumb. Receiving consequences is how people learn. What I am saying is, that it is unhealthy to denigrate or attack a person in any fashion in an attempt to make him or her better.

A mid-to-late 1800s philosopher, Friedrich Wilhelm Nietzsche, had this to say about punishment, although his words are equally true for blame:

> "Distrust all in whom the impulse to punish is powerful. The broad effects which can be obtained by punishment in man and beast are the increase of fear, the sharpening of the sense of cunning, the mastery of the desires; so it is that punishment tames man, but does not make him 'better.'"

Chapter 24

Undoing Blame

For as long as I can remember there have appeared to be topics that are generally not open for discussion in any social setting, such as religion, politics, abortion and the death penalty, among others. It has been clear to me that once a person's mind is made up, it closes down to opposing views. Rarely are there exceptions to this. It does not matter how sound and thorough one's logic may be, if another person has made up his/her mind with an opposing view, facts, logic and rational thought have no place in that discussion.

A large number of people even seem rather intolerant and get angry when another person has a contrasting opinion. It amazes me that we are shocked more by a person making a blunder or faux pas in etiquette than by a person making a mistake in logic and reason.

If you are one among the great majority who is almost literally addicted to blaming yourself or others, I encourage you to discard your unwarranted blaming philosophy and adopt a healthier, more sensible, effective and functional strategy. To eliminate the blame philosophy, it is important to do three things on an ongoing basis until blaming concepts have been exorcised from your thinking:

1) Stop subscribing to the concept of blame
2) Rethink and challenge the notion of blame every time you use blame or even think about it
3) Practice talking and thinking in ways that illustrate a separation between a person and his/her behavior (e.g., I don't know Jim very well but I do not like what he is doing).

Blame is immoral.

If unnecessary violence done to others is immoral, verbal violence, too, is immoral, both to yourself and others. You are human and as such are allowed to make mistakes. Charity and forgiveness apply to all people and not just a select few. We all behave badly from time to time and with this as a given, it's important to allow ourselves to be human and then to forgive ourselves, receive the outcome of our behavior, hopefully learn from it and then move on.

We are imperfect.

None of us is God. We are fallible and will continue to make mistakes...all kinds of mistakes. This is why they put erasers on pencils. To err is human; to forgive is divine — not a bad philosophy. This does not imply that we should continue to blindly put up with transgressions. Of course it is important to act and correct the wrongs and ills of society, but to preoccupy our present with self-condemnation is distracting and a waste of our time.

Blame is anti-religious.

All major religions throughout the world remind us that we have sinned and that condemnation — judging the person along with his behavior — is wrong.

"Blessed are the merciful..."
Mathew 5:7

"Judge not, that ye be not judged."
Matthew 7:1

*"He that is without sin among you,
let him first cast a stone at her."*
John 8:7

When we blame, we judge, *and* we throw that stone.

Blame perpetuates bad behavior.

If you believe you are a bad person for doing a bad thing; well, what do bad people do...more bad things. When we denigrate ourselves or someone else, there is a tendency to feel bad. When we feel bad and focus on the bad thing that we did, we are distracting ourselves from focusing on the solution. Also, when we feel bad, we tend to have less confidence and tend to feel weaker. If we are going to challenge a bad habit or behavior then this is exactly the opposite of what is normally required: feeling stronger and more confident.

Blamers offer a poor role model.

People who utilize blame as a philosophy or display contempt habitually in life tend to have children that will also adopt this belief system. Just as alcoholic parents have a higher incidence of raising alcoholic children or depressed parents raising depressed children, so too with blamers. Children imitate and adopt their parents' belief systems regardless of what the parents say. Children pick up on the smallest of nuances developing accents, tone of voice and facial expressions. It is little wonder why blamers raise self-critical, contemptuous children who could be spared years of distress if the parent assumed a different and less judgmental position in life.

Attempt never to judge people to be good or bad.

It simply does not make sense to judge people at all. Judging their behavior makes a lot of sense. In fact, it is important to judge our behavior as right/wrong, good/bad, practical/impractical, functional/non-functional or beneficial/harmful. People who do good things are simply that, people who do good things. These same people may occasionally also do bad things. This does not suddenly make them bad people, just people who did bad things. It is an over-generalization and illogical to judge a whole person based on a few select behaviors. In this way we avoid both pride and vanity and work toward our goal of enjoying a happy, productive and fulfilling life.

<u>NOTE</u>: Judgment and judgmental are two different things.

Some people have come to believe that judgments and being judgmental are the same thing. The common or informal use of judgment is: "In my judgment..." Thus, "judgment" is commonly used as the capacity to form of an *opinion* after consideration; to assess situations or circumstances and draw sound conclusions. It is important that you make judgments, which differs sharply from being judgmental.

When one is being judgmental, it implies the person is stating a moral imperative; an over generalized absolutistic *moral fact* without sufficient information, understanding, wisdom or appreciation of the situation.

"Judgmentalness and
self-righteousness go hand in hand.
Unless you are perfect
and without flaw, abandon both."

"What do I do?"

1. Remind yourself that the people you interact with are simply expressing behavior that you either like or dislike. This behavior does not encompass who they are.
2. Do not use labels (e.g., jerk, idiot, genius, etc.) with others or yourself.
3. Realize everyone has a mixture of good and bad qualities.
4. Eliminate any putdowns, name-calling or denigrating comments from your thinking and your speech.
5. Practice praising yourself and others, even small seemingly insignificant but positive behaviors. Praise the attempt, irrespective and independent of the outcome.
6. Speak in terms of "he behaved badly" or "I don't like what she did," instead of "I don't like her/him for doing that."
7. Explain the concept of blame — that a person and his/her behavior are not the same thing — to others.

SECTION HIGHLIGHTS

➤ The evaluation of human worth is a faulty and dangerous practice.

➤ It is impossible to fully rate a person, but it is relatively simple to evaluate any particular behavior.

➤ Both pride and shame are flawed concepts that rate a person based on his/her behavior.

➤ A person is never good or bad based on behavior or anything else; a person just exists with various behaviors.

➤ No matter how badly a person behaves, it does not make *him/her* bad.

➢ No matter how well a person behaves, it does not make *him/her* good.

➢ There is no blame, although there may be responsibility.

➢ Unhealthy Blame: making a bad decision means the person is bad.

➢ Healthy Responsibility: making a decision and being responsible for it, good or bad.

➢ All people are a mixture of good and bad qualities and behaviors.

➢ Saying that you *are* a "teacher" is a gross over-generalization; you only exhibit those behaviors some of the time.

➢ If unnecessary violence is immoral, then verbal violence is also immoral, regardless of whom it is directed to.

➢ Minimize any form of criticism; practice praising often.

➢ Self-blame is a form of conceited fascism.

➢ Blame is immoral.

➢ We are imperfect.

➢ Blame is anti-religious.

➢ Blame tends to perpetuate bad behavior.

➢ Blamers offer poor role models for others to follow.

➢ Never judge people to be good or bad, only label their behavior that way.

Section VI

Depression Entrapment

Section Preface

In general, people seem to have a lot of neutral emotions or "blah" emotions. Unless there is a distinct emotion like happiness, excitement, anxiety or anger, a lot of people tend to be just "okay." Sort of flat-lined. No particular emotions going on at the time. They are not distinctly happy or sad, at peace or in turmoil. Just okay. This simple "okayness," more often than not, is a low-level depression. They aren't crying in the corner or contemplating suicide. Just sort of okay.

Over the next week, notice when you are having this emotionally neutral or blah time. Then, notice what you're thinking during that time. Pay special attention to your thoughts. They may have become so routine as to have become mundane and almost unnoticeable, but they are there. Notice if your thoughts reflect self-criticism, feeling tired and frustrated with your situation or feeling sad for another's problems.

I'm going to talk about depression in more general terms — feeling blue, down, dejected, blah, numb, indifferent, detached, apathetic, disinterested, aloof, dead, emotionally dull. These are all expressions of depression, usually in its most common and mildest form. This section will, however, apply whether you are seriously depressed or just feeling "down in the dumps."

It's time to address the depression that plagues huge segments of our population. Most people are not even aware that they are mildly depressed. Here's a little test: If you are not feeling distinct happiness or some other specific emotion, chances are you are depressed, either mildly or significantly.

Depression is energy-absorbing, so people simply find themselves doing less over time; being less involved in life as they get older, being less active, less creative, less enthusiastic, bored. Without knowing it, this melancholy that has produced so many TV watchers, has become the opiate of the people. This emotional blandness has become the norm, and few recognize the seriousness of this state of being.

Who do you think typically laughs more, children or adults? Right. Children. When you were a child, you did not think, "Boy, I can't wait to grow up and laugh less!" But somehow, that's what has happened to you or someone you know.

There can be many biological causes for various degrees of depression. <u>ALWAYS CHECK WITH YOUR DOCTOR</u>. Whether your melancholy is caused biologically or not, there will be a change in your thinking, and that is something you do have some control over. This is what we are going to look at in this section: the types of thinking that most commonly cause depression.

Whether depression shows itself in its mildest form of just laughing less or whether one is crying throughout the day and is severely depressed, it is important to apply several approaches at the same time. You will want to combine new philosophies or thinking strategies with practicing those behaviors that support these attitudes. When the attitudes and the behavior coincide for a period of time, the emotions begin to change. Practice new thoughts. Practice new behaviors and the emotions follow.

Certain specific types of fallacious thinking apply to all emotional entrapments. Pay special attention to recognizing these unsound beliefs and eliminating them.

NOTE: Please re-read the Section Highlights of the three previous sections (pages 117, 153, 181) as these relate strongly to depression. This section will be more targeted, filling in the gaps so you can learn to eliminate that "down" feeling from your daily experience.

Depression Entrapment

Chapter 25

Self-Denigration

Psychologist Dr. Paul Hauck in his exemplary book called "Overcoming Depression" does an outstanding job at ripping apart depression (available at the Albert Ellis Institute), and is a "must read" for anyone experiencing the doldrums. With biological determinants of depression left to your physician, psychologically speaking there are four interrelated causes of depression:

1. Self-Denigration
2. Feeling Sorry for Yourself
3. Perceived Immobility
4. Feeling Sorry for Others

The beliefs that are associated with depression are:

1. An earnest belief in one's personal inferiority
   (see Sections I & V)
2. Believing that not getting what one "needs" is
   "terrible" (see Section III & IV)
3. Believing that things are "awful" the way they are
   (see Section IV)

Self-Denigration: the beginnings of depression

The beliefs associated with self-denigration and self-condemnation are:

1. I have sinned, failed, hurt someone or otherwise
   acted badly.
2. I *should* not do bad things and *never* make
   significant mistakes.
3. As a result, *I am* a bad person and *deserving* of
   pain and punishment.

The previous section — Worth Entrapment — details the most common initiator of depression: Blaming, condemning and denigrating oneself. When you denigrate yourself for anything, you weaken yourself. You are hassling yourself. Dishonoring yourself. You will feel like the world is ganging up on you or that your problems are becoming insurmountable. This will tend to lead to feeling sorry for yourself: the second cause of depression. When feeling weaker, making decisions will become more difficult as you doubt yourself more. You will have a sense of immobility, being stuck, unable to take action. Helplessness sets in. Believing that your life has become a tragedy, and speaking of tragedies, you see them occurring for others as well and hopelessness takes over.

This is not an uncommon series of steps for the etiology or creation of depression. Depression, more often than not, begins with a sense of self-condemnation or self-criticism. It is difficult to feel good about yourself when you are constantly being criticized. This is true whether you or someone else is doing the criticizing.

Self-denigration will get you depressed as surely as the sun sets in the west. Learn to let yourself be human and make mistakes, regardless of what those mistakes may be. If you do not like repeating your mistakes, you can forcefully attempt to minimize them in the future. Or you can ignore them and let them keep happening. Either way, getting angry with yourself will not eliminate errors, correct wrongs done or help you to be happier. Remember that your happiness remains the goal. Why? Because happy people tend to make fewer mistakes, concentrate better, be more creative and are normally personally and socially responsible.

Self-denigration and guilt are virtually synonymous, but *feeling* guilty and *being* guilty are two different things. You can be guilty of doing something wrong, but not feel guilty about it. One is an act and one is a feeling. Now, I am not suggesting that people act badly and have NO feelings about it — that is usually more descriptive of the sociopath. (Sociopath: One who is affected with a personality disorder marked by aggressive, antisocial behavior and who is void of remorse.)

An appropriate emotional expression when having behaved

badly would range from mild concern or disappointment to intense feelings of grieving or regret. For most people committing most types of errors, mild concern, frustration or disappointment are appropriate. These feelings will help to motivate and inspire one to make the appropriate changes. Guilt and self-flagellation are not required and are never, under any circumstances, desired.

Feeling guilt is an unhealthy feeling created as a result of self-recrimination, self-anger or self-hate. None is healthy as each will weaken you, and you will never do better in life feeling weaker as opposed to stronger. And, feeling stronger is the key to handling life confidently.

Three reasons never to denigrate yourself

Remember that the essence of blame and denigration is to combine the *individual* with her *behavior*. When you berate yourself, you are basically saying, "Because I behaved badly, I am bad." Or, "Because I behaved like a jerk, I am a jerk." It is unfairly combining the deed with the doer. You are and will always be more than your deeds. To combine the two is a gross oversimplification and a recipe for depression.

There are three irrefutable reasons never to down yourself (or anyone else) ever at anytime. They are:

1. Physical impossibility
2. Lack of knowledge or skill
3. Judgement errors and emotional distress

Physical Impossibility: Let's say a mentally handicapped child takes his brother's pellet gun and shoots at passing cars. An accident occurs where several people die. Is the child a bad, wicked, evil person? No. He was not capable of knowing better.

What if a young girl is taking ballet, but because of an inner ear problem has poor balance and will never be proficient at ballet. Is she a bad person? Of course not. She is physically limited. You would say, "Nice girl, doesn't dance very well." YOU WOULD SEPARATE WHO SHE IS FROM HER LIMITATIONS AS A DANCER.

Lack of Knowledge or Skill: What if there is no physical limitation? Then is blame okay? No! There may be a lack of knowledge or skill and it would be completely erroneous to blame someone for not being talented, skillful or knowledgeable in all areas of life.

If we placed you in a jumbo-jet and asked you to fly it, my guess is that you would do a poor job. If during your first week of driving you forget to set the parking brake on your car and it rolls down a hill and kills someone, while you are definitely responsible, it does not make you a bad person. Meaning that you did not somehow suddenly become a bad person for not having the knowledge, foresight, skills or habits to behave better. If your best friend showed you his newly wallpapered living room and you noticed that the wallpaper was mismatched right down the center of the room, you would not think, "Bad wallpapering job; he must be a bad person." Not in a million years. You would be more likely to think, "Nice guy but not a very good wallpaperer." Here too, YOU WOULD SEPARATE YOUR FRIEND'S SKILLS AT WALLPAPERING FROM WHO YOUR FRIEND IS.

Judgement Errors and Emotional Distress: Okay, so the issue you might have with yourself is that you did something that you knew was wrong or you took a risk and it turned out badly. It is not that you were physically limited or that you did not have sufficient skills, you simply messed up royally. Well, there's still no rational, good, healthy or sane reason to denigrate, disparage or blame yourself.

Let's say that your best friend comes to your door late one evening. You open the door and he is standing there pale and shaking. My guess is you would invite him in and ask him what's wrong.

He tells you that it was a co-worker's birthday and the gang at work took him out for a celebration. Your friend tells you that all he had was two beers, but on the way home he mistakenly ran a stop light and killed a small child. He has just come back from the police station where they fingerprinted him and all and he goes into court tomorrow.

Of course, you would say to your best friend, "You did this bad thing, therefore you are a bad and wicked person." You'd spit at him, kick him and order him out of your house. Not on your life! You would be aware that he made a serious error in judgement, has killed another and has gotten himself into very serious trouble. You would console, comfort and reassure him that you are there for him.

Internally, YOU WOULD SEPARATE WHO THIS WONDERFUL FRIEND OF YOURS IS FROM HIS THINKING, HIS JUDGEMENTS, HIS REASONING and what is more personal than that?

Now the question is, "If you were the one who ran the light would you be as loving, compassionate and forgiving?" If not, why not? Why is your friend deserving of such thoughtful compassionate consideration and you are not?

The third reason for never berating yourself is 1) you are an imperfect human and will make errors in judgements or 2) as a feeling human, you will make errors driven by emotional distress. How would you expect a distressed person to behave? In a distressed manner, of course. We may not like our behavior when we get distressed, but it does not make *us* bad, it makes our *behavior* bad.

Humans make all kinds of reasoning, thinking, personal, social, relational and financial errors to name a few. These errors are more common and usually intensified when we get ourselves depressed, angry, fearful, jealous, embarrassed, etc. Blunders don't make us bad, they make us human. While we may make some very bad decisions when we get distressed and some unpleasant consequences may befall us, it's still no reason to castigate ourselves. You will never achieve anything of worth through self-denigration or guilt. Never!

The illogical connection

When you were young you were taught to be self-critical and to berate yourself. This is what happened — you were told one thing that was true and two things that were false:

1. "What you did was wrong." — True.
2. "You're a bad girl for doing that." — False!
3. "You should be ashamed of yourself." — False!

Basically this was said: You did something wrong, which may be true. Then you were told that because you behaved badly, you somehow magically became a bad person. This is absolutely false. Then you were told to be ashamed of yourself. This means that you should not like who you are because of something you did. This is the worst kind of manure you could imagine. There is never a good reason to dislike who you are. It will only help to increase bad behavior, emotional distress and greater mental confusion.

Did you ever have a pet that you absolutely loved? Let's say you have a puppy named Tanner.

While you are training Tanner, he wets on your rug. Do you stop loving Tanner? No. Why not?

You continue to love Tanner although he behaved badly. While you may discipline Tanner and not like his behavior, you think "I love my dog...don't like him wetting on the rug." You separate his behavior from your love for him.

You would never use the same steps for Tanner as others did for you growing up. What if your parent said to you:

1. Tanner wet on the rug which is wrong.
2. Therefore, Tanner is a bad, wicked, evil dog for wetting.
3. Therefore you should stop loving Tanner.

WOULD YOU STOP LOVING TANNER? Of course not. You would continue to love your puppy unconditionally as I would suggest you do for you! While you may do something wrong, you are NEVER a bad, evil or wicked person and NEVER are deserving to be hurt or feel ashamed or to dislike yourself. YOU HAVE THE INALIENABLE RIGHT TO LIKE AND LOVE YOURSELF ALWAYS — REGARDLESS OF WHAT YOU DO.

Here's a hint: re-read "What do I do?" and Section Highlights of Section I on self-love (pages 45 and 46). Attempt to always talk to yourself as lovingly as possible, much the way you would likely talk to your dearest friend and then treat yourself that way as well.

Chapter 26

Feeling Sorry for Yourself

The beliefs associated with feeling sorry for yourself are:

1. I want to get my way.
2. It is *awful* when I do not get my way.

Feeling sorry for yourself is a mental or an emotional form of suffering known as self-sorrow or self-pity. It is most often derived from the weakness that grows out of self-denigration.

Feeling sorry for yourself is a "condition" we all have under the right circumstances. If your family and partner reject you, your boss fires you, you lose all your money, society ostracizes you and your dog growls at you, somewhere in there, you will start to feel sorry for yourself. For most people, there is a point where they develop a "poor me" attitude. If you listen to people who have just had a significant problem develop in their life, they frequently ask, "Why me?"

Well, the question is, "Why not you?" There's a sense of grandiosity in asking "Why me?" Others have bad things happen to them, why not you? You may think it is unfair or wrong that bad things happen to you — and this may be true. But the question remains, "Why not you? What makes you so special as to be the only person who should avoid these things?"

I am not taking a harsh or cold approach, just one that conforms to reality. Life can be difficult and unfair. If life was fair, we would not need a justice department. Whoever told us that life was going to be fair or easy? It's just not that way.

We have grown up watching Westerns, cop shows, Disney movies and the like that give us the illusion that life is fair. The good guy rides off into the sunset on a white horse with his lady, while the bad guy is face down in the dirt wearing black. The message is that good things happen to good people and bad things happen to bad people. When bad things happen, we ask "why me" under the assumption that we have been a good person. It's a healthy understanding that, yes, sometimes bad things do happen to people who have attempted to do everything right, but that you *are* strong and *can* withstand it *and* grow beyond it.

Overcoming self-pity is the ability to roll with the punches, to realize that you are strong, that you will survive and that you can make things better. Believe it or not you can overcome, handle and stand anything. The basic belief system that gives power to feeling sorry for yourself is the amplification of negatives as described in Section IV, Awful Entrapment. Please review it to discover or find how it applies to you in this regard.

Remember what Nietzsche said, "Anything that doesn't kill me, strengthens me." This is a lesson well worth remembering when you are starting to feel down because of wallowing in self-sorrow. You will get through it and you will be stronger because of the adversities you face in life. In fact, some of your best learning experiences have been derived from unpleasant and unexpected experiences.

If you compare with others on television or your family or next door neighbor you may be comparing up — comparing with people who you believe are doing better than you. This is a colossal mistake because there is no comparison. They are different people with separate goals and desires and outcomes. Whatever comparison can be made remains problematic. There is no value in it — it will leave you feeling superior or inferior.

Feeling Sorry for Yourself: external sources

Be careful of believing in the criticism of others. When others criticize you they may be stating a truth or an opinion. If your parenting skills are criticized and you believe that you are a bad parent, then attempt to improve your parenting skills. Don't sit there and feel sorry for yourself. If it's true then it's true. Now do something about it!

If you believe that the criticism is untrue, then you simply have a difference of opinion. Let it go. Not everyone will always agree with your assessment of yourself or your skills.

Some people will feel sorry for themselves for not being loved enough. This leads us back to the first section on self-love. While it may be desirable to have more love or that special connection with another person in your life, it is hardly necessary and definitely not a catastrophe if you do not currently have what you want.

Feeling sorry for yourself can come from believing that you need or must have another's love to be happy or fulfilled. While this is completely erroneous, it is one of the most common and prevalent beliefs. In part, a frantic search for love comes from your lack of self-love — most evident in the sharpness of your self-denigrating skills.

To overcome feeling sorry for yourself requires a fair amount of enthusiastic energy in shredding self-weakening beliefs, trusting that you are strong and you can stand anything...always followed-up with lots of action! Have faith in yourself! Believe in yourself! Treat yourself wonderfully and take consistent, focused action toward your goals. Never say die.

Other feelings that promote self-pity

Trapped Feelings: Self-pity can develop from trapped feelings. If you tend not to be assertive, you will find that you get your way a lot less. People will tend to simply do things their way assuming you want or condone it if you do not speak up. With a lifetime of unassertiveness it can be easy to believe that 1) you're just not worth it or 2) that you don't deserve to have your way or 3) that other people are more important and 4) letting them get their way will make you happy. While all of this is rubbish, it has been my experience that people can convince themselves of almost anything. Do not buy into this nonsense.

It is important that you speak up assertively. If you do not express your thoughts and feelings freely to those around you, how will they ever get to know you? Of course, that's some people's fear: "If they get to know me, they'll find out what a crumb I *really* am." If you think about it, this is never true.

In over twenty years of doing therapy, I have never known a person that others didn't like once other people really got to understand and to know who he/she is...deep down. It is the façade, the pretence and the inappropriate unpleasant emotional displays that most people dislike most. Unmask the genuine you, and you will naturally find the people who like the real you, and then you will both win.

Attempt to assert yourself with others, a little at a time, until you have learned to express your thoughts and feelings appropriately and freely. In doing so, you will become a stronger person (and other people like strong individuals), you will get more of what you want, and feeling sorry for yourself will be minimized.

Fear of Feelings: Emotional discomfort is part of our emotional richness. While excessive emotional reactions can be most unpleasant, many people fear any emotional discomfort to the extreme. These people tend to live a life of emotional blandness fearing their own emotions. Usually, unassertive people have the belief that "I might feel bad so I do nothing."

Taking risks is part of the wonderfulness of life. You roll the dice and take what comes up. Life is about risk. Every time you try something, anything, you take a risk. I have never met an elderly person who said, "I really wish I would have done less in life."

People who fear their emotions and tend to live their lives in a state of unconscious self-pity are missing out on so much of life, to what degree they will never even know. If you are one of these people, Escaping Emotional Entrapment was written for you. It is important to get a handle on your emotions so that it is you who is in control and not random circumstances in life.

People traditionally say, "take care" at the end of a letter or conversation, I like to say, "take risks" because that is how we grow. It is impossible to grow if you do things the way you have always done them. Take one step at a time so long as you keep taking that next step. People who are risk-takers are not self-pitiers.

"Rapid Intolerance"

Dr. Albert Ellis will be long remembered by many for being the first to condense emotional disturbance to simply whining and complaining about the way things exist. As oversimplified as it may sound, he is essentially correct.

We, as a modern culture, tend to moan and grumble about not getting enough approval, respect, money, admiration, job opportunities, sex, you name it — we whine about not getting our way. Now, most people do not whine about everything, just certain things unique to them.

Two centuries ago there seemed to be a lot less griping though times were tougher. There was, by all accounts, also a lot less time and little focus on fun, pleasure and personal fulfillment. Nevertheless, either you tended your fields when necessary or you and your family starved to death during the winter months (in the northern climates of course). There was no welfare and no expectation that anyone was going to provide for you. Like it or not, life fell squarely on *your* shoulders. Today, people bellyache about not getting their way and how tough life is.

Rapid intolerance is just that: becoming intolerant to problems, disappointment and dissatisfaction rapidly. *Discomfort intolerance* is similar but relates to one's intolerance to any form of discomfort. Both are the essence behind self-pity, anger, some depression, procrastination, anxiety and most fears and that only starts the list. When depressed, one's poor skill-set at handling disappointment and dissatisfaction most often comes across as, "Poor me. My life *should* be the way I expect it to be: easy and effortless, and it's *awful* when it is not. I *must* do everything in my power to avoid difficulties, unpleasantness and discomfort because *I couldn't stand it* otherwise."

Listen to *"poor me"* in that almost-whining voice. Sends shivers down your spine, huh? When we are feeling sorry for ourselves, that is the whine that others hear: "Poooor meeee!" That is why people who feel sorry for themselves have a difficulty keeping friends. Who wants to listen to that? Most people will want to tell you plainly, "shit or get off the pot."

Rapid intolerance was epitomized in the humorous quip I heard as a kid: "God give me patience. But, HURRY!" Not having sufficient patience in life often leads to fast and usually thoughtless behavior. People often re-act by striking out (anger) or withdrawing (anxiety and depression).

The way to become happier and more satisfied is always "thoughtful action." And that's the hard part because depression is so energy absorbing that it *appears* there's no energy to take action. The key word here is "appears" because there *is* energy to spare. Always! If you are sitting there watching television and you notice the curtains suddenly catch fire — you would have an abundance of energy in a flash.

When something does not go your way, one path to overcoming the withdrawal, agitation or irritation caused by discomfort intolerance is not to consult your feelings. This may sound odd at first, but it is something you do a thousand times a day. You likely don't consult your feelings as to whether or not you are going to brush your hair, put on underwear or tie your shoes. You just do it. For the most part, you do not consult your feelings when you fill your car with petrol. You know that either you put fuel in your car or it stops on the highway.

Imagine if difficulties were the deciding factor in how our world ran. When was the last time your teacher said, "All those who find writing exams easy, come and write the exam"? Wouldn't that be absurd? Either you write the exam and get a mark or you don't and you get zero. Difficulty is not an issue. Either you do or you don't.

Anytime someone starts off with, "That's *so* hard" or "That's *too* hard" or "I don't *feel* like it," you can bet that it's likely discomfort intolerance or self-pity that's taking hold.

"So it's hard? So what?" Either you do it or you don't. You will get a different outcome either way. The outcome doesn't care, but you do! Difficulty is not the issue. Admittedly, if it's fun to do or easy, then life is grand. But so often that is not the case. Do not consult your feelings when you have difficult things to do that you know are good, healthy or appropriate to do. As Nike® says, "Just do it!" and without consulting your feelings. It will get easier and more enjoyable if you are not consumed with your whining and complaining about the way the world is.

You can also try focusing on a good past or a good future if you do not like the present moment. It may help to distract you from an unpleasant "now." If you are getting a root canal, focusing on another more pleasant time will help you through the unpleasantness.

When possible, think about how you can improve and make more enjoyable the unpleasant task at hand. Work on making your time more pleasurable. Focus on the benefits of the outcome or the satisfaction you will feel. Do not let yourself get stuck in the rapid intolerance mode of self-pity. Trust in yourself that you can do it, will survive it, and flourish with enjoyment, fun and fulfillment as you develop increased tolerance to problems and displeasure.

"Believe that you can make a positive change in your life and then act on that belief."

Chapter 27

Perceived Immobility

The beliefs associated with perceived immobility are:

1. I *have to* get my way.
2. I *must* find a solution.

Perceived immobility is really a derivative of feeling sorry for oneself, but is characteristically different enough to be given it's own category. This form of depression occurs when a person is feeling stuck, immobile or in a conundrum.

Remember that feelings are just that: feelings. People often believe that there is no solution or that they are stuck in a problem but this is virtually never true. There is a solution, but one that they cannot readily find; or the solution is not ideal or does not sit right with them emotionally.

A man of 45 has an argument with his father and they part angrily. That night the father has a heart attack and dies. The son may find a lasting depression from perceived immobility or the inability to solve a problem:

"I *have to* tell my father that I'm sorry and that I love him,
but I can't because he's dead."

The problem is two fold: 1) believing he *has to* tell his father something and cannot, and 2) believing he *must* solve this problem. What goes on in his mind is: "I have to, but I can't. I have to, but I can't. I have to, but I can't. I have to, but I can't." So he drives himself into a depression. He is stuck. Immobilized.

If you ever find yourself in this type of depression the way out is abundantly simple, but not always easy: eliminate the insistence, the "have to." Or, make a decision in another direction — symbolically in this case by talking to his father at the gravesite, as an example.

Another possibility is that this man could also come to the conclusion that his father really understood the love that was shared between them and having one unresolved argument is inconsequential to a lifetime relationship. Not all problems have nice neat solutions, nor do they always need to be resolved. Closure does not have to happen with the other person, but is about coming to terms with reality.

Whatever the problem, it means either letting the problem go realizing there is no solution or sidestepping the problem and finding a different, maybe less satisfactory, solution such as in this example:

> I *have to* get a job, but I cannot because
> I can't afford daycare.

Either make do as is and struggle to get by or possibly start an in-home business so you can work from home and still make money. Neither may be necessarily desirable, but either will help to eliminate any depression caused by perceived immobility.

The key here is that the immobility is not factual, but perceived. Once a solution is found or a movement in a particular direction occurs, the depression lifts. There tends to be a strong element of frustration in this type of problem and when combined with rapid intolerance it's common for one to start feeling sorry for him/herself.

Chapter 28

Feeling Sorry for Others

The belief associated with feeling sorry for others is:

"I *should* get upset over other people's problems
or world conditions."

Feeling sorry for others is another offshoot of feeling sorry for yourself, only aimed in another direction. The sorrow felt can be aimed at oneself or others, and both will get you equally depressed.

From childhood there are subtle messages conveyed to you that you are *supposed to* get upset when things go wrong. To show caring, you *should* also get upset when things go wrong for others. "If you don't get visibly upset then you don't care" is the flawed thinking. But of course you can care about the plight of others and not get yourself distressed in the meantime.

I was speaking to a mother of a son whose marriage was ending. The mother was very distraught about the marriage ending, her grandchildren's fate and the distress her son was in. While caring, sadness or empathy would all be appropriate, feeling down and depressed over her son's problem was helping no one. In fact, it likely worsened the problems her son was experiencing because now there was no one to lean on — as he surely could not turn to his depressed mother for support.

People who feel sorry for others fail to recognize certain obvious facts: 1) Things could be worse and 2) there are virtually always positives.

Her son and grandchildren could easily be worse off in innumerable ways. There were many positives associated with the ending of *that* particular relationship. A few of the positives were: the kids wouldn't see fighting parents daily; both parents could pursue other healthier relationships; separation could be an impetus for growth; it would provide an opportunity to model for their children how to healthfully deal with the ending of a relationship, among others.

People who feel sorry for others for their plight in life can easily, though not meaning to, come across as condescending to others: "I'm so good that this couldn't happen to me," or "He's so weak, he couldn't possibly enjoy life with this problem." Condescension is not intended, but from the recipient's perspective, that's the way it sometimes feels.

Sorrow for others sometimes develops out of one's own fear of particular circumstances: "I'm so lucky it didn't happen to me." Because we think it would be a tragedy for it to happen to us, we erroneously believe it is a tragedy for others.

When you feel sorry for others, you'll get yourself feeling down and depressed — simply adding to the pain felt in this world by one extra person: YOU. A rule of thumb would be: If you want to help the suffering of the world, begin with yourself. In the words of Richard Bach in Illusions:

> "If a man told God that he wanted most of all to help the suffering world, no matter the price to himself, and God answered and told him what he must do, should the man do as he is told?...And what would you do...if God spoke directly to your face and said, 'I COMMAND that you be happy in the world, as long as you live' What would you do then?"

The impact from other pity is substantial, though never intended:

✦ It weakens others as they trust in you that their situation truly is horrible

✦ It increases the pain in this world by at least one person: the person doing the pitying

✦ It distorts reality by focusing only on the negative and ignoring the positive

Depression Entrapment

✦ It nurtures negativity and breeds fear

✦ It will distance you from others encouraging them to feel inferior to you or a burden to you

✦ It will help to increase your fear of pain and suffering

"Distress honors no one.
Do that which will help you
to be happier each day."

"There is nothing in this world <u>worth</u> being upset over."

Albert Ellis, Ph.D.

"What do I do?"

1. Praise yourself, accept that you make mistakes and errors in judgement; do not berate yourself and continually encourage yourself to do better in the future.
2. When things don't work out, take charge and actively work at making yourself or your life better.
3. Know that sometimes you are required to take action before feelings change. Avoid feeling self-pity by being proactive.
4. When feeling stuck in your life, make a decision and take any course of action and you will tend to feel better.
5. Provide caring and support for others, but don't "experience" their feelings. Things could be worse. Focus on the positives.
6. Do something fun and playful each day for the next week. Only you can find out what that is for you. Try anything.
7. Get out and socialize. Praise, compliment and be involved with others.
8. When accepting a compliment, look at him/her directly and say, "Thank you."

SECTION HIGHLIGHTS

➤ For the treatment of *clinical* depression, medication *and* psychotherapy often work best — see your physician.

➤ Many people suffer from a chronic form of mild depression generally displayed as emotional blandness.

➤ It's important to eliminate those thoughts that cause depression then to think *and* act in ways that promote happiness.

➤ The four psychological causes of depression are: Self-denigration; feeling sorry for yourself; perceived immobility; feeling sorry for others.

Depression Entrapment

➤ Self-denigration and guilt are synonymous, but *feeling* guilty and *being* guilty are two separate things.

➤ Guilty feelings tend to weaken you and help promote worse behavior.

➤ Three reasons not to blame: physical impossibility; lack of knowledge or skill; emotional distress/judgement errors.

➤ Blame assigns responsibility (good), and then it degrades the person (bad).

➤ Blame and it's cousin shame get you to stop loving yourself, and that's <u>NEVER</u> healthy.

➤ Self-pity is simply feeling sorry for yourself for not getting your own way.

➤ Bad things do happen to *all* people regardless of how well they have behaved in the past.

➤ Bad things will happen to you, *but* you are strong *and* can withstand them.

➤ Don't internalize other people's criticism of you, it is only *their* opinion — whether you agree with the criticism is up to you.

➤ Don't like something? Change it or learn to live with it (hopefully happily).

➤ You need what you need, but you do not need what you want.

➤ Perceived immobility is being mired in a problem that you believe has no escape: "I have to, but I can't." The way out of this depression is to make a decision or compromise which allows for movement.

➤ Care about, but do not feel sorry for another's predicament.

➤ Feeling sorry for others ignores two facts: things could be worse and there are virtually always positives.

➤ Feeling sorry for others increases the pain of this world by one person: the person doing the pitying.

➤ Pitying others nurtures negativity and will increase the fear of pain and suffering.

➤ Feeling sorry for others helps to weaken them not strengthen them.

*"You have the power to choose.
Choose to be happy."*

Section VII

Worry Entrapment

Section Preface

Do you worry? Get anxious? Many people are not aware of their worry or anxiety but it often shows up as: agitation, stress, mental preoccupation, restlessness, sleep difficulties, frequent irritation and problems managing weight, difficulty quitting smoking and eliminating other addictions or dependencies.

More people enter the therapist's office for reasons of anxiety than any other problem. Worry, fear, anxiety, panic and phobia are all kissing cousins of one another. In fact, there is a lot of crossover from one to another, and exact definitions separating them are clumsy at best. One thing is clear: When a problem of anxiety or worry develops, the focus that is on this feared event can be all encompassing and debilitating at its worst or distracting and counterproductive at its best. Because the feelings are so distracting, there is usually little attention paid to one's own thoughts or the process on how they create their anxiety. The next time you feel anxious, carefully examine your thoughts — all of them — from shortly before you started feeling anxious until after the anxiety subsides. Pay special attention to the "awfuls."

This section will be relevant to all future-oriented emotional entrapments such as Anxiety, Worry and Fear. I will blend these three emotions under the acronym of AWF and largely, discuss them as one.

The theory that I would like to put forth is: Feelings of

apprehension occur when we believe our happiness or well-being is being threatened. AWF may show itself when we anticipate future pain or displeasure, foresee a potential for loss of love and approval or when envisioning a failure that produces a lessening of self-acceptance.

Tangible fears are usually relatively easy to deal with. If you are afraid of dogs for example, you can avoid the dog or you can eliminate the fear. How? By slowly approaching dogs — first with pictures, then on TV, then with live dogs at a distance slowly bringing them closer. Pairing the dog with a pleasant "something," challenging self-weakening beliefs, while thinking healthy reasonable thoughts is called "desensitization" and works very well.

Some fears seem obvious and simple to identify, but are actually quite tricky. Take the fear of bridges for example. Seems pretty clear cut. "Fear of the bridge, the height of the bridge or crossing the bridge. What's so complicated?"

I was on a talk show a few years ago discussing fears, and the host of the show declared that his wife had a strong fear of bridges. The fear was so strong that there were places nearby that she had not been to in over 20 years because she would have to cross a bridge to get there. He had said that she had been to many therapists but nobody was able to help her significantly with her fear. I told him, while on the air, that there was no such thing as a "fear of bridges." He looked puzzled and assured me that his wife did have a fear of bridges. I guaranteed him it was quite impossible. This is what transpired:

"If I gave your wife a magic pill that would get rid of all of her bad feelings when driving over the bridge, would she then drive over the bridge?" He acknowledged that if the pill really did work, then she would drive over the bridge. "Then she isn't afraid of bridges," I said, "*she's afraid of her own feelings* when driving over the bridge. The bridge did not change, only her feelings. She's likely made little progress with other therapists if they've been working on her fear of bridges, instead of *her fear of feeling bad* when driving over a bridge." The point is, she was actually afraid of her own emotions but nothing dangerous or tangible.

There are only two things to fear: 1) physical harm or 2) emotional harm (i.e., being upset). The focus of this section will be on the latter.

NOTE: Sections III & IV relate strongly to displeasure anxiety while Sections IV & V relate most to acceptance and achievement anxiety. Please re-read the Section Highlights of all three sections (pages 117, 153, 181) before reading further on how to escape the worry entrapment.

"When faced with a neutral,
such as the future, assume a positive."

*"When you exaggerate negatives,
you reinforce, intensify and
deepen your negative emotions."*

Chapter 29

Identifying the Fear

Defining anxiety:

> A state of intense apprehension, uncertainty and fear resulting from the anticipation of a threatening event or situation, often to a degree that the normal physical and psychological functioning of the affected individual is disrupted.

Defining worry:

> To feel uneasy, anxious or concerned about something; be troubled with a persistent mental uneasiness.

Defining fear:

> A feeling of agitation and anxiety caused by the presence or imminence of danger; a feeling of disquiet or apprehension.

Physiological responses for anxiety and fear may include increased heart rate, altered respiration rate, sweating, trembling, weakness and fatigue. Psychological aspects include feelings of impending danger, powerlessness, apprehension and tension.

Anxiety, worry and fear (AWF) are a result of future-oriented cognitions. You would not feel guilty about the future because guilt, along with shame, embarrassment and anger are past-oriented emotions. Anxiety suggests feelings of fear and apprehension such that a person *might* not know exactly what he or she is anxious about. A common underlying cause is the "fear of being afraid." Worries and fears can range from the specific and isolated to the pervasive and unspecific. More people have the "fear of rejection and failure" than all other fears combined.

Think about something that you might become anxious about. Being in a cabin where you might encounter spiders or snakes? Flying? Or maybe something as safe as riding in an elevator? What you get anxious about could be virtually anything. It does not have to pose any real or physical threat, such as the case of the woman mentioned earlier who was afraid to drive over a bridge. What do you needlessly preoccupy your mind with? Do you have something in mind?

See if you can identify exactly what you are afraid of. Maybe you already know. But don't be too sure. Check it out and let's see.

Whatever you have in mind, whatever you are imagining, examine the steps you go through and play the movie out in your mind. Move it forward to the end. Here is an example:

I had a client who was telling me how she was afraid to ride in elevators. Since elevators these days are extremely safe with five times the cables needed, brakes and redundancy anti-falling features, safety was not in question. But she was still terrified. I had her advance the "movie in her mind." I asked her...

What would happen if you got into the elevator?

I just couldn't.

Of course you could, it'd just be unpleasant. So what would happen if you got into an elevator?

I would just die. I would be so anxious. I just couldn't handle it.

Well, you would not die, and we know you could handle it, though it might be extremely unpleasant because you would be so anxious. But what bad thing would happen *to* you?

If the elevator got stuck, I'd just panic.

Worry Entrapment

So let's say that the elevator gets stuck and you panic. You start crying and pounding on the door. As unpleasant as that is, nothing bad is happening *to you*. What bad thing will happen *to you*? (She looked at me somewhat bewildered and confused. She had not thought of it that way.)

What if other people were in the elevator? Then they might panic...

So let's say that there are a few others in there and you are all yelling, crying and pounding on the door. What bad thing has happened *to* you?

(She paused dumbfounded. She had never moved the movie forward enough to realize that nothing bad would occur, she'd just make herself unnecessarily anxious and upset over a "non-event." My client would make a big thing, a huge catastrophe over getting into the elevator thinking something horrible will happen, but it stopped there at her getting anxious. She never looked beyond that point.)

But I'd feel trapped! That would be horrible!

You would be trapped — that's not a feeling but a fact. To put it plainly, facts don't make you anxious, it's your evaluation of those facts that make you anxious. While, in all likelihood, you'd only be trapped for a few minutes, you have attached the label of "horrible" to being trapped. It is this label that is causing your distress and not the fact that you are trapped in an elevator. While being stuck in an elevator may be unpleasant and inconvenient, I want you to notice that still nothing

bad has happed to you. It is *you* who is needlessly
distressing yourself because of the way you label
the situation as horrible, awful and intolerable.

Move *your* movie forward and find out if there is something
else you might even be more afraid of. Or, are you simply afraid of
your own feelings of anxiety and that's what you are avoiding and
not so much a situation or thing? Like the woman in the elevator or
the person afraid of driving over the bridge, so often the real fear is
one of feeling bad or anxious.

Your prescription for eliminating anxiety

In the most general sense, anxiety is an internal warning system
that one is in danger of not getting or losing something that is
needed. While anxiety can be uncomfortable, it is absolutely not
dangerous. In fact, your bodily reaction is entirely natural; it's
merely out of context — meaning that you are acting as if you are
in danger, when in fact you are not.

Before I discuss three common forms of anxiety — displeasure
anxiety, acceptance anxiety and achievement anxiety — I would
like you to have an understanding of how to overcome all types of
fears. I am going to discuss "fear" in general for simplicity, but the
process is equally true of anxiety and worry. As complicated as the
process can be, the steps are basically simple.

1. The more you are internally motivated to overcome your
    anxiety or fear the better. For most people, overcoming
    fears is like walking across hot coals: It is uncomfortable
    or painful and very scary. So, it's tough at the start to keep
    doing that which you are afraid of and going places or
    doing things that will precipitate your anxiety. Keep your
    goals in sight and you will get there.

2. Identify, then *challenge* and argue — with gusto and vigor
    — any self-limiting, nonsensical beliefs that you have.

Make sure to follow any challenge to self-limiting beliefs with positive self-strengthening statements, the same kind that you would use to help encourage and motivate a dear friend to succeed.

3. Do it slowly. Very slowly attempt to approach that which you are afraid of or do that which you fear. Let's say you are anxious around large crowds. Go to a shopping mall on a low-traffic day and stay in the outer, lower-traffic areas. Your goal is to make yourself *mildly* anxious where it is still very manageable. Make sure you have control. In other words, a method of escape or a way to avoid the crowd easily and lower your anxiety at a moment's notice. The goal is not to terrify yourself, but to get you to feel comfortable and confident around groups one small step at a time. Each time you repeat this exercise, attempt to take it a little further and make yourself just a little bit uncomfortable. At no time is it a good idea to let your anxiety escalate. Make sure, though, you stay in there until the anxiety has subsided. Have endurance. In this way, you can travel miles, one small step at a time. Much like losing weight. It seems like a huge problem to lose 80 pounds but to lose 1 pound 80 times is a lot easier. As each exercise becomes comfortable, move forward until you find yourself somewhat uncomfortable again. Pursue this strategy until you have moved all the way to the end and the problem *and* the anxiety no longer exist.

4. While performing your exercise practice shredding self-weakening beliefs (as described in Chapter 19, page 145). Stay there until the anxiety or fear has subsided. If the fear jumps up in intensity at anytime, back away for awhile until you can try again, only letting yourself get slightly anxious each time.

5. After the exercise, make sure you celebrate, regardless of how well you did. That is what you would do for your child or your best friend. The idea is to CELEBRATE THE ATTEMPT and not the outcome. Many attempts will bring about a positive outcome, that is not in question. Simply encourage yourself to continue making attempts by celebrating your efforts.

6. Make sure to shred self-weakening beliefs and to do self-strengthening after each exercise. Do not let fear and trepidation creep back in. Keep on top of it.

7. Practice visual imagery first thing in the morning and last thing at night, always seeing yourself the way you would ideally like to be. This visual image can be a strong reinforcement and companion to the verbal shredding of your self-weakening beliefs. So you are now seeing yourself in a strong and confident manner (sans anxiety), talking to yourself in a strong and confident manner and behaving in a strong and confident manner. When these elements come together over a period of time, a new skill develops — anxiety leaves and confidence stays.

8. Practice the steps above until the anxiety has left completely. Make sure to practice the above 7 steps, ideally, daily. Remember the three elements for progress: frequency, duration and intensity.

Worry Entrapment

Chapter 30

Freud's Pleasure/Pain Principle

Sigmund Freud is the grandfather of "talk-therapy." He introduced a theory: We have a drive to achieve pleasure and to avoid pain as our chief motivating force in behavior. A person who experiences "Displeasure Anxiety" is anxious about an upcoming event that he/she finds unpleasant or painful to deal with, thus minimizing pleasure and happiness, thus motivating avoidance acts.

There are three beliefs that lead up to displeasure anxiety:

1. *"Some bad thing might happen."*
    Meaning, <u>you anticipate that something adverse or obnoxious is impending</u>. As a rule of thumb, the more distant the event, the less anxious you will likely be about it. Anxiety is less likely for those situations that can be postponed or avoided all together.

2. *"If it does happen, it would be awful and catastrophic."*
    This suggests that <u>if there is a loss, this loss would be of great enough importance to rob you of happiness</u>, now and in the future. In other words: "If 'x' happened, then I couldn't be happy." This statement is the essence behind anxiety. People tend not to get anxious about things that don't impact negatively on their happiness.

3. *"Because it would be catastrophic, I must find a solution to it so that I can control it."*
    <u>The inability to find a solution to a problem that is believed essential to be solved</u> is a key factor within anxiety. When anxious, there is a sense of helplessness or inability to cope with the identified concern. As there develops a mastery

and an ability to control conditions, anxiety is minimized. Another way to minimize anxiety is to *abandon the self-weakening beliefs* associated with anxiety *and* to actively and pragmatically deal with the concern to the best of your abilities.

Displeasure Anxiety

The belief that you "need" to be happy and content at all times will cost you greatly in life. Much of the time you won't even know how much this belief will be a detriment to you.

It may be uncomfortable for you to ask the woman across the dance floor to dance. It might be unpleasant to discuss a family member's rudeness. It might be stressful to ask for a raise or promotion at work. Most people who are skilled and successful in any area of life push through or tolerate the momentary loss of happiness and displeasure that those who fail do not.

There's an old adage: "When it is easier to change than to stay the same, people change."

This is so often true. People often give up far too early and are not persistent enough to put up with the disappointment of repeated failures. As the story goes…"You don't want to have your dreams go unfulfilled just because you gave up too soon. Imagine the forgotten nameless gent who gave up after his sixth attempt to create a delicious soft drink and 6-Up was a failure."

One problem behind displeasure anxiety is Discomfort Intolerance: poor tolerance to any form of discomfort. The problem is in two parts. First the person whimpers about the hardness, difficulty or unpleasantness of some aspect of life. Then, the person *insists* that the unpleasantness not be there or a solution be found because security and happiness *must* always be present. When a solution is not rapidly found or is not likely to be found, then displeasure anxiety results.

Displeasure anxiety is the real culprit behind a lot of anger, all forms of procrastination, jealousy, very often a lack of progress in one's life and virtually all addictions. When there is an unpleasant situation to face, the anxiety drives the person to escape the uneasiness, instead of dealing effectively with it. Avoidance behavior is a highly developed skill by those who have had years of displeasure anxiety. This is why it is important to be sincerely dedicated to overcoming it — because years of training will want to kick in and have you avoid the agitation and hard work of overcoming this form of anxiety. The way through displeasure anxiety is to WORK THROUGH IT!

"Apply yourself and you can overcome any adversity."

*"Self-reliance and interdependence
work together to produce
confidence and assertiveness."*

Worry Entrapment

Chapter 31

Never Be Lonely

Have you ever felt alone in a crowd? Or at peace while being all by yourself? *Being* alone is very different from *feeling* lonely. The essence of "lonely" is lack of a connection. Many people believe that this connection *has to* be with another person, but it doesn't. The most vital connection is with yourself. Self acceptance and self-love is the key to banishing loneliness forever.

If you are in short supply of self-love and self-acceptance, then you are in danger of developing anxiety or the fear of not being loved, appreciated or accepted by others. When people are in jeopardy of not receiving the love or approval they think they *must have* in order to remain happy and content, then acceptance anxiety kicks in.

There are two beliefs that lead up to Acceptance Anxiety:

1. *"I might not be liked, loved or appreciated the way I want or otherwise might be rejected."*
   While not being loved or being rejected may not be desirable, generally, it's a minor, practical frustration. If you are simply not getting the acceptance and loving you desire, it leaves you free to continue looking for it where you will receive it in abundance and in just the way you would like to receive it. Until then, you may feel slightly disappointed or mildly frustrated.

2. *"I must be loved and appreciated at all times and never get rejected as it would be awful and horrible if it did happen."*
   As soon as a person believes he/she *requires* love to be happy or fulfilled, then anxiety looms. It is putting one's own happiness in the hands of others. If the tides of fate flow favorably today, anxiety lowers. If the tide ebbs or

Worry Entrapment

recedes, the anxiety peaks. Believing that you *require* love, and if you don't get it, it is truly *horrible* will leave you constantly waiting for when the tides — you believe — will eventually turn. Anger, jealousy and permissiveness or acquiescence are common with acceptance anxiety.

Acceptance Anxiety

Acceptance anxiety can cause a dramatic display of intense emotions that are seldom seen with displeasure anxiety. Few people are truly free of acceptance anxiety. As long as one stays within her safety zone, this anxiety may appear non-existent, but in reality, it lies dormant waiting to be awakened the moment the safety zone is breached.

One of the strengths of a cognitive-behavioral approach to change as has been discussed and more specifically, Rational-Emotive-Behavior Therapy is the *active approach* to dealing with emotional problems. REBT's famous "shame attacking" exercises are indispensable to helping individuals actualize the desired change.

In essence, the shame attacking exercise is designed, in a controlled and predicable fashion, to get a person to stop mind reading and to tackle the idea that he or she needs to be loved and approved. The exact exercises are limited only by one's imagination.

Here's an experiment: Get into a busy elevator, walk right to the back, go up several flights then get out. Sounds simple enough? Do you think you could do it without any discomfort of what people might think of you? Maybe, you really do not have any acceptance anxiety lurking in the background. But, it is important to follow the directions: Get into a busy elevator — one with several people. Then walk straight to the back of the elevator. Don't turn around, just stand there with your nose up against the back wall. It is at this time people start to become uneasy about really doing this exercise in any serious way.

Imagine that. Just by standing in another direction from the crowd, you'd start to get anxious. Assuming you're not fearing someone stabbing you in the back, your fear is completely being driven by you thinking that you are being made fun of, thought badly of or otherwise rejected. This is representative of your belief in the necessity for love or acceptance. You have put your self-worth on a platter and handed it to strangers to either accept or reject. This experiment demonstrates complete mind reading on your part, as you don't even know if anyone has even noticed that you did not turn around.

The way out of this anxiety is to challenge the idea that you require another's love or acceptance for your worth or happiness. Understand that when you do not get the love you want, it's <u>NOT</u> a tragedy, but only disappointing. Re-read Section I on self-loving and Section V on self-denigration to refresh your memory and sharpen your skills in the self-love area.

Just in case this experiment did not get you anxious, try singing in the elevator or standing with your back to the door looking in and smiling at everyone. Do this with importance and politeness. The idea is not to make a joke out of it, but to do it naturally. This exercise can be escalated to the point where few people would not feel anxious about what others might think of him or her. The point being illustrated is that most of us have this irrational *need* — not just a desire — for love and acceptance. The weaker that *need* is, the healthier you will be.

<u>NEVER</u> put your sense of worth in the hands of another. Better yet, eliminate the idea of self-worth altogether and focus on self-acceptance, self-growth and happiness. In this way you will never feel lonely, but at peace within yourself.

*"Fear and anxiety can motivate us
to be a traitor to our
better judgment."*

Worry Entrapment

Chapter 32

The Spirit of Perfectionism

Here's a little test to see if you are perfectionistic: Can you name three things that you do with some frequency, that you enjoy doing and that you do poorly? Most perfectionists won't do things and definitely won't enjoy doing things that they do poorly.

The mood of the perfectionist is believing that he must behave properly, rightly or effectively to think well of himself. If you think that you must achieve to your predetermined yet arbitrary standard or you're a louse, then you will tend to remain perpetually anxious — as you may fail or make a mistake at any time. This is achievement anxiety.

It's not uncommon for people to tell me that they are perfectionistic yet do not down themselves. The question is, do you feel crummy when you perform less than perfectly or even poorly?

This form of anxiety will heighten, especially when you attempt a task that is new, there is likelihood of failure, or you have your identity dependent upon its success. Like with acceptance anxiety, achievement anxiety is strongly connected to one's sense of identity.

If you think of yourself as worthy or unworthy, you are already standing on a slippery slope. If anything threatens your sense of worthiness, value or rating, then anxiety ensues. As discussed in Section V — Worth Entrapment — it is better to discard the idea of worth altogether and focus on unconditional self-acceptance.

There are two beliefs that lead up to Achievement Anxiety:

1. *"I might not do well, might not succeed, might make a mistake or otherwise fail in some form."*
   The truth of the matter is that you will, from time to time, fail at almost everything in some way. No matter how much you practice writing, you will make a mistake. That

is why they put a backspace key on keyboards. While you will not like messing up, it is a fact of life, and I guarantee you that you are not so special as to never make a mistake. Besides, wouldn't *that* be boring.

2. *"To make mistakes or to fail would be terrible and prove that I am not a worthy person."*
Achievement anxiety will often be behind emotional entrapments such as: perfectionism, jealousy, anger, depression, shame, guilt and embarrassment. You, and only you would ever get to determine your worth — if you really believe that worthiness is a concept you wish to maintain in life. A healthier approach would be to sidestep the construct of "worthiness of a person" entirely and focus on self-love, fulfillment, enjoyment and self-acceptance. Combine this with the fact that it is only inconvenient, frustrating or a hassle to fail, and you have virtually eliminated this form of anxiety.

Achievement Anxiety

A few friends of mine were going out bowling just for an evening out. Light-hearted and playful was the planned atmosphere. I called a friend to see if he would like to join us and he told me that he wasn't a good bowler. I told him that his score didn't count, we were just going to grab a beer, talk, laugh and push the big black ball down the lane. His response was that he hadn't bowled in years. I reiterated that it did not matter if he had ever bowled before, we were just going out for a fun time. He restated that he was not skillful at the game and did not enjoy it much.

You can see what was happening here. He was basically saying, "If I don't do well at it, I can't enjoy it." How sad. If we are only going to do those things that we are skillful or proficient at, we will limit ourselves to only a handful of activities in a lifetime. Unfortunately, that is what many people do. How many new activities do you try a year?

Worry Entrapment

An ex-client of mine told me of this story shortly after she developed a sense of enjoyment just for enjoyment's sake: She was at home sculpturing with clay. A friend of hers came over to visit, noticed the sculpture and when asked what she thought said, "You know, your choice of texture isn't very good." "*I know*" my client said. "I don't mean to be critical but your proportioning isn't close to reality." "*I know*" my client acknowledged. "And, you know your balance and symmetry is way off." "*I know*." "Then why do you sculpt if you know that you don't have a talent for sculpting?" "*Because I enjoy it*," my client said confidently.

It is very possible to be atrocious at some activity and enjoy it thoroughly. Unfortunately, most people have a very difficult time enjoying or deriving any satisfaction from an activity that they do not perform well at. This limits their enjoyments to only the relatively few areas where they are competent.

One way to avoid "achievement traps" is to avoid risk by doing nothing. In that way, it is harder for you to get upset with yourself for making mistakes. The other way is when you do something, you do it perfectly or outstandingly well. Unfortunately, this would be a rare individual who could enter any arena of activity and perform well right from the start. One way to minimize achievement anxiety is to do anything just for the fun of it, independent of the outcome. Focus on enjoyment and on having fun *doing* instead of *doing well*. Continually challenge this notion that to feel good you must behave optimally. Do not amplify negatives and make a big thing out of potentially failing at anything and you will be much calmer.

Interacting Anxieties

While one area is usually the primary culprit, the three anxieties interact. As an example, I may believe that *I have to* perform well at my next lecture (achievement anxiety). This belief that *I must*, will tend to make me anxious. If I don't do well, especially because I happen to be anxious, then others will notice and think badly of me (acceptance anxiety). This potential failure, lack of acceptance and resulting infamy would be catastrophic to me, and thus my anxiety would go up fearing a loss of happiness, contentment and increasing emotional pain (displeasure anxiety).

It is important to be aware that when you try to eliminate one form of anxiety that one or both of the other anxieties may be lurking in the shadows. When you confront one form, explore the possibility of challenging the other two. Be relentless in challenging and eliminating anxiety.

"Doing is more important than doing well."

Worry Entrapment

Chapter 33

Overcoming Anxiety

If you understand the process to overcoming anxiety and fear that is outlined on pages 216 to 218, you have a good handle on what to do. Here's an example from my client files of a 45-year-old man whose job, in part, was to climb the stairs of a huge four-story oil reserve tank. The stairs circled around the outside of this enormous oil drum starting at the bottom going around to the top where the measurements were required to be taken.

1. Although my client, "Peter," was terrified of climbing the stairs, he was highly motivated to overcome his anxiety and fear as he enjoyed the rest of his job immensely.

2. Peter believed that he *must* feel comfortable to climb the stairs and by not climbing the stairs, that *made* him flawed, weak and unmanly. The stairs were safely enclosed with a guardrail and there was no real danger. He believed he *could not* climb those stairs. But the reality is that it *was* possible, although it might have been scary and unpleasant. I got him to forcefully challenge the notion that he *couldn't* climb the stairs. Peter also spent time countering his belief that having certain fears *made him* less manly, weak or flawed. I pointed out to him that it was these ideas that kept him from feeling stronger and more confident. He was to enthusiastically praise and encourage himself for every effort he made to overcome his anxiety and fear.

3. Peter then started on a daily exercise of climbing the stairs until he would start to feel anxious and then stop there. He would only go as high as to keep his anxiety — on a scale from 1 to 10 — down to about a 2 or 3, where it was very manageable. The plan was to go a few stairs higher each day until he could comfortably reach the top.

4. He would then sit on the stair where his anxiety was at a 2 or 3 and challenge any self-limiting beliefs until his anxiety subsided to a 0 or 1 — then he would go back down. Occasionally, his anxiety would start much sooner and he would only get half way from the day before. He was not to make a big deal about it but confidently persist with the exercise, knowing he would continue to progress and that backsliding is part of the process.

5. Immediately after climbing the stairs he would loudly cheer his attempt for that day. Later in the evening, he was to take "special time" to celebrate his courageous attempts to overcome his anxiety.

6. Shortly after the exercise *and* later in the evening, Peter would practice challenging any self-limiting beliefs and do an abundance of self-strengthening, congratulating himself on his attempts and encouraging himself for the next day's exercise to go even higher.

7. Each morning just upon awakening and shortly before he would fall asleep at night, Peter did visual imagery. In the morning, he would see himself doing his exercise calmly and confidently. At bedtime, Peter would review his exercise for that day, enhancing and fine-tuning the mental image to make it a little better than reality actually was. In this way, he tends to remember the previous day's exercise with these improvements and this will simply escalate his confidence and his progress.

8. Peter practiced these steps above daily for weeks even after he could reach the top confidently. This helped to ensure success-longevity and minimize the possibility of backsliding. He was aware that spontaneous backsliding is common with anxieties and fears, and if it should occur, he was to simply repeat the above steps *immediately* to get himself back on track.

Chapter 34

The Value of Persistence

When facing fear and anxiety there will be times that feel tough, as if you are not making progress or that you are backsliding. Do your best to push through all obstacles and persist because you will succeed if you follow the procedure outlined earlier. Of course, it will be important that you creatively adapt the process to your individual circumstances but the basic method will remain the same.

Here is a story that will illustrate *most* people's attempt at overcoming anxiety:

A man wanted to know the secret to obtaining serenity, confidence and fulfillment. So, he visited the wise old sage of the woods.

"Tell me old sage" the man asked, "which path do I need to take to find serenity, confidence and fulfillment?" The wise old sage, sitting contentedly, looked up and silently pointed down a path. The man, a little uncertain, started to walk down the path the sage had pointed to.

Splat! The man was bruised and beaten.

Staggering back to the sage, believing he misunderstood the directions, he asked again, "Wise sage, which way to serenity, confidence and fulfillment?" The sage pointed down the same path but remained silent. The man decided to walk down the path again, following the sage's directions.

S-P-L-A-T! The man was bruised, beaten, cut and bleeding. He could barely remain conscious, walk or keep balance.

Angry and irate, he returned to the meditative man and yelled, "Enough of this silence. Tell me old man, which way to serenity, confidence and fulfillment? SPEAK!"

The wise old sage slowly looked up, pointed in the same direction as before and softly but firmly said, "Just past splat."

To overcome fear and anxiety, success only comes AFTER "splat." Some people believe that "when I get confident, then I will do XYZ." Don't shoot the messenger, but it does not work that way. *First* you do the work, and *then* the anxiety goes. Other people encounter splat and back away, only making the subsequent attempts even more difficult and unpleasant. Tackle the hard times right away, up front, and you will succeed more quickly. And if you think about the earlier quote by Nietzsche "Anything that doesn't kill me, strengthens me" it really is true.

Do not run from your fears; learn to challenge them on a regular basis. Embrace them and understand that unless the fear is of physical harm, you are simply afraid of feeling fear — basically afraid of your own emotions. Learn to get a handle on your emotions and the world opens up to you in ways that you never thought possible.

In my own life, I figured that if I'm going to teach this "stuff" I had better live what I teach and just not preach.

I have had a fear of heights most of my life and I am aware that there is nothing in the "height" that causes my fear — it is all in my thinking. Because I know this and because I have a high desire for adventure, I haven't let my anxiety stop me from skiing, skydiving, rock climbing, hang-gliding, taking 7-story sheer-drop waterslides, walking across suspension bridges, riding Space Mountain at Disneyland and leaning over the fence at the Grand Canyon. Because of my internal motivation and persistence, I embraced my fear and have largely overcome my anxiety about heights. You, too, can conquer your fears.

P.S.: Just in case you are wondering…Yes, I am from the human gene pool and have all of the same emotions as others. I have made all the mistakes that are of the common variety and survived them, and even more importantly, learned from them. But after working diligently and now living what I teach, my emotional range is primarily in the positive and my negative emotions are normally mild and short-lived. The unhealthy range of my negative emotional repertoire goes largely unused. In this way, I get to derive greater enjoyment than those who fret and stew about the reality over which they have no control.

"Enjoy yourself while you're here,
because when you're there
you won't be here anymore."
Ziggy

"I've had many worries, most of which have never happened."
Mark Twain

"What do I do?"

1. As fears are future oriented, focus on the "now" and be proactive about the future — doing what is required to reasonably ensure your desired outcome, when possible.
2. When confronted with a task and unpleasant feelings, focus on the task and on ways to make doing it more enjoyable.
3. Practice an abundance of self-love, reassuring yourself that while having others love and respect you has its benefits, it's not required for you to enjoy yourself or your life.
4. Practice being more daring and self-loving to combat any possible rejection you may receive because of doing things differently.
5. Praise your attempts, learn from your mistakes, and be forgiving and accepting. Reach for that "brass ring" and risk failure.
6. Be persistent. Do not let failure or difficulties stop you.
7. For the next three days, intensely practice challenging all self-limiting beliefs; remind yourself not to amplify negatives and that you are strong and can handle anything.
8. Practice exaggerating positives and reframing any negative into a positive, when feasible.

SECTION HIGHLIGHTS

➤ It's very important to become acutely aware of your thoughts just prior to and during the time you're anxious. Challenge any thoughts that are self-limiting or irrational in nature.

➤ There are only two things to fear: 1) physical harm or 2) emotional harm.

➤ Most anxiety centers around the second fear, which is developing a fear of one's own emotions or feeling bad.

➤ Identify, as specifically as possible, what you are afraid of.

➤ Make sure to move the "movie" forward and notice that you can handle anything.

➤ Realistically, if the worst thing happened, could you survive it and eventually find happiness? A "No" answer is what helps to drive anxiety, but the answer is virtually always "Yes" in reality.

➤ Make sure you understand the basic steps to eliminating anxiety on pages 216 to 218 and 231 to 232.

➤ Displeasure Anxiety develops out of believing that you must be happy and content at all times.

➤ Acceptance Anxiety revolves around *needing* to be appreciated, loved and accepted.

➤ Achievement Anxiety is oriented around believing that your performance determines your value.

➤ Challenge what you are afraid of today! Don't wait or put it off — that's an indication of Displeasure Anxiety.

➤ To overcome anxiety or fear, first you do the feared activity, combine it with rational self-talk and the challenging of amplified negatives and self-limiting beliefs, then the anxiety leaves and not the other way around.

➤ Backing away from fear reinforces it, making it more difficult to overcome — repeatedly go through SPLAT and it gets easier.

Section VIII

Anger Entrapment

Section Preface

The problem with anger is that it is self-justifying. People feel justified in their indignation and self-righteousness. I cannot ever remember someone saying, "I really made myself unnecessarily angry and foolishly hostile when things didn't turn out my way." It is virtually always the other person's fault. We heard it growing up. We hear it from our peers today. And many of us have said it to our children: "YOU MAKE ME angry when you do that!" But, our angry emotions are NOT the responsibility of others.

The next time you find yourself irritated, hurt, angry or enraged — look for that insistent "should" hidden in your language or style of thinking. Try to speak in first person singular: "I"...as in, "I MADE MYSELF unnecessarily angry when that happened." It is harder than you think and also feels better than you'll imagine.

Introducing...ANGER!

Self (sèlf) — **cen·tered** (sèn-terd)
The total, essential focus on a singular person, the individual.

O·ver·bear·ing (o´ver-bâr-îng)
Domineering in manner; arrogant

Ar·ro·gant (àr-e-gent)
Propensity to make claims of unfounded significance or importance out of conceited pride.

Con·ceit·ed (ken-sê-tîd)
Characterized by or holding an inordinately high estimation of oneself; vain.

Fas·cist (fàsh-îst)
Acting in a dictatorial manner.

Dic·ta·to·ri·al (dîk´te-tôr-ê-el)
Insistent on dictating; domineering, autocrat.

Au·to·cratic (ô-te-kràt´ik)
Acting in a grandiose manner with unlimited power or authority; a tyrant.

Ty·rant (tì-rent)
An oppressive absolute ruler who exercises power in a harsh, cruel manner without restrictions.

Gran·di·ose (gràn-dê-os´)
Characterized by greatness of scope or intent; grand.
Feigned grandeur, pompous.

Anger is an intensely strong emotion of displeasure, antagonism or hostility. *Anger* stresses the bias to take authority in a peremptory manner characteristic of a dictator. *Anger* will behave in an authoritarian manner that demands unquestioning obedience. Being rigidly dogmatic, *Anger*, imposes will or opinion as though it were beyond challenge, and thus is oppressively and rudely domineering. This *is* Anger.

Anger's credo is: "You must do as I want, when I want it, the way I want it or you will be responsible for making me upset and will be deserving of any wrath that I believe should befall you."

This section is about winning our struggle to calm the beast.

NOTE: This section will focus on two forms of anger: Rapid Intolerance Anger (see Sections III & IV) and Self-Worth Anger (see Sections III & V). Please re-read the Section Highlights of all three sections (pages 117, 153, 181) before reading further on how to escape the anger entrapment.

Additional Reading: For hard-hitting full-length books on anger, contact the Albert Ellis Institute for Rational Emotive Behavior Therapy. Dr. Albert Ellis and Dr. Paul Hauck have excellent books on this subject matter, and they are well worth reading.

"Winning by using anger usually results in a pyrrhic victory."*

*A victory won where the costs outweigh the benefits.

*"It is an error to use force
when reason and tolerance
are required."*

Anger Entrapment

Chapter 35

The Value of Anger

Evolutionarily speaking, anger was a functional emotion. Biologically it helped the animal to fight better, which meant it had a better chance of either *having* dinner or avoiding *being* dinner.

In the wild, moments of anger would be useful. Today, *unless attacked*, moments of anger can be deadly. The biggest argument against having guns at close reach is: when people get angry, sensible rational thought goes out the window. If it didn't, people would surely make another choice than to angrily shoot — essentially murder — another person. When I first started taking Kung Fu, my teacher said, "I'm the master of the oldest self-defense known to man...Running!" There's an important lesson in here for all of us: Win by avoiding direct confrontation whenever possible. It would be foolish to risk injury for an inanimate object or for reasons of ego.

Regardless of the style or form, anger is imposing absolute arbitrary demands. When we get angry, we get stubborn. We get single-minded. We get close-minded. We get self-righteous. We get aggressive. We become punishing. And then we attack! This is *not* a good combination of traits when guns are at hand.

We have progressed technologically at a faster rate than our philosophies. Albert Einstein noted this predicament when he stated: "The unleashed power of the atom has changed everything save our modes of thinking, and we thus drift toward unparalleled catastrophes."

It will be a long time before aggression will be eliminated from our gene pool. As there is a biological tendency to become aggressive, there is also a similar tendency to be calm and rational. Until aggression is eliminated, it is our responsibility to model for our younger generation and others, how to deal with disappointments and problems in a manner that does not include anger or aggression.

Anger may seem like the best solution at the moment, but aggression does not reap consent, though it may force compliance. Get angry with your secretary and she will conform out of duress, but as soon as your back is turned, you receive a knife in it, and most likely, you will never even know it. As an example, an important message never gets to you or gets delayed; you end up paying more money on your next flight, and you have to take the red-eye as the other flights are booked solid...so your secretary informs you. This is known as being "passive-aggressive." It is a sneaky kind of anger or retaliation. Remember that a war does not prove who is right but who is strongest.

Anger tends to beget anger. This makes sense in a "survival-of-the-fittest" kind of world. It just does not work well in large societies. Displays of anger are not required in societies, although cooperation and compromise are. To date, there is no strong evolutionary development in our genes for cooperation that replaces anger and aggression. While we definitely have both qualities, hostility is still far too easy to express *and* to rationalize (i.e., meaning to make a false excuse for it).

Watch for the signs of growing aggression or anger. Look at your thoughts. Pay attention to subtle physiological clues like increased heart rate, breathing or tension. Be aware of the emotional escalation of agitation, tension or aggression. Some people will go from calmness to hostility in almost a heartbeat. It is important to pay special attention to the progression of anger so you will be able to slow your reaction and control it.

Steps of Anger & Aggression

These six steps will lead you from a calm state to one that could land you in jail. In any given situation the first two statements may be true and correct; the last four are irrational, insisting on compliance, downing others and threatening violence.

1. I want something.
2. Someone or something has stopped me from getting what I want.

3. I *must* get what I want.
4. This difficulty *must* not occur and is awful when it does occur.
5. Anyone who interferes with me getting what I demand *is* bad, evil and wicked.
6. This wicked person *must* be *punished* and taught never to do this again.*

*While not all six steps are necessary to produce anger, to varying degrees of intensity all six are commonly displayed. Some people punish by withholding love, sex or attention, while others will become obstinate. Some will get you while your back is turned. There are those, too, who will subtly express their anger toward you by such means as giving you coffee in the chipped mug or by slightly burning your toast.

*"The force of anger, like war,
may prove who is stronger
but NOT who is right."*

Anger Entrapment

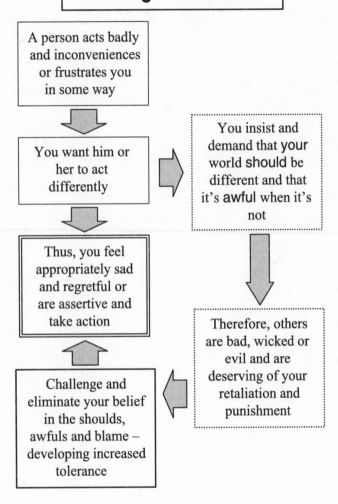

The Anger Schematic

A person acts badly and inconveniences or frustrates you in some way

You want him or her to act differently

You insist and demand that **your** world **should** be different and that it's **awful** when it's not

Thus, you feel appropriately sad and regretful or are assertive and take action

Therefore, others are bad, wicked or evil and are deserving of your retaliation and punishment

Challenge and eliminate your belief in the shoulds, awfuls and blame – developing increased tolerance

Anger Entrapment

Chapter 36

The Experience of Anger

Anger is an emotion and like all emotions you create, managing it is easier said than done. Anger is partly instinctual and partly learned. Without a doubt and with a lot of diligent practice, you can learn to greatly minimize instinctual anger and undo learned anger as both are tied to your thinking.

Anger is a controversial emotion. Depending on who you ask, some will say it is essentially a good emotion as in when fighting off an attacker or motivating yourself to take action against an injustice. Others will tell you anger is negative and destructive causing arguments, fear in others, violence and wars.

Anger is usually created when some transgression has been paid to you — someone has behaved contrary to your moral code, ethics, desires or wants. Not only do you not get what you want, you do not get what you *insist on*...and therein lies the real problem.

Anger not only contains insistence and a sense of blaming or condemning others as bad, but also displays the tragic horribleness of the offence in question. One might say that if things went wrong but were tolerable then the appropriate emotion would be frustration. But if having something go wrong that is truly awful, horrible and catastrophic then full-blown anger would seem justified. Of course, since the problem is *NOT* awful or catastrophic, and there is *no* reason why you *must* get your way then anger is *not* justifiable!

Anger also contains elements of feeling sorry for yourself. If you were to listen carefully to an angry person rant and rave, you can clearly hear the "poor me, I didn't get my way." Anger comes across as rough and tough, but that is the external bravado. Internally, there's a whining, whimpering and screaming child feeling sorry for himself.

Anger, to many people's surprise, is painful *and* physically destructive to oneself. Some people are so familiar with anger that they are unaware of their own pain. Look at someone enraged. Not a pretty sight. They sure don't look like they are having fun. No one ever said, "I am having a really good time, can't wait until I get angry again." Biologically, a series of events occurs inside your body when you get angry, and with sufficient repetition, over many years will kill you via a heart attack.

The experience of anger tends to be particularly self-defeating. First your desires are thwarted then you *foolishly* and *unnecessarily* make yourself upset and angry, potentially giving yourself a coronary. This is a double jeopardy. You lose twice.

Beneficial Anger

Anger has few benefits that cannot be realized through effective assertive action driven by frustration and desire. Some people believe that anger is beneficial because it is motivating. They believe that anger can get people off their tuff to take action, but this is inaccurate. It is the *desire* to right a wrong and the resulting *frustration* caused by that wrong that motivates action. Anger is an unnecessary stress that can actually interfere with one taking action or the *manner* in which one takes action, may *decrease* the chance of obtaining the desired change.

Anger — either toward oneself or others — is a form of threat, intimidation, aggression or violence. Violence is problematic morally, spiritually, ethically, psychologically, physically, biologically and socially. All *unnecessary* violence is immoral because it causes needless and gratuitous pain and suffering along with an attempt to restrict another's freedom of choice. The key word here is "unnecessary."

"Is all anger bad?"

No. Not all anger is inherently bad.

There are forms of anger that are beneficial: self-preservation anger and pseudo-anger, which are not *real* anger but only displays of anger. There are also two other forms of anger that are *unhealthy* — Rapid Intolerance Anger and Self-Worth Anger — and will be discussed in detail in the following chapters.

Self-Preservation Anger: If you are being attacked and get angry or enraged it may help you to muster the strength to ward off your attacker. As most people do not live in a war zone, this type of anger does not create the health threat that daily anger will cause.

Experienced boxers and fighters will tell you that anger is a deterrent to winning a combative engagement. Instead of fighting with cold, direct, objective skill, the emotional fighter can be provoked or angered into fighting foolishly, flailing his arms around and missing his target. Most of us are not experienced fighters, and anger may serve us better than not having it in defending against physical aggression. Fortunately, this form of anger is rarely required and is not what I will be referring to throughout the rest of this discussion on anger.

Pseudo-Anger: This form of anger is not real anger at all but simply pretending to be angry. The image of an angry person can be intimidating and thus, when used occasionally and in the right circumstances, can motivate others to action. If pseudo-anger is used infrequently and judiciously, there is some value in it.

Let's say that your small child is about to do something, like dart away from you and run toward a busy street. If you angrily yell at your child to stop, your anger may instill a warning not to move. When used sparingly and wisely, pseudo-anger has its benefits.

Remember that pseudo-anger is just pretending and does not constitute a real emotional experience of anger. You look and act like you are angry but may be as calm as can be inside. But if pseudo-anger or real anger is overused, others will tune you out, learn to fear you or become aggressive toward you, all of which you don't want.

*"There never was a good war
or a bad peace."*

Benjamin Franklin

Chapter 37

Qualities of Anger

Anger contains grandiosity. When angry, you act as if you are the king of the world. You not only want something but believe that you absolutely *should* get it. All anger says, "If you would only do as I want (demand), then I wouldn't have to get upset and angry with you." Again, the two parts are 1) the insistence and 2) faulting others for your distress.

Let's face it, you want what you want, but you do not absolutely *need* what you want. Insisting you get what you want changes nothing and simply gets you upset. Anger does not make people agree with you. In fact, it generally does the opposite. When you get angry with people, they will tend to resist you more. This is a normal reaction as people do not like their freedom of choice usurped. Some people will *disagree* with you simply to exert their own individuality, whether or not you are correct.

It is not uncommon for parents to tell their teenagers hundreds of times to turn off the lights when leaving a room. Do you really think teenagers are that forgetful? Teenagers are rebelling and expressing their freedom to act as they wish in spite of their parents' insistence.

When a person gets angry, seldom does he/she comprehend the magnitude of the emotional response — fear — in the recipient. When an adult gets angry with a child or a large man with a small woman for example, the fear is real and one of self-preservation. If the parent decides to attack the child, there will be no contest, and the child knows it. Fear does not instill respect for the other person but appreciation for the angry person's ability to inflict harm.

The other person frequently misses the message, but hears the anger. The message may be: "It's important to study hard now to ensure future success," but the message heard is: "Dad thinks I'm stupid and can't do anything right." Anger will confuse the message being delivered by instilling fear or implying an attack on the person's sense of esteem. Either way, the intended message is usually muddled.

When others do learn to comply, seldom is it out of reason and understanding but to avoid your anger in the future. The only thing learned was how to act submissively and fearfully in an attempt to keep you calm. In essence, your anger conveyed the message that:

> "It is your job to give me exactly what I want so I can remain happy. It is your job to take care of me emotionally as I am far too incapable of looking after my own emotions. If I ever become unhappy, it will be entirely your fault, as I take no responsibility for my own emotions, and you will thus deserve to be degraded, humiliated, punished or otherwise hurt as I see fit."

Now isn't this an image of a person out of touch with reality? But when you get angry, this is the *essence* of what is displayed. Don't believe it? Ask the people you get angry with to read the above passage and ask them if they agree. They will.

I had a client, Gary, come into my office rather irate. I asked him what was wrong. He said someone had just sideswiped his brand new car in the shopping mall parking lot. While I understood why he wouldn't like it, why he'd find that annoying and frustrating, I asked him why he was angry.

"Because someone hit my car and didn't even leave a note."

I asked him how long he had been driving…about 25 years. I asked him when was the last time his car was stolen or broken into? Never. I asked him when was the last time someone sideswiped his car? Never, again. I tried to convey to him that he had been living on borrowed time. He had been fortunate up to this moment in time, as most people have a number of problems involving their cars in a 25-year time frame. Rarely do people avoid such unfortunate experiences for such long periods. I reminded him that it was *his choice* to get a driver's license and put a car on the road where he knows that there are inconsiderate and bad drivers. Did he really think that he was exempted from having bad things happen to his car when everyone else has these problems? A little grandiose, I would say.

Wanting, even expecting things to go your way is not the problem. It is when you *insist* and *demand* that you get what you want or expect...that's the problem. You then become, in essence, a whining, demanding spoiled brat who thinks that life damn well *should* treat you fairly and justly to the exclusion of all else and everyone else.

Would you agree or disagree with the following comment?

"We all have the right to be wrong."

Almost everyone agrees to that statement, at least in theory. Every time you get angry with someone, you are abandoning this philosophy. Let's say that the other person is as wrong as wrong can be. When you get upset, you are saying that...

> *They shouldn't have done that!*

> Why not?

> *Because it's wrong.*

> I agree that it is wrong. Why shouldn't someone do something that is wrong?

> *Because it's immoral and might hurt someone.*

> Let's say I agree with you that it is immoral and someone might get hurt. That would be wrong. But don't people, by virtue of being flawed and fallible human beings, have the inalienable right to be wrong?

You see, no matter what, everyone has the right to be wrong — whether we like it or not. You and I cannot do anything about this fact. While we can take action when someone wrongs us, we cannot do anything about the fact that people will think differently and behave differently than we would prefer. While you may not like it, unnecessarily upsetting yourself when things do not go your way is the mark of emotional immaturity and a lack of a healthy emotional skill-set. By the way, most people in our society fall into this category, so you are in good company.

Whether you are angry or a child is angry, the dynamics remain the same. Let's say the father comes home enraged that he was just unfairly fired because someone lied about him at work. On his way home, he forgot to pick up a chocolate bar that he promised his child earlier in the day. When he gets home his child is angry with his dad for forgetting. The dad will likely downplay the child's anger by thinking that his child is just having a temper-tantrum because he did not get something he wanted. He is being childish.

What the father likely does not realize, is that *he* is doing the same thing as his child: insisting that the world turn out as expected. The father expected to be treated fairly and honestly and wasn't. The child expected to receive a chocolate bar and didn't. While the object of the anger is different — being fired versus not getting candy — each is insisting that he gets what he wants and is whining because he didn't. The steps involved are the same and that's what is producing the anger. The cause is not the severity of the real-life consequences of either situation.

The way out of anger or to avoid it in the first place is to become your own personal expert on anger. Fully understand the craziness that goes into the formation of anger. Attempt to truly appreciate the absurdity in the grandiosity and see it humorously for the preposterousness that it is.

Review "Insistence Entrapment" Section III and attempt to dismantle the awesome "shoulds" that became part of your philosophical foundation growing up. Attempt to speak in terms of wants, likes and preferences. Question every "should" spoken or thought. Remember that others have a right to be wrong, even when you don't like it. Take action and be assertive.

Chapter 38

Self-Worth Anger

Anger is usually considered the mirror image of guilt. Guilt is being angry with oneself, and anger is that same emotion directed at others. Guilt and self-worth anger have a strong connection in that they relate to how the person feels about him or herself. Self-worth is what's at stake.

On the surface, self-worth anger looks like other forms of anger that contain a lot of insisting and condemning. Just below the surface though, is a boiling cauldron of insecurity, inferiority and other self-worth issues.

People who exhibit self-worth anger have a proclivity to generalize the actions of others as an attack on their own self-worth. They tend to be egocentric, as if everyone and everything revolves around *them.* Instead of dealing with a transgression by directly turning inward and feeling guilt and condemnation for themselves, as the depressed person would, they become hostile toward others. This is a defensive reaction to protect themselves from facing their own feelings of inadequacy and worthlessness.

As an example, John gets angry with Mary when she disagrees with him. Instead of seeing this disagreement as a simple case of differing points of view, John believes that if Mary really liked him or valued his ideas, then she would agree with him and thus would substantiate his worth. In this way, John sees Mary as directly degrading him. He also views the disagreement as a confirmation of his deepest suspicion — his essential worthlessness.

The irrational concept behind all self-worth anger is: "Your behavior proclaims that you regard me as insignificant and unimportant; therefore I must be insignificant and unimportant, and you are a jerk that must not ever do that."

Many people believe that to feel good about yourself, you must obtain a certain level of love and approval from others. This is highly problematic as it relies on another for your sense of self-worth. Instead of maintaining one's own level of worth as a constant or ignoring the concept of "the value of a person" altogether, it's common for people to place their "value" in the hands of others. This is precarious at best.

Here is an excerpt with a past client Judy:

Judy: *I am really angry that I was left to wait in that restaurant for twenty minutes before Dave showed up.*

Therapist: Dave showing up twenty minutes late might be somewhat frustrating or disappointing, but why are you so angry?

Judy: *Because I have better things to do with my time than sit in a stupid restaurant. We could just make our lunchtime for twenty minutes later if that's when he's going to show up.*

Therapist: While I definitely understand the annoyance with him showing up late, you seem to be upset with him not valuing your time.

Judy: *That's right! If he respected me at all or cared about how I felt, he would be more courteous.*

Therapist: So you see Dave showing up late as not valuing you, not respecting you or caring for you less?

Judy: *That's right. If he cared, he would respect my wishes.*

Therapist: I think you may have made an error in your reasoning. I assume Dave isn't just late with you but most likely is late with many appointments. You seem to think that because Dave has a different concept of time than you, that that somehow relates to how valuable you are to him. Isn't it just as likely, and probably more likely, that this is simply how Dave functions generally and is not a statement about you? In fact, it seems to me that you are being rather self-absorbed and self-centered in thinking that you should be, or ought to be the center of Dave's life. While he may have been discourteous, he, too, might have his reasons, if for no other reason than the simple fact that Dave has a bad habit of being constantly late and this is <u>NO</u> reflection on you, his caring of you and is <u>NOT</u> a statement about you.

This is only one of thousands of cases files where a client is believing that the other person's behavior is a statement about or a reflection of him. Most people are who they are with no great hidden message behind every action. In fact, no matter what *you* do, they will continue to act the way *they* do.

I had a client say something that is all too common. My client sat down in front of me and said, "I just found out my husband is having an affair. That means I must be a bad wife."

The real issue in this statement is not what seems most obvious, it's what is behind it that is seriously at fault. This woman demonstrates a strong sense of grandiosity and self-centeredness. I bet that wasn't the route you thought I would take, but it is one of the most serious problems in this case.

I tried to have my client understand that the world doesn't revolve around her and that she does not get to control her husband's behavior nor does she get to dictate his desires. She was angry about many things, but the one that stood out above all the rest was, "How could he do this to me?"

This question is really best dealt with as a statement, "He *should not* do this to me! And if he does, it tells me that I must be a bad wife and a flawed human being."

I went on to explain that she could be the Wicked Witch of the West and he could worship the ground she walks on or she could be Miss Perfect and he could have countless affairs. She is not powerful enough to determine his wants, his ethics, his morals or his behaviors. He gets to be his own person…always. The most she could ever hope to do, unless at gunpoint, is to encourage one behavior over another. She can cheer him on in one direction, but the final decision remains his.

While she may abhor his behavior, it's *his* behavior and he gets to decide for himself how he will behave. She, too, has the inalienable right to act as she wishes, which might include ending the relationship. But that will be her choice, just as having an affair was his. There are, of course, countless other alternatives.

Behind much anger is a feeling that what happens in the world is a reflection on ourselves. In a general sense and for the most part, people and the world will be as they are, independent of us and regardless of what we think or do. We are not powerful enough to determine the wants and behaviors of another.

If someone treats you badly at any one moment, that is a reflection on *him* — NOT you! How *you respond* to that treatment may say a lot about *your* concepts, values, ability to love yourself or your conflict-resolution skills. How you react to bad behavior will make a statement, *and* it will set your boundaries as to whether or not you will allow such treatment in the future.

How you act or re-act is a reflection on *you* just the same as how others behave is a reflection on them. If you find yourself being *consistently* treated in ways that you don't like, you are promoting, encouraging, condoning or otherwise allowing that treatment to continue. While you are *not* the cause of their behavior, you can be an advocate for, or rally against, any behavior of theirs by your response.

If you find yourself angry with others and find yourself using phrases that include a lot of "I's" or "me's" in them, there is a good possibility the anger just might be self-worth anger (see Section I on self-love and Section V on blame).

Chapter 39

Rapid Intolerance Anger

Residing behind anger is often a strong *need* to avoid hassles, frustration and displeasure. When displeasure occurs, the person gets angry. Because there is such a powerful aversion to displeasure, many problems of life become even more apparent. The person may procrastinate, be less assertive or attempt to escape the discomfort of frustrating situations by drinking, taking other drugs or using other forms of distraction.

Like with self-worth anger, rapid intolerance anger contains the main anger ingredients: insistence, amplifying negatives and condemnation. While self-worth anger is fueled by the belief that there is an affront to one's self-worth, rapid intolerance anger is driven by the belief that:

"Life should be hassle-free, easy and convenient,
especially for me, and I must remain happy and
avoid discomfort at any cost."

Rapid intolerance anger is common with passive people. "It's simply too much hassle to take charge. Too risky. To try something new might mean — usually means — some amount of discomfort, physically or emotionally and that would be awful and must be avoided." Because these people are passive, they control their life less and thus fewer things go their way and their frustrations actually increase because of their lack of control. When this happens, anger results.

We often see rapid intolerance anger expressed by the tyrant, insisting that everyone do his bidding. If anything in life fails to go his way, he is outraged: "How dare life treat me differently from what I expect and demand." The problem is that the dictatorial Napoleon-type person really *believes* this statement.

People with rapid intolerance anger frequently fail to realize that there is usually "little gain without pain." If you are going to achieve your goals in life, almost certainly you will need to put in the effort and time to do so and this includes putting up with a certain amount of discomfort, displeasure or pain.

Road-rage, where drivers get furious, is usually a result of rapid intolerance. When we do not tolerate the imperfection of others well or the frequent randomness of problems in our lives well, rapid intolerance anger is often the result. The depressed individual turns inward, feeling sorry for himself. The angry person displays hostility toward others or the situation, with his own special brand of self-pity, whining and complaining.

If you find yourself getting angry when things do not go your way and you don't feel personally attacked or offended, then rapid intolerance anger is likely the issue. Rapid intolerance anger is virtually identical to the child having a temper-tantrum because he did not get his way.

One of the main problems with rapid intolerance anger is that the individual truly believes that these frustrations should not happen. "If only" is a common justification for the anger.

> If only people would drive properly...
> If only she would have called earlier...
> If only the quality was better...
> If only people would park correctly...
> If only people would be more courteous...
> If only...
> 　　　...then I would not be so frustrated and angry.

Anger, again, condemns the *other person* for the outburst. "It's not my fault. If only life would go my way, then I wouldn't have to be angry." As in self-worth anger, the grandiosity and self-centeredness is immense.

The ways out of rapid intolerance anger is done by solidly disputing the ideas that 1) you *must* get your way so you will be constantly satisfied, 2) that life *should* be easy and convenient,

3) that you *must not* ever have to apply effort or be uncomfortable, 4) that the frustration *should not* exist and 5) that experiencing this frustration is *awful*, and that *you can't stand it.*

It is important to follow up this challenge with action by handling the frustration. When possible, stay in the frustrating situation and then challenge until your levels of emotional hostility subside and you prove to yourself that you can handle not getting your way, that it's not awful and while displeased, there are no bad or wicked people.

*"When I despair, I remember that
all through history the ways of
truth and love have always won."*
Mahatma Gandhi

"An 'eye for an eye'
leaves the whole world blind."
Mahatma Gandhi

"What do I do?"

1. Remind yourself that everyone has a right to be wrong in judgement, attitude, emotional expression or behavior.
2. Watch how your emotions develop in intensity and talk yourself out of anger before you get there and while you are only feeling frustrated. Start early to talk yourself out of anger.
3. Practice assertively and respectfully speaking your mind, expressing your desires. Avoid using any "shoulding" words.
4. Speak in first person singular:
   "I MADE MYSELF unnecessarily upset and angry."
5. Look at other people's behavior as a reflection of them, not you.
6. Expect that some things will not go your way. Counter any developing anger by realizing that this is a fact of life, and focus on what can be done to make things better.
7. Leave an anger-provoking situation promptly if you are not able to get a handle on your own anger quickly.
8. Attempt to be less serious. Focus on being more easy going and playful. Almost guaranteed, the "problem" isn't *that* important.

SECTION HIGHLIGHTS

➢ Anger is an intensely strong emotion used in various forms of offensive or attacking behavior.

➢ Anger consists of absolute insistence: requiring getting one's own way.

➢ Anger produces either more anger in others or fear.

➢ War doesn't prove who's right but who's strongest.

➤ Irrational thoughts drive and sustain anger.

➤ Childishness and feeling sorry for oneself underlie anger

➤ Used sparingly, pseudo-anger can have benefits.

➤ Insisting that others or the world be different doesn't change reality.

➤ An adult's anger and a child's temper-tantrum are the same: whining and screaming about not getting one's way.

➤ Become aware of your physiological responses in your anger development and arrest your anger early.

➤ Stop the anger early on before it escalates — the more intense the anger, the harder it is to stop.

➤ Challenge, argue and shred the foundation of anger: "I *should* get what I want."

➤ Review Sections III, IV & V.

➤ Self-worth anger is thinking that another's actions are an attack on your self-worth and is based on your *need* for acceptance.

➤ Like all forms of anger...self-centeredness and grandiosity are at the core.

➤ Remember that everyone has the right to be wrong...even when you don't like it.

➤ Calm, assertive action usually goes a lot further than anger ever will.

Anger Entrapment

➢ When assertiveness is a dominant skill, one rarely gets angry — practice being direct, open and assertive.

➢ Rapid intolerance anger is driven by the "need" to avoid all forms of frustration and discomfort, and to *always* be content.

➢ Rapid intolerance anger is a temper-tantrum about not getting one's way immediately and easily.

➢ Challenge the irrational belief that your life *must* be hassle free, avoiding displeasure at all costs.

➢ Take responsibility for creating your own anger regardless of how much you were provoked and want to fault another.

➢ Attempt never to down, degrade or otherwise blame another for his actions or your anger.

➢ Anger is often a sign of not loving yourself sufficiently — practice a lot of self-loving.

*"Decisions made
in anger are
most likely excessive."*

Section IX

Fun and Fulfillment

Section Preface

In general, adults tend to laugh a lot less than most children. Although adults have more responsibilities or pressures, that's not the reason for laughing less. Children, too, can see their world as filled with responsibilities and that can overwhelm them. Most entered adolescence and quickly worked at being adult-like. Now it's time to recapture the fun and spontaneity of being child-like, but not childish, which implies lack of thoughtfulness and self-centeredness.

Today and for the next week, make the time to go to the park to play on the swings and teeter-totters. Play in a sandbox. Hang upside-down from the monkey bars. Do something that is fun, child-like and playful and then do it again and again and again until it becomes part of who you are. It was once. That part of you hasn't gone anywhere. Revive it. Express it in your daily action until playfulness is a way of life.

Playfulness is exhibited in all children and in the young of the more highly evolved animals. One would think that there must be an evolutionary value to play. In fact, there is.

Play is a way of socializing as well as developing and practicing skills that will eventually be used as an adult. Playfulness helps to mold the character of the animal or the person. Without playfulness, there is noticeable increase in solitary or aggressive behavior.

When studies of happiness have been conducted cross-culturally there were a few surprising results. There was an attempt to compare individual levels of happiness of people in third world countries to those in first world countries. What do you think the results were? Who do you think was happier?

When those in the starvation-ravaged third world countries were asked to rate their levels of happiness, the question wasn't understood. Happiness was not a consideration. As psychologist Abraham Maslow suggested, there is a hierarchy of needs.* When people are having trouble surviving and are attempting to prevent their children from starving to death, happiness is not even contemplated.

For those of us that live in a first world country, we have the luxury of putting our energy into deriving more fun and fulfillment from each day. We do not have to worry about being eaten by wild animals or starving to death. Our nemesis is usually ourselves. As Walt Kelly stated, "We have met the enemy, and he is us." We complicate our world with psychological and emotional entrapments that ward off happiness and distract us from feeling content and fulfilled. Once free from negative thinking and unhealthy emotions, we cannot only generously drink from the river of life but also dive in and go for a swim.

As to be expected, people find it difficult to *focus* on being fulfilled and happy when they are depressed, anxious or angry. That is what the previous sections of <u>Escaping Emotional Entrapment</u> have been about. Now that you know how to minimize these entrapments, it's time to let yourself be free to be who you are and to reach for the stars.

We have been fortunate. We live in the 21st century and in a first world country. Two hundred years ago it was not possible to focus on fun and personal fulfillment as it is today. Fun and pleasure as a way of being is a rather new concept. Cultivate this idea and pass it on to your children and grandchildren. It is a legacy worth more than all the gold and glory in the world.

Fun and Fulfillment

Maslow's Hierarchy of Needs

**The psychological term "need" is used as a strong
motivating drive or tendency and not as "insistence."*

*"Most people are about as happy
as they make up their minds to be."*
Abraham Lincoln

*"The greatest use of life is to spend it
for something that will outlast it."*
William James

Fun and Fulfillment

Chapter 40

Running Life Your Way

There is no one correct and absolute way to run life. While there are countless ways to run your life badly, there is no single formula for the ultimate life. There are, however, two broad approaches to life, and depending on which one you choose, your overall experience will be greatly affected.

The Chess Board Approach to Running Life

Many people run their lives as if they were a chess piece on a chessboard. Whatever square they are on, they look around, weigh their options and risks and make the best possible move they can make at that moment to go to the next available square. Once on their new square, they look around again, weighing options and risks to make their next best possible move and so on throughout their life.

If you are proficient at analyzing your options, are exceptionally bright and with some good fortune, you can do a reasonably good job of running your life that way. Where you end up though, may be very different from where you were originally headed.

The chess board approach is the favored method for the vast majority of people, but think about it — did you really expect to be exactly where you are in life today? If you are like most people, your life turned out very differently from the way you thought it would. Maybe it's better than you thought possible. Maybe it doesn't come close to what you had hoped. Either way, you probably used the chess board approach to life, taking one step at a time, analyzing all options at each step.

The Pilot Approach to Running Life

Another way of running life is the pilot approach. Here is a familiar story to illustrate. Remember the story of "Alice in Wonderland"? Alice is chasing the little white rabbit through the woods and loses track of him. She comes upon this large tree with many signs posted all over it pointing in every possible direction all saying: "Take this way." There in the tree is the smiling Cheshire cat. Alice asks the feline, "Which way should I go?" The cat asks back, "Where are you headed?" "I don't know," Alice answers. "Take any path; it will get you there," the cat advises.

The moral of this illustration is that if you are going to pilot the plane, you had better know where you're headed. So...where are you headed? Do you know? If not, realize that if you don't change your direction, you will end up where you are headed. If you don't know where that is, you won't even know when you get there.

Most people do not have a good idea of where they are headed. One day blends into the next, they look up and twenty years have gone by. In their wildest dreams, they never expected to end up where they are.

As it has been said, "Life is not a dress rehearsal." It's important that you take charge and be the pilot of your own life, charting your own course, flying around thunder clouds, heading toward clear skies, landing and taking off when *you* choose. While there is no method for guaranteed success, the pilot approach to running life usually assures greater personal fulfillment and a better chance at success as you live your life your way.

What is your goal in life?

If you were to stop people on the street corner and ask them what their *primary* goal in life is, you would find two groups of answers. One group of answers would be like:

> To be a good parent.

> To be wealthy.

> To find a cure for...

> To be my best at...

The other group of answers would fall under this basic answer: To enjoy life or to have fun.

Any other answer, other than to "live a long and happy life," has missed the mark. In fact, this *had better* be your primary goal. If not, you are already in trouble. Why? If you are not focused on enjoying *your* life, who is? If you are not enjoying your life, you will be a liability to somebody...guaranteed!

Even the people with the first group of answers, if they were not happy being a good parent, not happy being wealthy, not happy finding a cure for some disease, then their level of success would almost certainly be lower. While not exclusively true, happiness tends to precede success.

Happiness is synonymous with emotional health. There is also a strong correlation showing that happy people tend to be more physically healthy as well. It's not that happiness is directly responsible for physical health but that happy people tend to be more active, eat healthier and do those things that promote better health.

When we say that our *primary* goal in life is to get married, have children, be a good parent, become a millionaire or whatever — we assume that achieving that goal will make us happy. But this is working the equation backwards. Happiness would be far more a certainty if *our goal* was to *be happy* getting married, *be happy* having children, *be happy* being a good parent or *be happy* becoming a millionaire. If happiness is our primary goal then why wait? And, why would we make happiness conditional on achieving something else?

We want to BE HAPPY ACHIEVING instead of *achieving* to be happy. Even if we never accomplished our practical goal, then at least we have been happy throughout. If our goal is to achieve something in order to be happy, what if that "something" never happens? Then we would never reach happiness. If happiness is our *primary* goal, do not place it second.

You may have heard of an old saying that "happiness is the journey, not the destination." This is what I am talking about. If you put fun, happiness and enjoyment first, then whatever you do, you will likely do better at because you are already starting from a position of enthusiasm and pleasure.

I would much rather consult a physician who absolutely loves and enjoys what he is doing than one who is in it for the money. Whether you require a plumber or tailor, a rule of thumb would be to hire people who love what they do. You will have a better chance of getting someone who is outstandingly proficient at his or her profession.

The Happiness Theory

While "hard work" has been a staple philosophy throughout much of history, major religions endorse the value and benefit to seeking pleasure and fulfillment:

> A man hath no better thing under the sun,
> than to eat, and to drink, and to be merry.
> Hebrew Bible. *Ecclesiastes* 8:15

Sigmund Freud called the tendency or drive to achieve pleasure and avoid pain as the chief motivating force in behavior the "Pleasure Principle." Dr. Albert Ellis refined this concept and eloquently encourages a healthy balance between, what he calls, short-range and long-range hedonism. Recommended reading: Ellis' book, Guide to Personal Happiness.

My original premise in writing this book is that fun and fulfillment are primary goals in life. When happiness is not our ultimate and primary goal, emotional entrapments arise. This is the "Happiness Theory" and can be defined as:

1. Pursuit of or dedication to pleasure and fulfillment is primary or distress will be forthcoming.
2. *Philosophically*...An ethical canon maintaining that what produces the greatest amount of overall pleasant consequences is intrinsically good.

3. *Psychologically*...The construct stating that behavior is motivated by the desire for pleasure, fun and fulfillment, and the avoidance of pain.

Escaping emotional entrapments and leading an enjoyable and functional life are both based on the concept of seeking pleasure and fulfillment. It is important to constantly adjust between immediate pleasure and expected future pleasure. It's a balancing act between enjoying your life now and planning to enjoy it in the future.

If you spent all your money today, it would leave you with none to enjoy for the morrow. The spendthrift is focusing on instant pleasures and this habit is a poor policy for long-term happiness.

The miser, on the other hand, makes an attempt at preparing for the future by hoarding all his money for "tomorrow." Unfortunately, tomorrow never comes and he never truly enjoys his savings. If he does learn to part with his money somewhere in the future, he has missed innumerable pleasurable moments by *only* investing in that undiscovered country: the future.

A compromise of trading *some* immediate pleasures to ensure long-term happiness is ideal. You, as an example, would spend some money today but also invest for tomorrow. When immediate gratification is used as a *primary strategy*, you do only that which is pleasurable and put off anything displeasing. This is usually a recipe for long-term dissatisfaction. When delayed gratification is the chief focus, rarely does the person years from now switch over to seeking present-moment happiness to enjoy the fruits of his labor. Our decisions are best made considering the pleasures of the "now" *and* of the future.

Normally our decisions are based on the desire for happiness, although we often pretend that some other logic guides our decisions. It's not uncommon to hear a friend say something like: "I took this job over that one *because* it paid better and gave more vacation time." But that is not why she took one job over another. If she was offered even *more* money with *more* vacation time, but she had to break rocks in the hot sun for eight hours a day, she would not take it. She takes one job over the other *because* she thinks she will be *happier* with more money and more vacation time. It is *not* about money and vacation time, it is about happiness.

When someone says that he has decided to get married, it is because he assumes he will be happier being married than being single. When a friend says that she is going to buy a car, she assumes she will be happier driving than walking. Again, it is a happiness decision.

Let's not kid ourselves. We generally make decisions based on the "happiness theory." If you were not happier overall, you would not do it. You might do something you detest but that would only be because there were greater rewards of happiness afterward. A student might skip a party to study, knowing that her overall happiness would benefit by getting her degree rather than staying another semester at school. While there may be a trade off of current fun for greater long-term pleasure, the goal remains overall happiness. It would not make any sense to say, "I'm going to do something that causes me pain and there are NO benefits." That would be absurd.

Emotional entrapments become apparent when the desire for happiness has been displaced by one's sense of ego: proving oneself as worthwhile. When you replace fun with ego gratification, placing your self-worth on the line, you have forgotten what is important: the experience of life *and not* to prove yourself correct.

I have had tennis partners who have smashed their rackets on the ground after having missed the game point ball. I asked them why they started playing tennis in the first place. The answer was unanimous: to have fun. I think they forgot why they started to play originally. The goal of having fun was replaced with the goal of winning or validating oneself.

You know you are deep in an emotional entrapment when pain avoidance is governing your decisions. I had a female client of 27, "Barb," who was about to marry a man she did not care for. Why? Because her parents just loved the guy. There wasn't a problem with her fiancée; she just didn't really care for him. To avoid her parents' anger and rejection, she was marrying him. She saw that marrying him would cause less pain in her life than confronting her parents with the fact that she was breaking off the engagement. The goal for Barb was to avoid as much pain as possible. Happiness, pleasure, fun and fulfillment were not in the equation. As you can imagine, to carry on with the wedding would be a foolish decision and likely produce a great deal of pain overall.

Anytime you find yourself in any serious emotional entrapment, you can probably bet that you are attempting to avoid pain instead of making decisions to enhance pleasure. Seeking short- and long-term pleasure is to be both self and socially interested, and thus would be an ethical as well as practical approach to life.

"Laughter: the best medicine."
Reader's Digest

"Live for today but plan for tomorrow."

Fun and Fulfillment

Chapter 41

Happiness: The Process of Life

There are two main styles of experiencing your life: outcome orientation and process orientation. One is commonly used and one is infrequently used. Guess which one tends to be the healthier one? You got it, the one that is used infrequently: process orientation. Let us examine both.

Outcome Orientation

Outcome orientation is predominantly taught in our culture. "Put your toys away." "Study hard." "Get good grades." "You need a degree." "Get married and have a family." "Work toward a promotion." "Save for retirement." These comments are representative of the intended message being delivered to us many times a day: "Get the job done!"

You do things to obtain a specific goal. You donate money to help starving children. You drive across town to get to work. You grocery shop so that you can make dinner. While all of these statements are true and they help to make life work, there is no declaration, suggestion or implication about *enjoying your life*, but rather "accomplishing your life."

The essential message delivered to us by the majority of parents was: Be responsible.

"Be responsible" usually meant "Postpone any fun thing to do until later." "I have no choice." "I'm not going to enjoy this." There was usually a direct or implied "*should*" wrapped around the idea of responsibility, and thus, resistance was common. A *should* is a hard sell at the best of times.

As an example: Let's say you are taking out the garbage. The goal is to get the garbage in the trash can outside. You are being outcome-oriented. You are focused on achieving a particular goal. The idea is NOT to enjoy the *process*, that is, smelling the aroma of the garbage, feeling the slosh at the bottom of the garbage bag, that sort of thing. When dumping rubbish, the goal is simply to dispose of it as quickly and efficiently as possible and not to necessarily relish the experience.

Process Orientation

When having a nice romantic candle light dinner, the goal is not to obtain the outcome, which would be to finish the meal. In this case, the process — dining, drinking, talking and sharing — is the goal.

Functionality and outcome orientation are not entertained during much of the time when being process-oriented. This is not to suggest that within any kind of activity there are no goals. Of course there are goals, it's just that the goal is not the focus of one's attention, it is the process. Hopefully the romantic couple is enjoying the food, the aroma, the music, the ambiance, the other's company, their feelings and the mood created.

The goal when you purchase a new CD is not to finish listening to it but to enjoy the music on the CD. You buy the CD to experience it, not to have it over with.

People act as if getting to work is an outcome. Then, getting that report in on time is another outcome. Then going to the luncheon meeting is still another outcome. But life is really an *ongoing* series of "now" experiences. It is an ongoing *process*. There *is* only one outcome to life and that's death. Do not get bogged down there but focus on experiencing your existence.

Remember when you were a youngster, you tried running up a down-escalator? (Bet you haven't done that in weeks. Okay, how about years or since you were a kid!) When you are in that playful mood, you may want to get to the next floor, but you decide that enjoying the experience is also important. You could quietly take the up-escalator but running up the down-escalator is so much more fun.

Generally throughout life, you want your focus of attention to be on the process and not the outcome — like during a romantic evening. Remember what is important: It is the experience of life that is most meaningful, so make that experience fun and fulfilling.

Time Travel: Escaping unpleasantness

When you are experiencing an unpleasant moment in time, such as having a root canal, and you are having an understandably difficult time enjoying yourself, then you will want to escape. How? By traveling to the past or the future. Imagine yourself in some happy, fun or pleasant situation in your past. Make this image as vivid to all of your senses as possible. Or, think of a wonderful future event and how you want things to be. Include sights, sounds, smells and touch in your imagery, if you can. Make it as real as possible. This will help you to deal with or avoid a bad "now" experience.

Focusing your attention to the past or the future is an excellent method of distracting yourself from an unpleasant experience but this is not what you want to do during pleasant, fun or highly enjoyable activities, such as making love. One major "arousal killer" for both sexes is to focus on practical, external situations of the past or the future. Unless the external focus is in the area of arousing fantasies that actually enhance and help you maintain excitement in the present moment, focusing on anything other than the now is anti-pleasurable. You do not want to be thinking about your taxes when you are at a movie. Be in the moment.

The rule of thumb is to focus on the "now," unless the *now* is unpleasant and apparently inescapable, in which case, focus on a pleasant future or past. With the exception of physical pain, which helps to keep you focused on a very unpleasant now, it is extremely difficult to sustain any serious emotional distress when focused on the here and now. When you are emotionally entrapped, you are almost exclusively focused on the past or the future.

What is your favorite movie?

The entertainment field is a multi-billion dollar industry. Disneyworld, the beach, the local movie theater or entertainment in many other forms, are all a part of our culture. This is also true of education and information, as we witness the success of CNN, the

Discovery Channel and the Internet.

If you were going to watch a documentary about sharks on TV, what might the reasons be? (See the chart below.)

There are two basic reasons you would watch a movie or a documentary: 1) you either find it enjoyable or fun in some way or 2) you find it educational or informative. Why else would you watch TV? Any answer you come up with, will fall into one or both of these categories.

POSSIBLE REASON TO WATCH A DOCUMENTARY ON SHARKS	
Reason One: Fun	Reason Two: Educational
You find it exciting	*You find it intellectually stimulating*
You derive vicarious thrills from it	*To test your knowledge of the subject*
It helps you escape, vegetate and unwind at the end of the day	*You learn about this fascinating animal*

Since your life is comparable to a documentary or a movie, then the same advice would apply. So...why *are you* in "your movie"? Are you enjoying your movie? Is it the best you've ever seen? Is it a fun and an exciting movie or a horror movie? When you are 90, are you going to enjoy watching the reruns? Will you be happy with your production, direction and participation?

What you may not truly appreciate, is that you actually get to write *and* direct your part. You do not get to write for others that appear in your movie, only you. Is your movie going to be a tragedy, a comedy, a romance, a thriller or maybe an action movie? Is your documentary about emergencies or about magic or meditation? You always get to decide your role.

You are, hopefully, either enjoying the majority of your life's experiences or you are learning from them. If you are not learning or having fun, why are you there? Just to be functional? To earn that paycheck? To be polite and appropriate? To be responsible? If so, you missed the boat. There is virtually always an opportunity for learning as well as making the best of things by being more playful and fun-loving.

Without going to extremes like torture, you can escape practically any situation so that it will become more fun and enjoyable or you can learn from it making that time valuable. The choice is ultimately yours.

"Your role in life is one that you script.
Write a blockbuster."

Fun and Fulfillment

"Make having fun a theme in your life by being more childlike."

Fun and Fulfillment

Chapter 42

Be Childlike

Couples who have children often relate stories of how they have rekindled their own childhood by having children. They get down on the floor playing games with their child, forgetting all the woes of life. For a moment, they once again become children.

Children have this wonderful ability to be fully and completely engrossed in the moment. So often this complete absorption is lost as they reach adolescence and adulthood. The "shoulds" start and they find themselves mentally or emotionally distracted with other *responsibilities*.

Children tend to focus completely on one thing at a time. Sometimes that focus will change from one moment to the next, but they are completely focused during that moment. Watch a child in a sandbox. She would sit there playing, ignoring the world around her until the spirit moves her to do something else. You want to awaken this ability to absorb yourself completely in any playful activity.

While children have this ability to be so self-absorbed, there is a down side at that young age. Children and adolescents can often disregard the impact of their behavior on others. Frequently, they do not look beyond the moment to what the long-reaching effects will be to themselves and more often, others.

On his way to school, a kid may knock over garbage cans on the front lawns of his neighbors. If he is not being malicious, he is negligent of how his behavior will impact on the lives and the emotions of others. Foresight and empathy are poorly constructed at early ages for most children.

The adult, on the other hand, will quietly and uneventfully walk down the street on his way to work. This "walk" time, for many people, is full of "work" and they are not even at work. The emotions are either neutral or the person may very often be getting somewhat tense in preparation for doing battle at the office.

There seem to be two stages that most people go through from childhood to adulthood. The problem is that it seems that we forgo one stage for the other, instead of combining them.

As a child, you were fun-loving and natural. You burped, made all kinds of bodily sounds, attempted to do as you wished and expressed emotions freely. As you grew up, you were taught manners, how to socialize and "be proper" in order to get along and how to be functional and practical so that you could achieve. Unfortunately, much of this "adult education" was put across to you in a serious fashion and that took the fun right out of most activities.

When I was a teenager, I was working in an electrical shop cleaning electric home power meters. I was cleaning the meters as instructed, being very thorough and efficient. While sitting there performing this rather mundane and monotonous activity, my work buddy and I started talking and telling each other jokes. When the supervisor of the shop walked in and heard us laughing and talking, he immediately reprimanded us and told us to focus on the task at hand.

The moral of this story is that if you are being playful and fun-loving, others will sometimes see you as if you are not treating the activity as important. While it is possible to be playful and irresponsible, one can also sit quietly, focus on the task, execute it successfully but be bored to tears and feel apathetic about the *quality* of one's work.

As mentioned earlier, people who are having a good time generally tend to do better at their work. Adults would be wise to understand this. It would be a sign of erudition or wisdom to do our utmost to keep playfulness in the learning process for both children and adults. Generally, people are not afraid of others who are playful. Seriousness, on the other hand, often produces great trepidation.

The ideal situation is to combine common sense, rational foresight, self-interest and empathy for others with the spontaneity, creativity and playfulness of the child. Instead of kicking over garbage cans or solemnly walking to work, the adult could be playfully jumping *over* the garbage cans or kicking a small rock down the street or pulling an occasional leaf off a tree that overhangs the sidewalk. No one is hurt and the time spent is far more enjoyable. The activities are limited only by one's own imagination. The point is to make the journey fun.

Let's say you are walking with a friend to some distant location. Both of you could silently walk there and in two hours you arrive. You have reached your goal. While this is functional, there is a better or at least more enjoyable way of going for that walk (or anything else for that matter). You two could talk and get to know one another better. You two could tell jokes along the way or share knowledge about your favorite interests. Knock on doors and see who lives in the neighborhood. Window-shop. You can do whatever you want to enjoy the time more thoroughly.

When you arrive at your selected location, not only have you achieved your desired outcome but you have also enjoyed the process of getting there. What would happen if a bus hit you minutes before arriving? At least you fully enjoyed your last hours. So even if you do not achieve your original goal, you still win by having enjoyed your life. If you just silently walked there — no matter how you look at it — you did not enjoy the process to the fullest…whether or not you arrive at your goal.

Time dollars

You were born with a finite amount of "time dollars." Every minute of everyday, you are spending these time dollars. No one knows for sure how many time dollars you have in total, but one thing is for sure, you do not have an endless supply of them.

Imagine that you had $86,400 dollars given to you, but at the end of the day, this money would be written off. Use it or lose it. Well, that's what you have: 86,400 seconds to use or invest each day. Invest it wisely, and it will pay you long-term dividends in health, skills, knowledge and relationships. You can't save it directly, but you can spend it so that it pays you for a lifetime.

It's been said that "time is money." But that is not true. Time is not money. You cannot put time in the bank, save it and then borrow on it in your later years. People will use that phrase when they are trying to stick someone with a bill, but in reality time is not money. Your time is much more valuable than money!

Once spent, you can never get that time dollar back. The question is, "What will you spend your time dollars on?" Misery, depression, anxiety and anger? If you are going to be spending time, it is better to spend it on fun and fulfilling activities. While it is left up to you to make *your* activities enjoyable, you could have no better challenge than to make your life fun and interesting. Let's face it, if you don't, who will?

Making NOW fun!

There is an old saying that "money can't buy happiness." While this is literally true, money sure does allow you to do things or obtain things that will greatly *add* to your happiness...and you don't need a lot of it. But let us be clear in this area, if you aren't happy without — you'll have a hard time finding happiness with. Why? Because happiness does not come from acquiring, it comes from within. If you don't know how to generate happiness from within, then having the riches of the world will not help you find it because you'll be looking in the wrong place.

People so often seem to work hard at minimizing their pleasures in life while others revel in them. Where you place your money will indicate where you are on this continuum.

A guy buys the best lawnmower on the market. He definitely loves his tools, so he gets the best. Good for him. To me, it seems odd that he will have a cheap hundred-dollar stereo in his house though. Where will he derive the greatest amount of pleasure, with his lawnmower or his stereo? The greatest lawnmower in the world will give him 30 minutes of pleasure a week while the stereo will provide countless hours of pleasure year round.

People pay huge amounts of money for a car that they will spend many hours in each week commuting and then be conservative in spending money for the sound system that is in it. So often we are using a false economy. What looks like a savings is really costing us. Although the cost may be in enjoyment and pleasure, it is important to work within our means. It's the disbursement of our income that is in question. Is the money you spend now best used in such a way as to encourage your happiness in life?

*"The future is guaranteed to none of us,
so make enjoying the 'now' a priority."*

Fun and Fulfillment

"God is a comedian playing to an audience that's afraid to laugh."
Voltaire

Chapter 43

Happiness as a Style of Living

Happiness is not obtained by doing any one thing. It is not obtained by doing any particular number of things. Happiness is a style of living life. It's a combination of an attitude of living each moment to its fullest, doing things that please others in the process of pleasing oneself and frolicking in the emotional expressions of life. It is learning to push aside the fears and take risks, going for the gusto in life.

A Positive Attitude

An unbelievably large part of happiness is determined by your attitudes. If you have been applying the lessons of the previous chapters, then you are primed for developing a greater positive mental attitude. It is important that happiness be a central focus of your life.

On a recent radio talk show it was quoted that behavioral scientists have concluded that people who are the happiest are the people who make happiness their primary goal in life. Well, duh! Of course. Whatever you focus on and practice the most, will be what you end up with. It will become your strongest skill-set. Unfortunately, most people focus on their worries and anxieties, problems in their lives, tasks and chores and paying the bills and thus, they are very skilled at that. While these things are important to deal with, one *had better* be in the process of enjoying life *while* living life.

If you have your taxes to do, you could just take a Saturday afternoon to do it. Or you could make yourself nice and comfortable, pour a glass of wine, pull out your favorite chair, put on some soft mood music and then do your taxes. Sound strange? Not for people who look for ways to enhance every minute of their lives.

A client of mine was telling me how she would watch a half-hour of news before going to bed each night. I asked her *how* she watched TV. She seemed confused so I gave her an example. Did she sit on the couch and watch the news or did she curl up on the couch in candle light with a few pillows propped up behind her with a hot chocolate in hand while watching the news? She stated she just sat and watched the news but said that the second example would be much nicer.

Most people don't have an attitudinal style of making each moment the most pleasurable possible. Too bad, because that moment in all of history will never come again. If you do not make happiness a primary and important goal in your moment-to-moment existence, when will you be happier? Are you going to plan for a day of happiness next month? Ask yourself how can you make the next hour of your life more enjoyable than it might otherwise be?

I'm a big kid at heart. I truly enjoy Disneyland. On one trip I was entering the grounds and noticed the car ahead of me had two adults in the front seats and two kids in the back seats. The father seemed awfully "ticked off" as he was waving his hands and banging the steering wheel. The mother was leaning over into the back seat wiping something off the little girl. I inadvertently ended up following them and parking beside them and then through the ticket lineup and on into the park. Right up to the moment that they got into Disneyland, the parents were annoyed and griping about a multitude of things. When they got into Disneyland, everything seemed to change. It was as if something magical happened and everything was now okay.

What so many people don't realize is that nothing special happens when on vacation or in Disneyland. What is almost magical is the attitude transformation. All of a sudden, the "shoulds" disappear. There are no "awfuls." There is an attitude of wonderment, tolerance, excitement and playfulness. All of their problems in life still exist but now, they live more in the moment. If people would only apply this attitude more often to their daily lives, they would fare much better in life.

Fun and Fulfillment

Positive Self-Expression

Practice, practice and more practice until the focus on fun and happiness become a reflexive attitude. Express yourself behaviorally by being more playful and childlike. Sit on some swings, play in a sandbox and simply be more playful. Let your hair down. Stop watching and wondering what everyone else will think of you. Become more animated. Put yourself out there and take risks.

When you express yourself verbally, put a positive spin on everything. The essence of your message remains the same but is put forth in a *positive light*. Instead of childless, you might be "child-free." Instead of dateless, you are "date-free." Being single means you get to be involved more deeply in personal pursuits. If you have the flu, you now have time to rest and catch up on your favorite television shows. The ending of a relationship means you get to spend more time with friends, engage in sports, reading or hobbies. Being laid off means you get to find a more enjoyable career.

Negatives will be self-evident. Do not ignore them. Focus on the benefits that these negative events bring along with them. If you cannot find any positives, you know that you are already entrapped and better work hard to escape that entrapment because there are *always* positives.

Make sure you talk to yourself positively and strongly. Be more lighthearted with yourself. When you are clumsy around others, humorously say, "Excuse me. I'm just practicing my clumsiness." Don't look at every mistake or social faux pas as a tragedy or a major embarrassment. Let yourself be human and have some fun with this idea.

It's okay not to have everyone like you. It's okay if others don't understand you. You will be in good company. Many groundbreakers throughout history were not understood well in their day: Socrates, Buddha, Christ, Galileo, da Vinci, Edison, Einstein and tens of thousands of other notable figures.

Appreciate the Little Things in Life

When was the last time you stopped to smell the roses? I mean this literally. Most people just walk by the flower shop display on the sidewalks without even stopping. How sad. There is pleasure waiting to greet the next passerby, but few will take advantage of the opportunity.

When was the last time you actually took extra time to enjoy the aroma of baking bread or freshly cut grass? You surely enjoy a campfire, but do you really *experience* the campfire — the various colors, the multitude of sounds to the variations in hot from the fire and cool from the night air?

Do you know how many sounds go into that first rip of an orange or the bite of an apple? Have you ever felt the softness of a rose petal on your nose and cheek? How often do you take the time to really listen to your favorite piece of music? How about a luxurious bubble bath with a fine glass of wine? Or walking barefoot on the cool grass on a warm summer's evening?

Exaggerate Happiness

"Anything worth doing is worth overdoing" — well, at least until it becomes a negative. There is a tendency to parcel out happiness. Without going to such extremes as to be a negative, learn to splurge and indulge in life.

While too much of a good thing is literally too much of a good thing, be careful of selling yourself short. The bubble bath directions say a cap full, unless skin allergies are a problem, but maybe you might want to try several caps or half the bottle. If one is good for you — how about eight? Don't take foolish risks but don't play it so safe as to waste your life away. Reach for what is just beyond your grasp. It gives you something to strive for.

Push the limits at times and see how it feels. Put a little boldness in your personality. Vincent Van Gogh said, "What would life be if we had no courage to attempt anything?" Reach for that brass ring and do it with enthusiasm and excitement. Develop a passion for adventure and the unexplored. Put fire into your daily living. Vacuuming? Crank up the stereo and cut a rug while cleaning one. Do different things in different ways. Be creative with fun and play.

Practice talking in terms of exaggerated positives: Wonderful, terrific, amazing, superb, extraordinary, sensational, awesome, outstanding, astonishing, smashing, marvelous, grand, excellent, remarkable, impressive, spectacular, striking, breathtaking, great. Shall I go on?

When exaggerating positives, be appropriate. If your friend's child just died, you would not say "How wonderful, now you have more time to pursue your reading." I hope this goes without saying. But when you genuinely see positives, instead of saying blandly, "That is good," try expressing with an enthusiastic voice, "That's GREAT! What a wonderful idea. I really like that." Feel the difference? Practice it until it naturally becomes part of you.

The Theory of Variation

Balance is important but so is variation and variety. If you get up early everyday, then sleeping in late can feel decadent. Going out every night can get tiresome while staying in with a good book and a hot chocolate might be a way to pamper yourself. Spending the day in your sweats might feel cozy if you normally dress up for work daily. Being pampered with a massage might be a pleasure but so can pampering your partner with a massage.

Keep balance, variety and variation in your life. Variation and variety provide stimulation and enhance growth. Too often we are striving for certainty in areas where there is little, if any. Certainty for a child is important for emotional health but is not required for adults to be happy and content. Do not confuse contentment with certainty. You can definitely be uncertain *and* content as long as you are not fearful. Certainty can be peaceful but too often turns to boredom and then soon after to depression. While small amounts of certainty can be beneficial, a large amount is harmful.

Make fun and playfulness part of your attitude, your being, your very existence. Remember that old saying, "All work and no play makes Jack a dull boy!" Learn to laugh at yourself and your own foibles and flaws. Treat yourself with less seriousness and so will others. There is little to ever be gained with seriousness. As quoted earlier by Oscar Wilde, "Life is too important to be taken seriously."

Make it a habit to learn from others. If you do not enjoy the opera when millions do, what are they enjoying that you are missing? Open your mind to new ideas, thoughts and ways of experiencing life. Anytime someone enjoys an experience that you cannot, they are one-up on you. At the end of life, will you be able to look back as you take your last breath and feel like you had a wonderful life or was that life full of hardship, dissatisfaction and pain?

Remember that it is the experience of life that is important. Your experience will be unique to you and also up to you. Talk with the elderly. You'll never hear them say, "You know, I really should have spent more time at work (or doing the dishes, cleaning up or that sort of thing)." You will hear many say, "I wish I would have spent more time with the kids (or my spouse, traveled more, went back to school, volunteered, etc.)."

One doesn't regret not being practical enough. The regrets are in the areas of fun, intimacy, closeness, the giving and receiving of love and pleasure.

Attachment and Individuality

While close connections with others are NOT required for a happy and fulfilled life, the vast majority of us have a powerful craving and desire to be intimately connected with one or more people. To preserve a strong sense of individuality while closely attached is difficult. It is easy to "adjust" yourself to the other person so that over time you lose "you" — stop wearing certain clothes, stop eating certain foods, changing friends, hobbies, sports and social activities. It's not that you add to what is already you but that you trade one aspect, quality or trait for another.

A sense of independence is important for you to feel unique, which you are, *and* to feel important and meaningful. If you are enmeshed with another person so much that you are a replica or shadow of that person, you will lose your sense of uniqueness.

Every therapist has heard a client say after the ending of a relationship, "I just don't know who I am anymore." Do not let this happen to you. Retain and respect your sense of individuality!

For variety, growth and many forms of emotional satisfaction and comfort, attachments are important. There are benefits from close intimate attachments that you cannot obtain elsewhere. There are also emotional risks unlike others. The more emotionally free and healthy you are, the lower the emotional risks are and the more likely you will develop the emotional attachments that are beneficial and healthy.

Share of yourself but do not "lose yourself" to the other person. Much of your uniqueness is your personal strength. Keep that. Be unique, outrageous, outstanding, average, mediocre, different and also the same as others at times. Be you and who you are. Practice self-disclosure: sharing more details of yourself to those you trust around you. It is good for the soul to be "naked" with another and still be accepted. Know your boundaries of what's appropriate, what's for public consumption and what you wish to keep private. When suitable, self-disclose; do not whine but share. As Mark Twain said, "When in doubt, tell the truth." It will help you to grow and to be close to others.

*"Self-interest is fused
with social interest."*

Fun and Fulfillment

Chapter 44

The Secret to Feeling Fulfilled

There is a difference between having fun and feeling fulfilled. If you were to move into Disneyland and live there daily, it would not provide fulfillment. In fact, it would not take long before the variety and originality of Disneyland would become old and stale.

People who seem to be the happiest *and* most fulfilled combine a sense of playful child-likeness, with personal goal setting, living primarily in the moment and a positive gracious disposition. There are two other qualities that seem essential to create a sense of fulfillment: growth and contribution.

FULFILLMENT IS WHAT GIVES HAPPINESS STAYING POWER. Some people say, "Well, you can't be happy all of the time." While this is literally true, you can virtually always feel fulfilled, and that will tend to make happiness a general daily experience for you. Without fulfillment, fun and happiness tend to be much more occasional and fleeting.

People who rate themselves as feeling highly fulfilled in life have two main qualities in common. Unfortunately, these qualities are not more common for the populace.

Personal Growth

You have an option: grow or die — either figuratively or literally. Many people think that their goal is to acquire enough money so they can quit work and *do nothing*. As the theory of variation mentioned earlier, this is not a healthy approach. It is important that you continue to grow, to develop, to evolve. There is no standing still in life, either your world is shrinking or expanding, either you are working on living or you are working on dying. Which is it?

Personal growth can take many forms, but all forms have one thing in common: There is a learning process. Take up sailing, a new language, go back to school, but this time take the courses that interest *and* challenge you. When was the last time you read a book different from your usual? Go to a movie that is different for you. Go to a museum or play. Learn to fly. Whatever you do, make it interesting and fun for you. Do not shy away from a challenge or the work involved — it's what helps you to grow. Growth is impossible if you do things the way you have always done them.

If you took the time to learn one new word a day for a year, at the end of that year you would know more words than the common vocabulary of the average person. If you missed one hour of television a day and studied any subject for that hour, within a short time your wealth of knowledge would grow far beyond 85 percent of the population.

Most people have largely just stopped learning and growing after they have entered their adult years. While learning to some degree is life-long, such as keeping up with current events, I am really speaking of the ability to develop in areas that are uncommon to you yet interesting. Soon these areas will become part of you and you can move onto other areas, always enriching and enhancing your life experience.

Contribution to Life or A Goal Greater than Yourself

A few years ago there was a study done on people who had won a million dollars or more in the lottery. It was found that nearly 70 percent of them had lost all of it *or more* within five years. And, that the winner's level of happiness went up dramatically for about 12 months, then it returned to it's original level or lower. Some people were actually worse off emotionally.

People so often believe that money will make them happy. While it can definitely add to happiness, money will never be the *cause* for happiness. All money really does is to provide you with a greater number of options in your life. You have an almost limitless number of options already. Money will simply increase your options in several new areas, but options do not cause happiness to suddenly occur. If you are having trouble being happy in your current lifestyle (pain or abuse not withstanding), then it's your attitudes that require overhauling, not your life or your bank account.

Money has this interesting feature of magnifying qualities. If you are conflicted within yourself, you will be more conflicted. If you are angry and demanding, you will be more so. If you are reclusive and depressed, then you can more easily hide. Money simply allows you to be more of what you already are; it does not create fulfillment.

In studies done on happy and fulfilled people, the first and foremost consistent trait is that they have a passion and a drive for something outside of themselves. What I mean by a passion for something outside or greater than yourself is that you give to others in some way — you contribute. For some, it may be being an absolutely wonderful parent and grandparent. For others, it might mean volunteering at a children's hospital or a nursing home. Other people love coaching little league or becoming a Big Brother or Big Sister.

Don't misunderstand, it's not the activity that creates the joy but the *honest desire* to share of oneself, to be involved and to genuinely give to others and encourage the betterment of their world. This is not about donating money but the donation of oneself and time. There is no axe to grind for these people. They do not have to prove a point or get their ego massaged. These people are not putting themselves out to get the reward of happiness or fulfillment — it is a style of living life — "Of course I volunteer." No question or doubt. It is just what they do.

Not all happy and fulfilled people volunteer. Some create, build or otherwise add quality to the world. Others have a passion for animals and work full-time in shelters. Talk with someone who has a green thumb and you will usually find a very happy and content individual. Be connected to earth, animals or children.

Learn about what's behind the science of dinosaurs, the stars and what makes our world tick. Learn about other cultures. Don't be too certain; be open-minded and ask a lot of questions. Explore other religions, opposing political views and attempt *not* to be too politically correct. Delve into the unknown. Be uninhibited. Be spontaneous. Learn. Think. Reason.

Psychologically speaking, as soon as you look to see what *you are getting*, you are already on thin ice. The happiness developed in receiving is short-lived with little or no sense of fulfillment. The pleasure derived from *giving* can last a lifetime. The child focuses on getting. The mature adult focuses on positive, creative, personal involvement.

If you are looking for a secret to happiness, it lies within you. Here is a synopsis:

1. As best you can, minimize your emotional entrapments, take responsibility for your emotions and your life and *everything* that happens within it. Be accountable, it will help you grow as a person. You know there are good times. During the not-so-good-times trust that the good times will return and make the best of things until then.
2. Trust in yourself. Believe in yourself. Treat yourself as you would your very dearest friend or better. Make this philosophy the standard in your life. Accept yourself and appreciate all of your wonderful qualities. You have a lifetime to work on the not-so-wonderful qualities.
3. Put yourself first so that you can remain healthy and strong, then place the people who mean the most to you a close second and give of yourself to them with great generosity and thoughtfulness.
4. Find your passion — only you can do that — then dive into it with your heart and soul. Learn, develop and grow a little more each day and share of yourself with the world around you.

For those who have read carefully, the message is to "be yourself." Let that child out. Be silly, bold and a little outrageous. Watch out for the following people who are "energy zappers" and will detract you from experiencing life:

Fun and Fulfillment

➡ The walking dead — those with no enthusiasm;
➡ The grave dancers — constant complainers;
➡ The fence sitters — they're uncommitted;
➡ The comatose — they do nothing and likely never will.

Surround yourself with happy, emotionally balanced people who encourage you to be yourself and to experience fully all that life has to offer you. Embrace yourself, your family, your friends, your ideals, your life. Most of all be happy because you are you!

"Your environment matters.
Surround yourself with happy people."

Fun and Fulfillment

*"A child of five would understand this.
Send somebody to fetch
a child of five."*
Groucho Marx

"What do I do?"

1. For the next three days, focus on being more playful, making every activity more fun and expressing a light-hearted attitude.
2. Go to the park and play on the swings; go roller-blading; wear flashy clothing; be silly, childlike and spontaneous.
3. Add the theme of fun, pleasure and enjoyment to any activity: bring donuts to a morning meeting, put on your favorite music when doing house chores, bring balloons to a restaurant luncheon. Be creative and playful.
4. Focus on making the process joyful and not only on the outcome or on avoiding potential negatives.
5. Make sure every event is fun or educational or both.
6. Be more childlike. Ask yourself, "How would a child have fun doing this?" As an example, when walking down the street as a kid, you tried to balance yourself as you walked along the curb or you swung yourself around a stop sign poll. Do it again as an adult. Loosen up. Relax, play and have fun!
7. Make play and fun a style of self-expression. Appreciate and exaggerate the positives in your life, praise a lot and be more lovingly demonstrative.
8. Learn, grow and develop yourself by becoming actively involved in your own interests, others and your community.
9. Encourage happiness in others with praise, respect and sincere appreciation.

Section Highlights

➤ Playfulness is natural to the human being, though it is often erroneously referred to as childish when displayed by an adult.

➤ To escape emotional entrapments more quickly, add a sense of fun, play and light-heartedness to your life.

➤ Your primary goal: To live a long, happy life.

➤ Focus on BEING HAPPY working toward any specific goal.

➤ Self-interest is fused with social interest as immediate pleasure is balanced with long-term happiness.

➤ Emotional entrapments ensue when happiness is not one's primary focus.

➤ Outcome orientation focuses one's attention on obtaining a particular result.

➤ Process orientation focuses one's attention on enjoying the process *while* obtaining a particular result.

➤ When experiencing a "bad now," focus your attention temporarily on a pleasant past or future event.

➤ At anytime during your life, you want to either be having fun, learning or both.

➤ Be childlike: combining playfulness and spontaneity with thoughtful, considerate foresight.

➤ Childish implies a lack of thoughtfulness and is marked by self-centeredness.

➤ Attempt to *deliberately* play more each day.

➤ Spend money in areas that will help you to enjoy life more, short-term and long-term.

➤ Develop a positive attitude and openly display it daily.

➤ Develop a positive self-expression, being more animated and expressive.

➤ Attempt to put a positive spin on everything.

➤ Learn to appreciate the little things in life that add so much, engaging all of your senses.

➤ Practice exaggerating positives: "wonderful, terrific, spectacular, awesome, striking, etc."

➤ Vary your routine, your lifestyle, your activities, your life.

➤ Make growing, learning and developing a daily experience.

➤ Develop a passion and put energy into something larger that yourself; give to your world, create, share, build.

➤ Be happy being you!

"Be committed to living your life with passion and enthusiasm."

Section X

Bringing It All Together

Section Preface

Within all of us, metaphorically speaking, there is a small child, an angry beast and a strong, confident person. It just takes the right combination of circumstances and thinking to bring them out. A mother can fight like a wildcat to protect her child and confidence can abound when coming to the aid of an elderly person who is facing injustice and vulgar behavior from a rowdy youth. These qualities are already inside of you but may have been untapped for sometime. Resurrect your strong, positive, valuable characteristics and learn to utilize them at will.

Think about a time in your life when you were feeling on top of the world. When you were feeling strong, competent and confident. A time when you felt that you could conquer any problem in your world. A moment when you felt invincible. It may have been when you were a child, right after winning a race or catching that winning ball. Maybe it was after coming out of an inspiring movie, lecture or seminar. Or, when you bought your new house, got married, had a child. Pick a time when you felt powerful, determined, courageous and confident.

Think back to this time. Remember (or imagine) what that feeling was like. Get it back now. You can. Do it. Generate it. Hold onto this image and the associated feelings. Now, stand-up. Position your body, your posture, your stance in a position representative of this feeling. Stand tall! Shoulders back! Chest out! Head up! Eyes forward and direct! Smile. Gesture. If shaking hands, make it firm and direct. Walk with briskness and life in your step.

Do not skip this exercise. Try it now. Get that feeling back and remember that time in your life when you felt exactly this way. Anytime you want this feeling again, think back to this "powerful" time and then snap your body, your mind and your attitude into alignment again. Now...stand up and do this. Now!

As a psychologically healthy person, you want excellent physical health combined with a strong sense of self-love and appreciation. You want to believe in yourself and to lead a long, happy and fulfilled life. To have few and infrequent negative emotions, spending a minimal amount of time in distress. You want to maximize positive emotions and to love, laugh, grow, learn and excel. You want to be a positive, productive, committed and valued individual within your society. You want to be confident, social and friendly.

You have all of these wonderful qualities within you and many more. Some may have been polished by experience, others a bit tarnished from disuse and still others may have been forgotten altogether over time. But they are there.

If you believe these qualities to be desirable, then make it your explicit goal to advance them within yourself daily. The endeavor to advance these qualities is commendable, and success attainable. Escaping Emotional Entrapment has provided you with much of the knowledge that will help you develop a skill-set to be happy and fulfilled.

This section takes the ingredients for happiness and fulfillment, stirs in the spices of imagination, belief and expectation and generously adds the qualities of effort, commitment and determination. Set the timer on "practice" to allow for the creation of an outstanding, flavorful and delicious life to be enjoyed immediately!

Chapter 45

Ways to Make Change Permanent

Every emotion you have exists because of a very specific set of events that occur inside of you. There is a different yet specific formula, recipe or set of qualities for each emotion that includes: beliefs (thoughts, values, standards, expectations, ideology, past conditioning) body/brain chemistry (nutrition, physical health) and physicality (body language, tone, rhythm and quality of voice, and countless behaviors). The unique sequence and relative strength of these qualities is like a specific combination that unlocks a particular emotion.

Emotions are somewhat mechanical. If you maintain certain thoughts and images in your mind, they will connect to various beliefs that impact on the brain to release certain hormones, and at the same time the body cooperates in movement and manner — all of which collaborate to produce what we call an emotion.

Each person is unique in the combination and amounts of these qualities that come into play when experiencing any given emotion. A few fundamental qualities impact more significantly on one's emotions than do others.

It is now considered common knowledge in the psychological community that thinking — your belief system — primarily and dramatically affects your emotions. Unless drugs and/or brain chemistry are in play, the *cause* of your emotions *is* your thinking. The other qualities will then help to create the variations of any one particular emotion.

Your Belief System and Emotions: One's belief system is extensive and complex by the time adolescence starts. Your belief system consists of a full range of beliefs, your ideology and in a general sense, past conditioning. We are conditionable animals. Much of the time this is good. If a child jumps in front of your car, you do not have to go through a "thinking process" to step on the brakes; you just slam your foot down.

Unfortunately, being conditionable can be negative as well. We pass by a favorite restaurant or hear a melody on the radio that is connected to a loved one who recently died, and we suddenly feel saddened. Someone says something that we are sensitive about and we instantly and without conscious thought, become angry. While there is a thinking process involved, it is so fast and the connection between the thinking and situation so strong, the emotions seem spontaneous. The way to change this "instant" reaction is to change the irrational beliefs to rational beliefs, then to deliberately enter "that" situation practicing the new thoughts, attitudes and beliefs.

Your Physicality and Emotions: Your emotions and your physicality are integrally linked. If you were to watch a short film clip with no sound, it would not take long for you to make an accurate assessment of a person's emotions just by watching his/her body language or physicality. While fine distinctions between emotions are difficult to simply observe, it is not difficult to know how another is feeling just by watching his/her movements and facial expressions.

An experiment showed how a deliberate change facial expression alters emotions. Two groups were asked to rate how funny a series of comics were on a scale from 1 to 10. People in one group were to read and rate the comics while holding a pen in their mouth in the same position as if sucking on a candy-cane, creating a frown. Members of the second group were to do the same thing except to hold the pen in their mouth sideways, making the face "smile." The smiling group rated the comics as significantly funnier than did the frowning group. If facial expressions alone impacted on emotions, imagine how altering your entire body language — your physicality can alter feelings.

If you deliberately force your body into a position of assertiveness when depressed, for example, it helps to lessen the depression. While this will not eliminate depression, it is one of many steps that help. If a person who is feeling anger intentionally relaxes his muscles, anger tends to dissipate. By changing your physicality, you can impact, sometimes dramatically, on the emotions you are experiencing.

Bringing It All Together

Practice positioning your body, including your facial expressions, mannerisms, gestures, tone of voice using the same composition of qualities as another time of your life when you were feeling the way you want to currently feel. Think back to when you were feeling really happy or content or assertive or excited or confident. What did it look like? How were you standing, walking, gesturing? Now try and replicate that now. Practice this until it is natural and easy to reproduce at will. In this way you can emulate the behavior while working on the thinking and feelings.

Your Brain/Body Chemistry and Emotions: Emotions and hormones have a relationship. This relationship is primarily governed by your thinking or belief systems. In some respects, you do not have an emotion…you "do" an emotion. Everything being equal, your emotions are under "thinking control."

Some self-help books and seminar gurus preach the possibility of ongoing, continuous happiness and bliss. This is highly unrealistic, largely because of brain or body chemistry. Our bodies do not work perfectly. Sometimes we get a twitch for apparently no reason. There's an occasional poor night's sleep. We get the flu or break a leg. We eat something that doesn't agree with us. Many women have PMS issues each month that are largely out of their control. Allergies, environmental sensitivities and genetic influences can throw our emotions into a state of flux. These things impact on our brain or body chemistry and that influences how we feel.

While we can attempt to eat well and take care of ourselves, sometimes there are little glitches and the brain/body chemistry is slightly off, and that will have an affect on our emotions. We don't have a "dipstick" that we can use to see if our vitamin B12 is a bit low and causing us to feel a little more lackluster today.

If your emotions seem to change for no particular reason and there is no preceding trigger event and nothing particular on your mind, suspect that the culprit might be a biochemical fluctuation. While there are other possibilities, this is a good place to look, so see a trusted physician if your emotions constantly fluctuate or remain negative for prolonged periods for no apparent reason.

Bringing It All Together

A biochemical change can help influence your thinking and you may find yourself more emotionally sensitive. You may become more irritable or snappy, moody or brooding or maybe fidgety and uneasy. Make sure you do your best to control the part that does remain under your direct influence, your thinking. If chemistry is the problem, it will be more difficult during these times to think clearly, but working at doing so will help to mediate the emotional oscillation and intensity.

Make your change permanent by:

1. Ripping up all unfounded beliefs (insistence, amplifying negatives and assessment of worth)

2. Deliberately behaving in the manner that you would be behaving if the change had already occurred

3. Following good dietary habits, getting plenty of rest/sleep, exercise and play daily

Challenge All Irrational Beliefs

Challenging our "nutty" beliefs is the leading step to permanent change. A common computer phrase is "garbage in, garbage out." This is also true with our human "computer." Think in rigidly negative and blaming ways and you will end up with emotions that reflect that style of thinking. It is of utmost importance that you practice, practice and practice thinking in ways that promote healthy emotions and productive and effective behaviors.

When someone fails to make progress, the first place to look is here: Are you strongly and frequently challenging, tearing up and shredding your old irrational ideas? If you are in distress or unhappy, it is due to your thinking. What thoughts are causing you distress? Those thoughts are guaranteed to be irrational, illogical and nonsensical because rational, logical thinking does not cause distress. If you think your "distressing thoughts" are sensible, there's the problem. Re-read Sections III, IV and V, keeping your current thinking in mind so as to locate your irrational beliefs. This requires work, but do not let discomfort intolerance kick in producing laziness and procrastination. While there is no free lunch, the meal is definitely worth it.

Every time you find yourself getting depressed, anxious or angry examine your thoughts and look for the shoulds, awfuls or blaming statements. Ferociously challenge the validity of these assertions and then replace the irrational thoughts with healthier, more realistic attitudes. Practice changing your speech from:

1. Should, must and need…to want, like, desire, prefer

2. Awful, horrible and terrible…to unfortunate, bad, unpleasant

3. "You are bad"…to "You behaved badly"

*"I do not feel obliged to believe
that the same God who has
endowed us with sense,
reason, and intellect
has intended us to forego their use."*
Galileo

Chapter 46

Making Common Sense Common

Some thinking is simply so rational, so logical and so reasonable as almost to defy debate. But, as the French philosopher Voltaire said, "Common sense isn't so common." Your goal is to make clear rational, logical thought common for you. You want your natural, spontaneous rational thinking to be reflexive. When you are thinking in irrational or illogical ways, use the associated arguments below to dismantle those fallacious beliefs and create a new healthier style of thinking. Do this repeatedly until your new attitudes become ingrained and habitual.

Self-Denigration
1. *It is illogical to judge yourself based on your behavior.*
    You are much more than any given combination of traits or behaviors. It would be an overgeneralization to say that you are either a good or bad person based on a few significant or outstanding behaviors. You are a highly complex individual with ever-changing qualities and skills. A gross error in reason is to judge the total you, to label you based on behaviors that only represent a small slice of time.

2. *The more one berates one's self, the worse one's behavior becomes.*
    If you think of yourself as a terrible person for having behaved badly, the question is begged: "How will you, as a terrible person behave?" In terrible ways, of course. Self-damnation or self-criticism encourages poor behavior.

3. *Anger and malevolence towards others and yourself is considered immoral.*
    We are all human and this includes you! Whether the violence is directed at others or yourself, it still remains unjustified. Do not

attempt to justify self-anger by saying that you should have known better. We all do things wrong, even when we know better — it's part of the human condition. You are NOT an exception. Stop thinking that you are the only human being that has ever lived who should not make mistakes in situations when you know better.

4. *All people make errors in reason, judgement and behavior. You are no different.*

It is a sign of great grandiosity to think that for some reason you should be perfect and not make the mistakes that the rest of us mortals make. Forgiving yourself for making a mistake of any kind, regardless of the outcome, does not let you off the hook — in fact, it helps you to feel stronger and face the consequences and your responsibilities, to right wrongs and to grow.

5. *When you focus on beating yourself up, you distract yourself from learning from your mistakes.*

There is no value in hurting for hurting's sake. If you have messed up royally, then correct the error and move on. You will feel the associated feelings of remorse or sadness for your error, but beating yourself distracts you from focusing on the problem and learning from it so as to avoid it in the future. One main lesson to learn is that the stronger you are emotionally, the less likely you will be to make rash emotional errors in the future.

6. *You have a moral responsibility to minimize the suffering in the world.*

When you degrade, down or castigate yourself, you increase your own suffering, and you also model this masochistic attitude for others to follow. In effect, you are teaching others how to hate themselves, also increasing the suffering of this world. Be a model for self-love, acceptance, tolerance and forgiveness.

7. *Religions of the world preach forgiveness and that God has made us imperfect.*

If you are angry with yourself for being imperfect, you are in essence angry with God for not having made you perfect. You are angry with one of God's creatures...you. Imperfect people do imperfect things, think imperfectly, reason imperfectly, make imperfect decisions, respond imperfectly and repeat mistakes because we learn imperfectly. Self-downing is a form of being anti-religious...going against your religious doctrine.

Self-Pity

1.   Your life at times will be difficult and painful, and things will happen to you that are unfair.

Feeling sorry for yourself when things don't go your way presupposes that for some unknown reason, things should go your way. Life is filled with trials and tribulations. This is reality. Fairness is in the eye of the beholder. If you are served first at a restaurant, then someone else isn't. What is fair for you is unfair for someone else. Tough, shake it off.

2.   Not getting what you want is NOT awful, horrible, tragic or catastrophic.

When you are deep into self-pity, you act as if not getting your own way is a tragedy. If you were to compare yourself with over half of the people in the world who live in third world countries, you would find that you are better off than they are. Many sad and unfortunate things will occur during your life. When you exaggerate these negative events, you only make your current situation worse and your present moments miserable.

3.   Self-pity weakens you.

When you belabor a poor position, you make your situation appear worse than it is, and you make yourself appear weaker. Feeling sorry for yourself is your response when you have already accepted defeat. Failing only really occurs when you give up and stop trying. Adversity can make you stronger or weaker depending on how you internalize it. As virtually all adversity can be overcome, you want to continue to learn and grow beyond where you currently are. The choice is either you give up and suffer or keep trying and eventually prosper. Making the wise choice will provide you with a rich, full life, that will not necessarily be easy, but is better than living in misery.

4. *The benefits are not worth it.*

There is a pay-off for displaying self-pity. Sometimes others will sympathize with you, do things for you or otherwise take care of you, since you are demonstrating that you are *so* incapable of taking care of yourself. This parent-child type of relationship will continue to weaken you. Instead of gaining healthy relationships based on mutual respect and reciprocity, this relationship is based on charity. It will help to weaken your sense of self-acceptance and opens the door to many other functional and emotional entrapments.

Pitying Others

1. *Pitying others helps to convince them that their plight in life is truly tragic and awful.*

Feeling sorry for someone else increases the suffering of the world by one: you. Pitying others helps to weaken them by convincing them that their situation *is* awful, basically saying, "You poor thing you. You could never be happy in such a situation. You are so incompetent to handle what life throws at you." Even with the best of intentions, you end up feeling miserable for them, which does no one any good *or* you get to feel superior to them because you are not in *their* situation. Behave in strong ways for yourself *and* as a model for others.

2. *Concern for another person is appropriate. Overconcern unnecessarily worsens the problem and thus, is immoral.*

It is important to have concern for others in your life. It is the mark of a high moral and philosophical development. Overconcern hurts and demoralizes others. You know that you have crossed the line from concern to overconcern when you feel the pain of the other person's plight. Keep the other person's problems in perspective and be strong and effective for him/her *and* for you.

Bringing It All Together

3. As bad as things may get, it could be worse.

It is important to realize that life could always be worse. Everyone has difficulties in life, and while it is important to deal with them effectively, pitying others encourages all concerned to keep focused on the negative as if it is the worst possible outcome. Any situation could be worse. Often people fail to recognize the benefits that already exist in their lives. When you feel sorry for another you tend to worsen the situation (as there are now at least two people feeling bad). You focus on the problem and you ignore the solution or the benefits that already exist.

Anger

1. All anger is a form of conceit and grandiosity.

Insisting that you get exactly and precisely what you want, when you want it is representative of a child having a temper tantrum. To insist that you get what you want, forsaking all others is the classic sign of conceit and selfishness. Be tolerant of situations where things do not go your way. Intolerance normally encourages others to resist you, and thus, you end up worsening your own problems when displaying anger.

2. Anger is only appropriate when used judiciously as pseudo-anger or in self-defense.

When anger is used to stir action in a dramatic manner, mock anger has some value. There are rare situations in which forms of intimidation with mock anger can be useful and responsible. If used to threaten or to demean, then *that* is irresponsible. If anger is used in self-defense, then you are doing only what is required to protect yourself or others from an immoral invasion.

3. Other people have the right to be wrong.

People seem to initially accept this statement and then add exceptions to it: "...except when it harms another person." Or, "...except when others are negatively impacted." These exceptions will often completely nullify — 90 percent of the time — the idea that people have a right to be wrong. Often, when people are wrong, they are not impacting negatively on others. Unnecessarily hurting others is socially and ethically wrong, but as wrong as it is, people remain fallible, committing socially wrong acts, whether or not we like it. All people have a right to be fallible because that is the *common denominator* that links all human beings.

4. *Either fear or anger is generated in the victim of anger.*

When you get angry, others will learn to fear, not respect you, or they will aggress against you and engage you in a war. Neither situation will help you minimize frustrations or provide a strategy for long-term happiness. On a rare occasion, others will give you what you want but will often sabotage your efforts in an act of passive-aggression. Anger is a poor approach in human interactions as inevitably both parties lose.

5. *Anger conveys the message that "you are bad."*

There are no bad people, although there may be an abundance of bad behavior. People display a full range of good and bad behaviors. Damning others for their bad behavior is failing to acknowledge their lifetime of good behaviors. While it is important to take action and to discipline or provide consequences when appropriate, anger toward others does not provide an impetus for them to change, but rather a reason to plot your demise.

6. *Punishment and denigration tend not to correct behavior but to worsen it.*

If punishment worked at rectifying behavior, we would not see a 65 percent plus recidivism or return rate to prisons. We have done a very good job at making prisons a very bad place to be. As bad as it can be to be a prisoner, crimes are still being committed after release. Why? Because punishing people doesn't make them better but more cunning and attentive at not getting caught the next time. To attempt to make others feel bad about themselves and then expect them to feel grateful and happy is absurd. The most common response to punishment is to retaliate, *not* to acquiesce or gladly summit. The ideal is to ignore minor misdeeds or to *appropriately* penalize bad behavior and lavishly reward good behavior.

Bringing It All Together

Anxiety-Worry-Fear

1. *Exaggerating negatives is the cause of most emotional entrapments.*

You, like everyone else, will have bad things happen from time to time. If you think about a potential bad thing occurring as a devastation or catastrophe, you intensify your healthy feelings of concern to one of the various forms of distress. A possible situation may be bad, inconvenient or unpleasant, but if you distort these negatives into awful, horrible or terrible, you will create depression, anger, fear, worry or anxiety, or you will tend to procrastinate because of discomfort intolerance. There are no healthy benefits to overstating negatives.

2. *A true catastrophe is rare to non-existent.*

If we are talking about the annihilation of earth by plague or something similar, and you insisted on referring to that as a catastrophe, so be it. Losing a leg, your child dropping out of school, your spouse having an affair or having your house catch fire are definitely bad but nowhere close to true catastrophes. While it may *feel* catastrophic, that is only because you *think* of it that way. Your thinking *does not* prove reality. If your goal is to be more functional and to feel stronger, then work hard at never amplifying negatives, and you will stay free of unhealthy emotions.

3. *Center your attention on a potential negative and you increase your chance of bringing it about.*

There is an old adage that we move in the direction of our most currently dominant thoughts. If you worry or are anxious about something, you generally increase the chance of making it happen. If you are anxious about failing on an exam, the anxiety will help you to develop a memory block. If you worry about getting in a car accident, your reaction time slows, making your driving more dangerous. Regardless of the situation, relaxed focused attention on a positive outcome will produce consistently better results than being consumed with the possibility of a negative.

4. *While fear and anxiety are part of the human condition, they remain self-defeating emotions.*

If you fear an upcoming event and are anxious about it, then you worsen your current situation and make it more difficult to prepare for the anticipated negative event. You make the "now" *unnecessarily* unpleasant. In essence, you have two problems for the price of one. It has been said that a coward dies a thousand deaths, while the brave die but one. To be concerned about the future and to take action is wise. To suffer the pain of anxiety now over the prospect of future anguish is like committing suicide because you are aware that someday you will die.

5. *Fear never stops you from doing anything; it just makes doing it unpleasant.*

To overcome anxiety or fear, it is important for you to face the feared object or event. People sometimes mention that when the fear goes away they will tackle the task at hand. That is like saying when I become an accomplished dancer then I will take lessons. It's backwards. First you face your fear and then you overcome it. The discomfort of fear and anxiety never stops you…you do!

6. *Fear is not required, common sense is.*

There is a misunderstanding that fear is healthy. This emotion is highly adaptive. While it may warn you from real danger, it also tends to spread. If you see a venomous snake while taking a hike and you feel fear, this might be protective. Unfortunately, the fear may spread and you find yourself months later fearful of going in your backyard or leaving your house. With our current evolutionary psychological development, we no longer require the emotion of fear to warn us of danger. If I pull a rope taut across Niagara Falls, you do not have to feel fear to tell you not to walk the tightrope. Your common sense will kick in and you will know it would be a foolish thing for you to attempt.

7. *People who obsess about possible negative futures are proficient at enduring pain.*

The vast majority of time, the anxiety created over the

possibility of something bad happening is far more intense and enduring than the anticipated event itself. People who worry or who are anxious fill their present moments with distraction and discomfort and become masters at tolerating pain. Mark Twain said, "I've had many worries, most of which have never happened." Focus on and enjoy the present and be proactive, when necessary, about the future.

Self-Love

1. *You have the right to like and love yourself for no reason other than that you choose to.*

You do not require any special reason to love yourself, regardless of what you do. We are all human and make mistakes...usually repeatedly. Being perfect is not a requirement or prerequisite to loving yourself or to enjoying your existence. The belief that "because I behaved badly in the past, I should *never* be happy, must endure self-punishment or *forever* express guilt for my sins" is excessive and infantile. It serves no useful purpose and only causes more pain and increases the likelihood of creating emotional entrapments. You have the inalienable right to like what you like, to want what you want, to fantasize what you fantasize, and to feel what you feel. This is and remains your business only.

2. *You have the right to enjoy your experiences in life even when making mistakes.*

Happiness and fulfillment are not reserved for the God-like elite who are perfect. We are all human and thus make mistakes of all kinds. You are allowed to be happy and enjoy yourself even when you are performing poorly. In fact, enjoying any activity is a good precursor to the likelihood that you will improve at it. We tend to do better at things that we enjoy. There is no nobility in being miserable. If misery produced better life results, I would suggest it, but it doesn't. When you make a mistake, learn from it and voilà, it's taken care of and there is no requirement to feel bad — you have taken care of the problem.

3. Self-interest is a moral position to take in life.

It is important to all those who rely on you that you be self-interested. When you are self-interested you will grow stronger and be happier as more of your desires are met. As a strong and happy person, you can give more to others. You can fully support those who depend on you. Self-interest is fused with social interest, and thus others benefit as you benefit. Giving in and cowering from the bully helps to make you weak and encourages the bully to become even more dictatorial. Go for what you want, and share the benefits of a self-interested attitude with others.

4. Inferiority and superiority do not exist.

In reality, there are no geniuses. There are only people who have genius-like qualities *in some areas.* You can never be unconditionally inferior or superior to anyone else. You can, though, have inferior or superior skills to another. But that's all that that means. The skill-set gets rated, not you! Everyone has certain strengths and weaknesses. It is a gross error in reasoning to *judge a person* by his or her actions or anything else for that matter. All we can ever do is judge the behavior alone.

5. Repetition does not prove fact.

Many people when told something (like "you're an idiot") will come to believe it through simple repetition. "He tells me I'm stupid so often and seems so convinced, that it must be true." Absurdity remains absurd regardless of how many times it is repeated. Repetition does not make nonsense true anymore than saying "lead is gold" a thousand times makes it true. Because we tend to believe that which we hear repeated, make sure you repeatedly tell yourself good, healthy, sane and loving statements about yourself.

6. Others will not always love you the way you want, so make sure you do.

If you want to be loved in a particular way at a given time, others frequently will not comply. They will give you loads of love

Bringing It All Together

and attention when you are possibly too busy or distracted to appreciate it. Other times, when you're feeling out-of-sorts, others won't notice and jump in with the loving support that you might like. If you want to be loved and appreciated at a specific time in any special way, provide that love yourself. In this way you will never be left wanting for love and appreciation. While it is always wonderful to get it from people you care about, unfortunately it's not always there. So, furnish it yourself.

7. *Loving you is your responsibility.*

It is not other people's responsibility to love you, it is yours. If you will not give yourself a bundle of love, why *should* others? Model for others how you expect to be treated, by treating yourself that way first. Never let anyone, for any reason, ever treat you shabbily, and that includes yourself! Always be a paragon of love, tolerance and forgiveness.

8. *Trust, respect and love promote good behavior.*

It is difficult, if not impossible to love someone that you do not trust and respect. It appears that respect precedes love. While there are no guarantees that if you trust and respect someone that he or she will behave well, it's a given that good behavior is more likely than if you don't provide that trust and respect. This also applies to you. It is important for countless reasons to trust in yourself. To respect yourself. To love yourself. Whether or not others do is up to them. Whether or not you do is up to you.

9. *Treat yourself wonderfully.*

Make sure you behave in warm, wonderful ways toward yourself. There is no good, rational or sane reason not to. You have *you* to live with yourself for the rest of your life. Make it wonderful. Do something wrong? Fix it. Make amends. Learn from it. And, in the meantime, treat yourself the way you would treat your very best friend…or better.

Still Not Sure of Your Thoughts...

Some people find that after having practiced rational thinking, there are times when they get distressed but can't find the area of thinking that is causing their distress. They understand and agree with the arguments and positions taken above, yet they are in distress. What could be causing this distress?

If you ever find yourself not sure of which *thoughts* might be *causing* you to be upset, but there is a distinct event that you are upset over, make a guess using some typical types of statements using shoulds, awfuls and blame. The statements that *feel* somewhat "true" at a gut level are likely the statements that are liable. Challenge these statements forcefully, making the assumption that these are your *subconsciously* TRUE beliefs.

It's easy to fool ourselves into thinking that we believe the rational, sensible thinking when we actually don't. We can tell ourselves that "there is no reason why I *must* pay my bills, but I do *prefer* to so I can maintain my standard of living," but we don't really believe that. Inside at a gut level, it *feels* like "*I must.*" If it feels that way, it's because you are thinking that way. It's a given that if you are in distress, you're using shoulds, awfuls or blame.

Here's another possible solution when you are unclear of what thoughts might be causing your emotions. Let yourself really get into the emotions that you are feeling. Let those feelings intensify. Start thinking about your current situation in detail and ask yourself these three questions:

1) What should be different?

2) What is awful?

3) Who is to blame?

Without a lot of thinking, what are your most immediate answers to these questions? Any answer is likely the problem area. Why? Because nothing should be different from the way it is.

Bringing It All Together

Nothing is awful and there is no one to blame. Be careful of snapping into the rational thinking that you have learned to parrot but not yet believe. It's easy to rhyme off rational statements, but believing them is a whole other issue. If distressed, *assume* an irrationality then challenge it forcefully!

There's no point in simply showing that you know what the rational, logical thinking is, if you are in distress. Remember rational thoughts won't make you upset, so look for the irrational thoughts. If you are upset, they are there! Find them, challenge them, eradicate them, and then add healthier, saner, rational thoughts.

"What appears obvious is not always true and what is true is not always obvious."

*"What we have to learn to do,
we learn by doing."*

Aristotle

Chapter 47

Getting Unstuck and Making Gains

There are times when people resist change and are frequently *unaware* that *they* are creating resistance. What they notice is that they are not making progress. If you are NOT aware that you are creating resistance, then you will look everywhere but where the problem actually comes from: YOU!

If you are not making the gains you would like, consider some of the following reasons and rationalizations:

"Nobody could really understand my problem."
Self-Pity: This attitude keeps the person stuck in self-pity and self-righteousness as *if his/her* problem is so unique and so special that no other person could possibly understand or appreciate the depth of his/her tragedy. This attitude is insulting and offensive to others, which usually results in minimizing the support you want so very much. Often there is a focus on the past, which of course cannot be changed, so the assumption is that nothing could ever be done to undo the feelings of guilt, shame, hurt or injustice. If you find yourself here, even if an infinitesimal amount of this is going on for you, challenge the idea that your experience truly is a tragedy or so special as to be somehow incomprehensible to others.

Self-Denigration: Forgive yourself if you did something wrong. There is no dignity, nobility or justification for continually beating up on yourself because you messed up royally. Make sure you understand what is *really* important: making your life better from this point forward. Self-flagellation will not benefit you, and you will tend to make life uncomfortable for those around you, whether they will admit it to you or not.

Fear of Failure: This is associated with self-denigration or what some people refer to as shame. "What if I *really* tried and failed? Then, that would prove what a worthless person I *really* am" is the unspoken belief behind fear of failure. It is a slight twist on self-blame but the outcome is identical.

Fear of Self-Discovery: Many people believe that if they looked in the mirror of their soul, what would be reflected back to them is a hideous demon. I have worked with a wide range of people from rapists to child molesters to top executives to homemakers, and have found that once the person looks inside himself or herself they find wonderfulness.

The anger, jealousy, hatred, depression and other forms of entrapment are the results of not loving and taking care of ourselves in the first place. Universally, people want to be loved and to love, to do things that interest them, to achieve and be respected, to have mutually satisfying relationships and to get along. No big surprise here. Trust in yourself that when you begin the journey of self-discovery, you'll be pleasantly delighted with whom you'll meet.

"I've been this way for so long, I just couldn't change."
Discomfort intolerance: If you adopt this attitude, it signifies that you do not believe that change is even possible so why would you work at it? Holding this belief is a sound indication of rapid or discomfort intolerance and an unrealistic attitude for yourself. Of course you can change! Do you really think that you will be the same 10 years from now as you are today? You *will* change. That is certain.

Since change is inevitable, why not guide your change to get what you want? Don't cop-out with a poor me attitude, as if you are the only person in all of history that could not possibly make a change. It is up to you, but it may require work. Debate the idea that work, even with an uncertain outcome, must be a horrible experience and that you should not have to apply effort to change. You do! Cop-out and you have already admitted defeat when success was there for the taking.

Bringing It All Together

"It just wouldn't feel like me."

Fear of Mediocrity: Some resist change because they hold themselves superior to others. The sense of superiority can bring about serious entrapments in the form of depression when not living up to one's superior standards. Being ordinary or mediocre would be the worst fate. The superior-inferior dichotomy misses the point. Life is not about comparing yourself to others; it is about enjoying your existence. If you accept others with *their* attitudes or failings and foibles but not yourself, then you have a fascist double standard: One standard for the ordinary peasant and one standard for the elite...you! It is okay to be below average, average and above. In fact you are all three, just in different areas of your life already. Lighten up and give yourself the break you hopefully give others.

Displeasure Anxiety: People sometimes fear change because of the uncomfortable feelings they initially feel. To make a positive change, it is common that one will need to progress through some unpleasant thoughts or feelings. It may mean admitting to themselves that they are not perfect or that they did screw up or that a certain bad reality does exist or that they are not loved as they would have hoped. But once through that admission, the healing begins and positive events seem to appear in droves.

Fear of Being Artificial: Some people refuse to change based on the idea that the change would be artificial and they would be a phony. The feeling of being artificial only occurs at the start when the change is new. If you have not dated in a long time, dating will feel awkward and artificial. But after you get to know the person, that artificialness disappears. You have found a new and improved comfort zone. This occurs when you attempt to make a change of any kind. Practice the new attitude and behavior and *it will* become comfortable. You will always remain you, just improved.

Fear of Being Cold: It is erroneous to think that being in control over your emotions will produce a cold, mechanized person. In fact, it is just the opposite. People who are in good control over their emotions, are not in constant fear of being hurt, are not plagued with anxiety or struggling to suppress their hostility. These people can be open, warm and forthcoming knowing that they are coming from a place of positive intent, regardless of how others perceive them. "Cold" people are cold as a result of protecting their emotions *because* the emotions are so out of control and easily wounded. As you gain control, you gain warmth and display the genuine you.

Discrepancy in Attitudes

A common reason for not making the gains you might like is because of a discrepancy in attitudes. Let's say you have a strong desire to visit the Mayan ruins in Belize, Central America. If you also have a fear of snakes, then you have two competing drives. One to see Mayan artifacts, and one that tells you not to go because there might be snakes there.

When there are two competing drives, the stronger one wins out. The way to solve any similar conundrum is to practice challenging the associated irrational beliefs *and* to practice the desired behavior (e.g., go to Belize). Make sure you perform both at once; in this way, the feelings change rapidly and the results are long lasting.

Ensure that you are not paying lip service to the new beliefs. Forcefully instill a new positive belief to replace the old belief. Talk to yourself in strong powerful ways that reinforce the rational, common sense thinking and the behavior that you are trying to achieve. Do not indulge yourself with the pernicious habit of irrational, negative thinking. Think, visualize, imagine, do...and repeat and repeat and repeat.

Chunk It!

One reason many people give up on their goals is because of early failure, convincing themselves that success is out of their reach. It's not. There will be backsliding. Expect it. It will happen and it's part of the growth-change process.

Backsliding sometimes occurs early on because the person attempted to take a giant leap forward, tripped, stumbled and fell. One way of minimizing (not eliminating) backsliding and making a consistent progression forward is to take "baby steps." Determine your goal and chunk out the steps to achieve it.

As an example: If you have been depressed and are not very good at loving yourself, start small. Practice saying, "Thank you" when someone compliments you. Then add some positive, complimentary self-talk. Start walking briskly with your head up and shoulders back. Make it a habit to smile and greet people offering your hand and name *first*. Make it a rule never to down or to degrade yourself, especially in front of others. Make it routine to treat yourself wonderfully and do things that add play, fun and love to your life. Then, continue to treat yourself as you would your dearest friend. Persist in this fashion.

You chunk out your progress continually adding to the list, ideally, for the rest of your life. Each journey begins with the first step. Enjoy the journey always taking the next step, as success and fulfillment have no end.

*"Happiness favors the flexible
and prepared mind."*

*"A person who has committed a mistake
and doesn't correct it,
is committing another mistake."*
Confucius

Chapter 48

Making It Happen

A certain magic seems to occur when an unshakable belief is attached to any pursuit or goal. Changes begin to occur, some almost imperceptible, others dramatic. Not with simple thinking or wishing, but when truly believing.

Prior to 1954 people believed the running of a 4-minute mile was impossible. Medical authorities considered it a physical impossibility by stating that: the heart, lungs and blood vessels could not withstand that level of exertion. And, of course, no one did run a 4-minute mile...

Until Roger Bannister in Oxford, England on May 6th, 1954 ran a mile in 3 minutes and 59.4 seconds. Breaking this self-limiting barrier changed world beliefs. Thirty-seven other runners ran a mile in under 4 minutes that same year. Over 300 other runners broke the 4-minute mile within the next two years!

Belief is the essential nutrient that all great change requires. Believe you can free yourself from negative thinking and unhealthy emotions. Apply consistently the lessons you have learned here. Be enthusiastic in your life and with everything you do. Play. Think positively and rationally and be proactive in your actions and you will achieve your goals in the shortest amount of time.

Imagine: What You See Is What You Get

Imagine the husband is putting the car in the garage and the wife is unlocking the front door. As she does so she sees a shadow of a man holding a knife. She freezes. Her husband comes up behind her and asks her what's wrong. She whispers, "There's a man in the living room with a knife." The husband in disbelief says, "It's just your imagination. Go on in." Will she?

Not on your life! The shadow on the wall may not be of an intruder, but as long as she believes there's a prowler, she will not go in.

Imagination can be so powerful that it will rule our beliefs, and our beliefs rule our behavior. When the imagination is total and complete, there is no difference from reality. For the individual, imagination is reality. If you want to make a change in your life, one of the most powerful tools to help ameliorate that change is your imagination.

Since you use your imagination anyway, whether you know it or not, why not control it so you can harness its constructive energy? Albert Einstein once said, "Imagination is everything. It is the preview of life's coming attractions." Start right now to picture yourself the way you would ideally like to be. Raise the bar, raise your standards, and reach for that unreachable star. It has been said that if you aim for the stars, you're sure to clear the trees. Aim high!

See life realistically, and then see it as being even better than it is. Exaggerate what is possible. All people who achieved greatness had lofty goals. There is no passion in reaching for your average. Reach for what is just out of your reach. Believe in yourself and that you will do what it takes to achieve your goals. Remember that your primary goal had better be happiness. See yourself the way you would ideally like to be and do not let that image waver in your mind.

If you find yourself thinking, "But I just couldn't achieve…" or "I'm just not that type of person," then you will never reach what you do not believe you can become. If you ever think, "I'm not…" then you are right. Not because it is not possible but because you have *that* self-limiting belief.

To simply attempt to use will power to make yourself change is not sufficient. Eventually your will power will fail you. What is essential, is that you change your self-limiting beliefs and that you raise your own personal standards. A self-limiting belief starts with the words, "I can't…" or "I'm not…" Raising your personal standards is reaching for that brass ring. Imagine your life the way you would ideally like it to be. Imagine how you would be in this ideal life. How would you look? What would you be doing? Include your emotions, your attitudes, disposition, style, mannerisms — everything that makes up this new image. Make it specific and detailed. Then make it a primary focus in your life to achieve; make every adjustment to your behavior, physicality, and think congruently and harmoniously with that image.

Imagination can be used both positively and negatively. If you are flying to Hawaii and you don't sleep well the night before because you fear the plane crashing into the ocean, this is called worry. It's the negative use of the imagination. If you don't sleep well because you can't wait to get going to Hawaii, then this is called excitement. Basically the same thing is occurring, but one is a healthy anticipation, and the other is distressing.

Your imagination is like a thermostat. If you perform above your imagined expectation, the air conditioner kicks in and your performance drops. It's common for golfers who perform uncommonly well on the front nine, to do poorly on the back nine. If you perform below your expected norm, then the heater turns on and you find yourself doing better on the back nine to match your anticipated score. So turn up your thermostat and raise your expectations.

You have tremendous control over your thoughts and your imagination. With a lot of practice, you can become proficient in using your imagination positively and constructively. Increase the clarity of your mental image, think and focus on what you want for yourself emotionally, mentally and experientially. Few things in life are as powerful as your imagination. Use it wisely.

What Do You Expect?

The sister of imagination is expectancy. What do you expect from life? What do you expect from yourself?

I know I will just flunk the exam.

I could never be a good artist.

Why try? I will never succeed.

I could never organize a seven-course meal.

I am just a klutz when it comes to sports.

I will never loose weight.

What do you expect of yourself? You can't? You're right. Not because you can't but because you believe you can't. Develop a different expectation of yourself and you will begin to rise to that level. Because you move in the direction of your strongest mental focus, do you focus on the fear of failure or the rewards of success? See yourself the way you would ideally like to be; believe you can be the person you want to be, then make every nuance of behavior congruent with this image, belief and expectation, and watch yourself achieve to that level.

Paying the Price

Everyone wants to be happy and fulfilled in his or her life. Unfortunately most people are unwilling to "pay the price." The colloquial phrase is "no pain, no gain" or in psychology it's called "high frustration tolerance, delayed gratification." No matter what you call it, there is always a price to be paid for the long-term happiness of tomorrow.

The price involved to escape emotional entrapments is time, energy, effort and the taking of emotional risks. Sometimes, there may be physical risks, though these are usually very minor.

Are you willing to give up the sympathy and attention you get from self-pity? How about giving up the self-righteousness and sense of superiority that goes with anger? Are you ready to sacrifice immediate short-term pleasures that go with abolishing discomfort intolerance and procrastination? There are payoffs to all emotional entrapments. The payoff is, at most, a short-lived benefit sacrificing long-term emotional and physical health.

Making a positive change in your life means making a *decision* to pay the price. This is a *conscious decision*. It is NOT a process.

Grieving is a process, with many steps. Controlling your emotions is a *decision* you make. You *decide* to lose weight or stop smoking. You *decide* you will gain better control over your emotions. Obtaining those goals may mean going through many steps or stages, but *it starts with an unshakable decision to make a change!*

Two Little Four Letter Words

Hard work.

Yuck. Phooey. What a *horrible* thought. Or is it?

Learning to control your emotions can be hard work. It's not breaking rocks in the hot sun, or working in a miserable job, but it is work. Hard? Yes; if hard means "with lots of effort." If you find taking emotional risks hard, then *hard* applies.

Those with discomfort intolerance tend to be most adverse to hard work. Putting effort into your endeavors is what makes what you reap so sweet. Geena Davis in the movie "A League of Their Own,", is trying to decide whether to stay in baseball or not and complains to Tom Hanks, "Why does it have to be so hard?" Hanks replies, "It's supposed to be hard. The hard is what makes it great!"

Hard work is still the cornerstone of all great achievements. It's also the avenue to developing excellent emotional control. For those who have developed a command over their emotions, it no longer *feels* like work, and that is because it has become natural.

It is better to think of the effort you apply to gaining emotional control as "effortful" as opposed to hard. Making love can be effortful — your heart pounds, you perspire, your body trembles but most people don't think of it as hard or work. The way you look at the energy involved will determine whether you see it as rewardingly effortful or hard work.

It is important to continue to apply effort, to develop and to grow. Leonardo da Vinci said, "Iron rusts from disuse: stagnant water loses its purity and in cold weather becomes frozen; even so does inaction sap the vigor of the mind."

Be Committed to the Process

It is important that you be committed to the process of enjoying your life, to applying effort to achieve your emotional and pragmatic goals and to feeling fulfilled. Commitment is a decision or a resolve. It is jumping in with both feet. No backing out. Fully involved.

I don't want you to allow yourself an out when it comes to treating yourself wonderfully or feeling anything less than terrific. Renew your commitment everyday to feeling the way you ideally would love to feel. Then make it happen!

An Old Story of A Real Commitment!

A pig and a cow were having a conversation. The cow said, "My commitment is to give one gallon of milk every day." "Commitment? Ha!" the pig exclaimed. "That's just participation. Try giving bacon. Now that's commitment!"

Commitment: without it, nothing happens! In every formula for success, commitment is a catalyst. The strength of your commitment will directly relate to two things: 1) the benefits of achieving your goals and 2) the consequences if you do not achieve them.

The secret to maintaining commitment is to constantly return to the "whys." "Why do you want to make a personal change?" What are the benefits to change? You want to focus on the benefits while understanding the consequences of giving up.

"How" is not an attribute of commitment. Commitment is simply, compellingly and without question, what you say WILL happen, what you KNOW will happen — regardless of circumstance. As an example, what is the chance of your children starving to death? "Zero. Absolutely no chance whatsoever!" "Why? You do not know the future. How can you say that?" Because you would do whatever it takes to make sure that that situation never happens. That takes commitment! Have that resolve that you will do what it takes to ensure you become the person you want to be.

Bringing It All Together

Unfortunately, convenience is the foundation for most people's decisions, not commitment. When obstacles arise or uncomfortable feelings are generated, as they inevitably will be, most take another direction and never get where they are headed.

Determination

Commitment and determination are brothers of one another. Determination is the active part of commitment combined with the refusal to quit. It is persistence and a stick-to-it-ness. It is the action quality and nothing happens without action. What is required is "focused daily action."

Little happens when actions or behaviors are not focused on a goal. You simply end up spinning your wheels. This is the epitome of anxiety and worry. When light is properly focused into what we know as a laser, it can cut through steal. Be focused and cut through problems and difficulties until you reach your goal.

If your action is not persistent (that is, on a daily basis) then the action becomes defused into the confusion and hecticness of life, excuses arise and, most of all, that behavior never becomes natural and reflexive. You want your behaviors to be congruent with the feelings you wish to promote. You want these behaviors to become reflexive and life long, so it no longer requires conscious effort and the emotions occur naturally.

The following story is one of determination: that "never say die" attitude, that refusal to quit combined with lots of work and effort.

A botched delivery with forceps in a hot charity ward on the Lower East Side on July 6, 1942, resulted in a facial nerve being severed.

His tongue, lips and chin were paralyzed and thus it made ar-ti-cu-lat-ing very difficult. Neighborhood punks tormented the oddball with the speech impediment, lopsided mouth and droopy eyes. They called him Sylvie.

"It was like Mr. Potato Head with all the parts in the wrong places," he says laughing, "and wanting to be anybody but me." Dad said, "You weren't born with much of a brain, so you'd better develop your body."

He struggled in New York, ushering at a movie theater and sweeping out Bronx Zoo lion cages in between reading about screenwriting and begging for bit parts.

"Swallowing criticism and rejection and despair and still being vulnerable as an actor is tough. I steeled myself against the terrible, terrible, terrible onslaught of rejection: 'You're no good, you're too short, you're stupid.'"

Hungry for success? "No. Starving! You have to be. Hungry people give up. If you're starving for something, you're absolutely dedicated to achieving it."

With only $106 in his bank account, he dictated the script he was working on to his then-pregnant wife, in three-and-one-half days.

Turning down $285,000 for the script that would not have used him in the starring role, he instead accepted $75,000 plus 10 percent of the net profits. Rocky, released in 1976, was nominated for two Oscars and earned $250 million. The rest is history.

What is responsible for Sylvester Stallone's success? "Hard work. I knew what I wanted; it had nothing to do with looks or muscle."

Determination means willing to go through "Splat!" and not be stopped by it. Your level of skill is not at issue. It is a psychological issue. It is having heart, an insatiable hunger, a passion, that refusal to quit…in summary: a burning desire. If you have that fire within you to make a change — you will! No one or no-thing will stop you.

Bringing It All Together

Chapter 49

Never A Conclusion

For some people, reading <u>Escaping Emotional Entrapment</u> will seem like they already knew this stuff, but it has now been put into words with ideas that they can utilize. For others, this material will seem new and inspiring. The concepts herein work. Making them part of your daily experience so they become a part of you, requires tenacity and endurance. Repetition is the mother of skill. Become skilled at rational thinking and controlling your emotions.

There will be many distractions to sidetrack you. Well-meaning family and friends may attempt to dissuade you…not because they don't love you but because they do. They may feel you changing and might feel that there is a distance growing in the relationship and they will encourage you not to change. But hang tight and remain steadfast to what you want to achieve for yourself. You know what it feels like to be you better than anyone. If you want to feel better, stronger, have more fun and feel more fulfilled than ever before — stay the course. In the words of Winston Churchill, "Never give up. Never give up. Never give up. Never, never, never, never, never give up!"

Excuses are like fingers; everyone has a number of them. Whether or not you apply yourself, you end up with the results. Other people have made changes within themselves and in their lives that have been truly astounding by all measures…and under some of the worst conditions. Acquiring personal growth and fulfillment in Nazi prisoner-of-war camps like Auschwitz and Dachau over and above simple survival would seem a near impossibility, but there are numerous accounts of just that happening.

One prisoner taught another to play the piano on keys scratched on a piece of wood, listening to the music played only in their minds. Another played 18 holes of golf every day in his imagination — improving his swing on every hole. One POW practiced sit-ups, and after the war held the record for the largest number of sit-ups without resting. Personal growth, fun and fulfillment are a choice. It is not always an easy choice, but think of the alternative.

Making your daily experience fun and fulfilling is a wonderful challenge, one that I encourage you to take everyday for the rest of your life. Remember what is important: you experiencing a wonderful life and sharing that experience with those you care about.

When you accept the responsibility for your feelings, behaviors and your own life, you become accountable; you develop and grow as a person. Even attempt to look at setbacks as an opportunity for growth. Just remember what you are working towards: a happier, better you. Here's a story that might make the point...

What are you building?

Masons were cutting and shaping huge blocks of granite in a stone quarry. A man was captivated as he watched from the side of the quarry and decided to take a closer look. As he strolled through the quarry he found that it was arduous, grueling work. Most of the men were sweating and cursing as they worked, chipping, splitting and cutting the stones with hammers and chisels.

The man spoke to the stonecutters as he walked. "What are you doing?" he would ask, and the men would abruptly snap back, "What does it look like I'm doing? I'm cutting stones!"

One worker stood out from the others. He seemed different. Smiling and cheerily humming a tune, he was happily cutting away at the gigantic slabs. The man was intrigued. Why was this worker so enjoying his work? He approached the man and asked the same question, "What are you doing?"

Bringing It All Together

The stonecutter stopped his work, looked up at the visitor and proudly replied, "I'm building a cathedral."

Just remember what *you* are building...a magnificent cathedral of life. Go with grace, happiness and Godspeed.

"It is not in the stars to hold our destiny but in ourselves."
William Shakespeare

*"Twenty years from now you will be
more disappointed by the things
that you didn't do
than by the ones you did do.
So throw off the bowlines.
Sail away from the safe harbor.
Catch the trade winds in your sails.
Explore. Dream. Discover."*

Mark Twain

Index